Let's Talk Toddlers

Let's Talk Toddlers

A PRACTICAL GUIDE TO HIGH-QUALITY TEACHING

Marie L. Masterson, PhD

Redleaf Press®
www.redleafpress.org
800-423-8309

Published by Redleaf Press
10 Yorkton Court
St. Paul, MN 55117
www.redleafpress.org

First edition 2018
Cover design by Lauren Cooper
Cover photograph by Kara Loman
Interior design by Percolator
Typeset in Whitman
Interior photos from iStock
Printed in the United States of America
25 24 23 22 21 20 19 18   1 2 3 4 5 6 7 8

CIP data is on file with the Library of Congress.

Printed on acid-free paper

This book is dedicated to early childhood professionals, parents, and families, who understand the indelible imprint of love, respect, and kindness, and who nurture, empower, and protect the hearts, minds, bodies, and spirits of our most vulnerable children.

Contents

Acknowledgments

Thank you to the Collaboration for Early Childhood and the toddler teachers and directors who shared their classrooms and inspirational journeys with me. I am forever grateful for the dearest toddlers in my life, both past and present, who are my greatest joys. Elle, Everett, Greyson, and Eisley: from you I understand the tender reality of each child's vulnerable spirit and sacred influence in the world. David, Tanya, James, Lisa, Sara, Steve, and Stephen: from each of you, I have learned the true meaning of emotional presence, kindness, compassion, and unconditional love.

Introduction

Whether you are a new teacher or a seasoned professional, this book is for you. As you begin this learning journey, you will recognize the special privileges and joys of teaching toddlers. You will also take a fresh look into the world of young children and discover why each activity, routine, and interaction in a group setting matters. You may read the chapters in order or turn to a topic of interest to find information that addresses your specific needs.

As you explore each chapter, you will gain insight into the unique traits and needs of your remarkable, lively, inquisitive, and highly sensitive toddlers. Bound by their developmental stage yet boundless in their expressive love and joy, they are absolutely dependent on you. In the months you are with them, the beautiful and stimulating setting you prepare will feed their rapidly growing brains and impact the rest of their lives.

Let's Talk Toddlers provides detailed information on preparing the environment for play. You will discover how to set positive routines and expectations. You will find strategies, tips, and skills to infuse your teaching with rich language experiences and effective behavior guidance. You will build a strong foundation for learning by nurturing secure relationships and important social skills. You will learn how to create meaningful partnerships with families and coteachers, which are essential for children to thrive.

This book offers easy access to practical, evidence-based information. The real-life scenarios show best practices in action, with words and strategies you can use in your own teaching. "Teacher Tips" offer successful approaches used by early childhood professionals. "Seeing from the Child's Point of View" reveals the perspectives of toddlers. "Fast Facts: Why This Works," "Strategies for Success," and "Resources for Growth" help you apply current research and best practices to create the highest-quality learning environment. At the end of each chapter, you will find "Quick questions" and "Simple solutions," which offer on-the-spot solutions for common challenges. You can use this book to jump-start conversations with coteachers. Together you can find answers to everyday questions.

As you read and reflect on each chapter, you will find encouragement to be your best self: a healthy role model who is invested in the success of every child. You will discover how and why your work makes such a profound difference for children and their families. *Let's Talk Toddlers* addresses the whole child in the context of family and community. It ensures the highest level of nurture for every area of children's development, including physical, social-emotional, language, cognitive, and self-regulation skills; personal skills such as emotion and behavior regulation and self-care; and mental health and well-being. As you embrace the philosophy of respect that anchors each page, you can be sure that your toddler setting will be a place of safety, security, support, and success for all children and their families.

Making a Difference in the Lives of Toddlers

High-quality care gives toddlers an early and lasting advantage in learning and life (La Paro and Gloeckler 2016; Ruzek et al. 2014). This chapter will focus on the remarkable influence you have in the lives of young children and their families. It will present the essential elements of responsive teaching that foster children's development. Examining the unique attributes of toddlerhood can help you anchor a strength-based perspective and renew your sense of purpose as you embrace the joys and challenges of toddler care.

Setting a Shared Vision

Ms. Loi is reading with Jack and Remy on the floor. "Look! The bunny is hopping around the flowers. Where did he go? There he is! I see the bunny peeking out from the yellow flowers." Ms. Loi covers her face with her hands. "Peek! I am a bunny peeking out of the flowers. Can you peek out of the flowers, too?" The boys cover their faces and peek out at each other. Pilar and Laura run across the room to see why the boys are laughing. Ms. Loi gives Laura a hug and says, "See the bunny? He is hiding in the flowers." The children's arms and legs touch as they lean on their teacher to see the pictures. The close emotional bond is evident. Ms. Loi asks the children about the bunnies they saw on their walk this morning.

Ms. Loi enjoys these moments together. She knows the children are learning much more than a love of books or animals. They are learning how to share happy moments, make room for friends, cooperate in activities, and feel good about themselves as learners. She treats them as her own and calls them "honey," "sweet pea," and "Laura-belle," names she has heard their families use. Smiles and encouraging words make the children feel special and loved.

As a teacher of toddlers, you know that that these rambunctious, loving, gentle, emotional, empathetic children are not at all like infants or preschoolers. The toddler years are a unique period of development that spans approximately sixteen to thirty-six months of age (NAEYC 2017). During this time, the rapid changes in children's skills bring many sweet moments of reading and cuddling as well as spirited times of bouncing, running, and active play. In a span of seconds, you may find that your entire group is following one child—screeching, running, or crawling under tables.

How can you meet the needs of multiple children on unique timetables? How will you provide appropriate cognitive stimulation and full inclusion for every child? Toddlers require routines for self-care, materials to boost learning, physical activities in safe spaces, and plenty of soothing and snuggling to ensure belonging. This is a tall order—with enormous rewards.

As an early childhood professional, your goal is to create the highest-quality setting for children. What toddlers experience with you has a direct impact on every area of their development. Nurturing toddlers requires deep understanding of child development and keen sensitivity to children's needs. You will need great patience with the children and with yourself. Flexibility, a sense of humor, and creativity will serve you well.

The attitudes, beliefs, and values needed for toddler teaching are anchored in a philosophy of respect for each child's worth and dignity. You will need to build trust and collaboration with families to ensure that you nurture each child in a consistent and meaningful way.

Exploring the Need for High-Quality Toddler Care

Mr. Desai grasps his six-year-old daughter, Priya's, and two-year-old daughter, Daryia's, hands. He says, "When we left home, the dog ran outside, and Priya ran after him. That was a lot of excitement, wasn't it, girls?" Ms. Tejal smiles at them and replies, "It sounds exciting to me. I'm glad you caught your dog. Does Priya have time to help Daryia feed the goldfish?"

The girls cross the room to the aquarium. Priya opens a small jar. She puts a pinch of fish food into Daryia's hand. Daryia drops the flakes into the tank. "Time to go!" says their father. The girls hug each other tightly. Mr. Desai kisses Daryia and says, "Bye-bye, butterfly," before heading out the door with Priya.

Transitions between home and school can be stressful for everyone. Successful partnerships between families and caregivers are essential. Families place enormous trust in you while they are working. The Desais are lucky to have a center close to home and two parents who can take turns at drop-off and pickup. Ms. Tejal taught Priya in her classroom before Daryia. This continuity provides security for the girls. But for many families, finding high-quality care close to home can be a challenge.

FAST FACTS: WHY THIS WORKS

Knowing What Families Need

Infant and toddler care have changed greatly over the last forty years. In decades past, mothers cared for most toddlers at home. By the mid-2000s, fewer than half of infants and toddlers were cared for exclusively at home. Most toddlers received part- or full-time care in settings outside the home (Laughlin 2010). By 2011, 88 percent of the 10.9 million preschoolers of employed mothers were in at least one child care arrangement (Laughlin 2013).

Toddler teachers are part of a growing and needed profession. In the United States, 73 percent of two-year-olds are enrolled in at least one weekly child care arrangement (Halle et al. 2009). Among mothers with children under age three, 61.4 percent are working and are seeking high-quality care (USDOL Women's Bureau 2016). The need for high-quality toddler care is expected to increase, and this demand is becoming a crisis in the economic and social lives of families (Hamm 2015; Child Care Aware 2016).

Defining High-Quality Care

Mr. Martin drops off a large cardboard box in Ms. Peloso's toddler classroom. He is impressed by what he sees. Low shelves hold baskets full of interesting objects, stacking toys, and puzzles. Children play in the colorful room with happy, calm, focused energy. Ms. Peloso is securing a tool belt on a child's waist. Ms. Abby is showing the children how to keep the stuffed animals from falling out of the strollers. Mr. Martin sees how the teachers respond to the children. The teachers notice the intensity level rising and channel the children's energy into music.

"I'm dropping off a box of books donated yesterday," Mr. Martin says. Carlo and James run over and hug his legs. He tells them, "I have some new books for you. I see *The Rainbow Fish* on top." Ms. Peloso smiles. "Thank you, Mr. Martin. I have two parent volunteers coming in this afternoon. They can sort the books. The children and I will enjoy reading them."

When you step into a high-quality setting, you feel a warm sense of welcome and belonging, with children exploring costumes and toys. You notice a low buzz of happy conversation, with teachers encouraging children in their play. This is a positive climate where children's personal needs, traits, and abilities are valued. You quickly sense that to the children, this experience feels like family.

FAST FACTS: WHY THIS WORKS

Understanding Why High Quality Matters

Providing a safe, clean, and nurturing setting for toddlers is not enough. Neurological research shows that the earliest years shape the development of lifelong skills that are critical to children's success (Braveman, Sadegh-Nobari, and Egerter 2008). High-quality settings are rich in interactions with children that positively impact development and learning (Center for High Impact Philanthropy 2014). In addition children need to learn critical life skills such as problem solving, persistence, and self-control. High-quality toddler experiences

▶ directly influence behavior, self-regulation, and learning (USDHHS 2006);

▶ have a significant and lasting positive impact on cognitive, language, social, and physical outcomes (Howard 2015; Weilin et al. 2013);

▶ improve children's school readiness and future academic success (Duncan et al. 2013; Yoshikawa et al. 2013);

▶ significantly benefit behavior, emotional competence, and cognitive development for the most vulnerable children, who can gain the most from high-quality care (Dearing, McCartney, and Taylor 2009; Vernon-Feagans and Bratsch-Hines, and The Family Life Project Key Investigators 2013); and

▶ act as compensatory intervention for children who experience risk factors, because these children benefit most from responsive and supportive relationships with caregivers (Sabol and Pianta 2012).

When you look carefully at what is happening in a high-quality classroom, you recognize a well-prepared setting. The structural components include the physical environment and materials, planned activities, group size, adult-child ratio, space and safety, and staff training. However, these ingredients are just a starting point for children's growth and learning (Slot et al. 2015).

A high-quality classroom also includes meaningful, positive teacher-child interactions called *process components*. These interactions are directly responsible for boosting children's social, achievement, and learning outcomes (La Paro et al. 2012). High-quality interactions foster language skills, increase opportunities to learn, and provide warm and sensitive emotional support.

Shifting Your Mind-Set

We have worked hard to shift our focus from *what* is present in the classroom to *how* we use materials and interact with children to help them learn. We now understand that our positive interactions make good things happen for children.

Creating a Foundation of Nurture

The children are running across the room, listening to their voices jiggle as their feet pound the floor. "Ah-yah-yah-yah-yah!" They reach the wall and turn around, grinning ear to ear, and start off in the other direction. "Here we go!" says Ms. Judy. She takes the hands of Eva and Miriam, who want to join in, and says, "We are making our bodies and our voices bounce!"

Across the room, Ms. Annie says, "Here comes the pancake man. Let's wash up and come to breakfast." She cheerfully asks Mr. Miller, "Did you bring *big* pancakes today for my growing children? Our hungry boys and girls are happy to see you." She begins to help children wash their hands, while Ms. Judy engages the other children in play. Ms. Annie helps the children roll up their sleeves and gives them time to enjoy the soap bubbles and sing a sweet "soapy bubbles" song. She gives them each a big hug before sending them to the table.

As the children come to the table, Ms. Judy asks, "Are we eating carrots for breakfast?" The children laugh. "No!" they say. "Are we eating zucchini?" asks Ms. Judy. "No!" "It must be potatoes!" "No!" Finally, Ms. Judy asks, "Are we eating pancakes?" The children shout, "Pancakes!" Ms. Judy smiles and says, "Mr. Miller brought us *big* pancakes to eat for breakfast."

Ms. Annie and Ms. Judy teach a group of younger toddlers. The group's warm connection is evident. Bubble songs and cheerful meals are familiar and comforting to the children. The classroom has a homelike atmosphere. Each child feels secure with the full attention and nurture of the adults. The children relax into the day, able to put all their attention on eating, learning, and playing.

Daily interactions with you help form a child's self-concept. Your relationship with each child creates a blueprint for relating with others. Your personality traits, such as flexibility, humor, and enjoyment of specific activities, help form a toddler's ideas about what is enjoyable, valuable, and fun.

The warmth and nurture you give toddlers can be life-changing. Your love, support, and acceptance enable them to give the same to others. When you treat them with gentle patience, they are more likely to be gentle and patient with themselves and others. This is how they develop an understanding about love.

Your attunement to children's needs for support, encouragement, and competence helps them feel accepted. They watch your expressions and listen to your words to form perceptions about themselves and others. This is how toddlers develop a sense of worth and security.

TEACHER TIP

Teaching Children to Ask for Help

I tried saying, "If you need help, call me." So when Miles needed help, he shouted, "Call me!" He meant "I'm calling *you*," but he said it backward. Now I tell the children to say, "Help!" or "Help me!"

Even when children experience inconsistency, poverty, or stress at home, your steady relationship can strengthen their resilience. Your consistency helps them bounce back from challenges and thrive. Because of their relationship with you, they learn what it means to feel loved and to be safe.

Caregivers as an Important Source of Attachment

Toby calls, "Push me higher." Mr. Aaron pushes the swing slightly harder. Toby whimpers, "I'm holding on!" Mr. Aaron asks, "Are you sure you want another push?" Toby responds, "Higher, higher." Mr. Aaron pushes gradually harder, making sure of Toby's comfort with each push. Toby laughs. "My feet are touching the sky!" he shouts, wide-eyed and clutching the swing with determination.

Mr. Aaron understands Toby's desire for increasing risk. At the same time, he hears Toby's anxiety. Toby asks to go higher even though he is worried. In the end, Toby's goal is stronger than his uncertainty.

The toddler years are a unique time of development characterized by intense connection and shared emotions while children test their skills and abilities. Children emerge from infancy with a growing awareness of self and others. They venture out with increasing independence but return frequently to a trusted adult for emotional comfort and physical reassurance.

The trust toddlers feel in their relationship with you is essential to their sense of security. Even though they are gaining physical skills, they can't yet manage self-care or social expectations independently. For example, observe the intense focus when a child pulls on sneakers and laboriously fastens the Velcro straps. This determination indicates increasing ability to plan actions and persist to accomplish them. A moment later, the same child may run around the room with abandon and may seem to lack control. Then you will need to guide the child to a safe and engaging alternate activity.

Toddlers may not yet have or be able to retrieve the words to express the way they feel. Tuning in to nonverbal cues is one of your primary responsibilities. By watching nonverbal cues, you can recognize fatigue, thirst, sadness, or frustration. You can step in before distress occurs. You can use your knowledge of toddlers to prepare materials and activities that match their needs. Over time you will become highly sensitive and attuned to their preferences, responses, and unique personal interests.

FAST FACTS: WHY THIS WORKS

Examining Attachment Theory

Secure attachment empowers children to explore their world, knowing that if they are threatened or upset, they can return to a secure base (Bergin and Bergin 2009). Secure attachment requires close connection with a caregiver responsive to a child's needs.

Richard Bowlby (2007) writes about the importance of caregivers as secondary attachment figures: "I am increasingly convinced that this is a fundamental necessity for all babies and toddlers if they are to tolerate daily separations from their parents" (308). Bowlby says that for toddlers to develop into emotionally robust and socially competent adults, they need "prodigious amounts of time and sensitive attention from trusted attachment figures" (308).

Richard's father, scientist John Bowlby (1969, 1988), introduced attachment theory as the foundation of children's well-being. Attachments create a blueprint for children that shows what relationships should look and feel like. The primary caregiving relationship becomes a model of the self as positive or negative. Children learn whether others are trustworthy or unreliable. Research explains the impact of attachment:

▶ Children's emotional experiences with their primary attachment figures shape their brain structures and lifelong mental health (Cozolino 2014).

▶ Attachment relationships profoundly influence development, including self-regulation, language, learning, and social skills (Bergin and Bergin 2009).

▶ Attachment security is associated with greater empathy in children (Panfile and Laible 2012).

▶ A three-way relationship among family, caregiver, and child is necessary to foster trust and security and to ensure healthy social-emotional development (Ebbeck 2015).

▶ Through healthy attachment, children develop a cognitive-affective representation of themselves that influences their relationships for the rest of their lives (Granot and Mayseless 2012).

Providing Security and Consistency

Mathias runs across the yard to Ms. Lauren. She bends and hugs him, leaving her hand on his shoulder as she talks with him. "Hi, Mathias. I loved watching you fly down the slide. You went so fast. Do you want to come help me hoe? We have some weeds in the garden." She takes his hand as they walk over to the garden, where kale and squash are growing. At one end of a row, she and Mathias pull their small garden tools through the dirt. Mathias says, "I am a farmer!" Ms. Lauren responds, "Yes, you are a farmer. You are helping the vegetables grow strong so we can eat them."

When Ms. Lauren stays at Mathias's eye level and talks with him about the garden, he feels her love and respect. As they hold hands and choose hoes, he feels important. Working with his teacher gives him a deep sense of belonging.

When you make children feel safe and secure, you help them believe they are worthy of time and attention. When you introduce new experiences and give encouragement, children feel they are capable of trying. When you share time together, they feel special and cared for. These psychological aspects of your influence are especially important for toddlers.

The toddler months are a time in development when children's curiosity and emotional inconsistency can elicit either frustration or support from adults. In a group setting, children watch to see how you react to them and to other children. Their sense of security or fear comes from the way you respond to their needs.

FAST FACTS: WHY THIS WORKS

Linking Security to Mental Health

The foundation for mental health forms during the toddler years (National Scientific Council on the Developing Child 2008/2012). This is when children are developing the ability to understand, express, and regulate emotions and take on others' perspectives (La Paro, Williamson, and Hatfield 2014). With long hours in child care, children learn these skills as much through you as through their families (Ahnert and Lamb 2011). A predictable, safe, and affectionate relationship with you is essential to a child's well-being, mental health, and resilience (Ebbeck and Yim 2009).

Toddlers who remain with the same caregiver for the first three years experience higher levels of involvement with their caregivers, and their caregivers rate them as having fewer problem behaviors compared with toddlers who don't have continuous care (Ruprecht, Elicker, and Choi 2016). Continuity of care supports attachment, security, and development in the most consistent way. To children, long-term relationships mean that they are well known and that you are invested in their success.

Toddlers also feel safer and adjust more quickly when expectations match. At home, family members may zip children's coats and put on their shoes. You may expect children to try these skills independently. Perhaps at home, children are allowed to walk around while eating, but you expect them to sit at the table. Your communication with families is a key part of coordinated care.

Creating a Positive Emotional Climate

Ms. Nia is sitting at a low table with several children who are feeding their stuffed animals bits of playdough. She notices Malik standing to the side and says, "I have a pan of green playdough. Will you help me make a leash for your puppy? He wants to go for a walk." She puts her arm around Malik and gently draws him closer. He leans on Ms. Nia's legs as he reaches for the playdough.

To figure out what children need from you, it helps to consider their point of view. Everything they know has come from their interactions with adults. Children are dependent on your example, your schedule, your responsiveness, your emotions, and your priorities.

Whether you are quietly reading a book, laughing, or cuddling to soothe a sad moment together, personal warmth is present. You express the quality of your relationship through endearments, verbal encouragement, and shared laughter. This connection is a zone of shared understanding and emotion.

Above all, children want to feel close to you, feel secure, and enjoy the moments they share with you. They watch your face and want to see the joy they bring you. The positive emotional climate you create teaches them that being with others and learning together makes them feel good about being themselves.

Making Common Routines Special

When toddlers experience your emotional presence, they in turn stay better tuned in to you. Toddlers can sense when you are happy and enjoying your time with them. They feel special when you are focused on them. Take time to make the most of common moments.

▶ **Practice smiling.** Children respond to your emotional cues.

▶ **Display pictures of children and their families.** Ask children about family members, pets, and activities they have done with their families.

▶ **Spend individual time with each child.** Caring connections, pet names, and hugs can make any moment special. Keep notes about what children say so you can remember to continue a conversation later.

▶ **Laugh and have fun.** Toddlers laugh almost constantly. They find common noises, facial expressions, and silly games funny. Share in the joy toddlers feel.

▶ **Enjoy special routines.** Good morning songs, "I love you" signs, and endearing names create personal connections. Toddlers remember when you tickle their knee or squeeze their toes before you change a diaper. They laugh at the "skit-skat-skiddeo" you say before you pull a shirt over their head. Repeated words and routines help children feel close to you.

▶ **Practice mindfulness.** Set aside distractions and be fully present with children. Don't miss the special words children say. Notice the details of how children respond to you and one another.

Using Developmentally Appropriate Practice

Lidia watches Ms. Wanda and Charlie playing with shells. Ms. Wanda says, "Lidia, will you help us put shells into the bucket?" Lidia picks up two big shells. "Shiny!" "Yes," says Ms. Wanda, "the shells are shiny." Lidia grabs another shell and pushes it into the sand in the bucket. Ms. Wanda comments, "Your shell looks like a house with a door." Charlie says, "I have a momma shell and a daddy shell." Ms. Wanda smiles and says, "So you do. Do you have a Charlie shell?" To Lidia, she says, "Do you have a Lidia shell?" Lidia pulls out a swirled shell from the bucket and says, "Here I am!"

Ms. Wanda lets the children's actions lead. She follows their play. Charlie and Lidia feel like Ms. Wanda is playing with them as she watches, listens, and asks questions. She uses this play to reinforce the children's sense of belonging to a family by personalizing the shells. Ms. Wanda knows that the way toddlers learn is different from children in other ages and stages of development.

Developmentally appropriate practice (DAP) is a framework for early care and education in which teachers understand the ways children best grow and develop (NAEYC 2017). DAP is the lens through which you observe children and reflect on how they communicate, interact, and respond. You match your level of support, the materials you use, and your interactions to create age-appropriate opportunities for learning.

Toddlers are not merely advanced infants who need a safe physical environment for play. They are not ready for an environment that a preschooler or kindergartner might need. The level of individualization needed in a toddler setting requires attention to detail, sensitivity to differences, and the ability to adjust approaches to meet the needs of each child. DAP requires you to be tuned in to each toddler's level of understanding, physical and emotional growth, cultural framework, and rapidly changing skills. You must be willing to learn as much from children as they learn from you.

Ensuring Each Child's Success

Sofia runs her fingers across the side of a blue feather. "It tickles." Ms. Teri responds, "Yes, your feather tickles. May I tickle your hand with my feather?" Sofia smiles. Ms. Teri tickles the top of Sofia's hand with a yellow feather. "Feathers are soft and fuzzy. Birds have feathers. When birds fly, the wind blows on their feathers." She blows on her feather. "Can you blow on your feather?" Sofia blows and watches her feather twist and wiggle.

Toddlers use all their senses to explore their environment. Ms. Teri is using the sense of touch and natural conversation to help Sofia engage in learning. At the same time, Sofia and Ms. Teri are enjoying a pleasant emotional moment together. Ms. Teri spends personal time with Sofia each day to monitor her developing communication skills.

Experts in child development have established milestones that show the sequence and timing in which children typically develop skills across a range of competencies. The Centers for Disease Control and Prevention (CDC) provides a set of milestones used by educators, health professionals, and others who work with children. These include social-emotional, language-communication, cognitive, and movement-physical development milestones. They are presented by age, and they

- show what children are likely to know, understand, and be able to do during the toddler years;

- give a sequence of skills over time through which children progress;

- provide common language and details to use when you talk with families and others;

- present a format to identify what children can do today; and

- draw your attention to how you can support children to reach upcoming milestones.

Developmental milestones outline the expected range of typical development during the toddler years, but development can vary in individual children. The following skills are listed separately but are interdependent. Each new skill builds on previous skills and capabilities:

- **Emotional awareness:** Toddlers experience intense emotions. At the same time, they are just beginning to use words and regulate their feelings. They express high excitement and delight and intense frustration within a few moments. They are gaining self-understanding and developing a preference for people, activities, interests, and experiences.

- **Personal traits:** Toddlers are developing a sense of themselves as separate from others. Their unique interests, personality, and sense of humor are evident.

- **Language acquisition:** Toddlerhood features an explosion of verbal expression and growing understanding of words and concepts. Children extend their ability to put words together into sentences and more frequently verbalize their feelings and needs.

- **Dispositions:** Toddlers demonstrate an increasing drive for independence and competence as they repeat what they see in others' behavior. They work hard to put on their own clothing or shoes, fit objects together, climb, balance, or open a container.

- **Relational needs:** Toddlers need reassurance, comfort, and security, yet want to take risks and try new experiences. They may be clingy one moment and full of bravado the next. They depend on moment-to-moment personal connection.

- **Regulatory skills:** Toddler self-regulation is just developing. Children need a sensitive caregiver to talk them through difficult moments and help them manage their bodies and emotions.

- **Cognitive growth:** Toddlers are making sense of the world by physically manipulating objects and by watching and imitating others' actions. They build their knowledge daily by opening and closing, splashing and pressing, rolling and sliding, and using their bodies. They begin to see cause and effect and can understand how experiences and objects are similar and different. Their brains coordinate their senses, emotions, words, and experiences.

- **Physical development:** With a drive to explore, toddlers show increased motor coordination and balance. From walking to running, jumping, climbing, rolling, and eventually riding a tricycle, toddlers need safe spaces and adult guidance.

While the sequence of development is predictable, toddlers follow their own timetables. Because of differences in individual needs, you need to know each child well. You must provide activities and materials that support each child's specific skill level.

RESOURCES FOR GROWTH

Developmental Milestones

Milestones provide a common language and framework to help families and teachers communicate meaningfully about ways to support children's development.

- ▶ CDC Developmental Milestones: www.cdc.gov/ncbddd/actearly/milestones/
- ▶ National Institutes of Health (NIH) Speech and Language Developmental Milestones: www.nidcd.nih.gov/health/speech-and-language

---

RESOURCES FOR GROWTH

Supporting Children with Special Needs

When children have special physical, developmental, cognitive, or emotional needs, nurturing their strengths and encouraging their unique gifts makes all the difference. Like all children, those with special needs thrive when you focus on building a sensitive relationship and fostering their skills.

When family members have questions or concerns about a child, encourage them to talk right away with their pediatrician. Regular testing of children's hearing and speech and early developmental screening can help families and teachers decide how to support children's development. Early intervention boosts outcomes for children, as it helps teachers and families know sooner what children are experiencing and what they need.

The American Academy of Pediatrics (AAP) recommends that children be screened for general development using standardized, validated tools at nine, eighteen, and twenty-four or thirty months and for autism at eighteen and twenty-four months or whenever a parent or provider has a concern. In addition the Individuals with Disabilities Education

Act (IDEA) states that children younger than thirty-six months who are at risk of having developmental delays may be eligible for early intervention treatment services even if the child has not received a formal diagnosis (CDC 2017).

Many resources are available to ensure the best possible development for every child. National, state, and local organizations can provide outstanding information to help you maximize children's adjustment and development. The more knowledge you have, the more you can provide the support children need to learn and grow.

- ▶ American Academy of Pediatrics: www.aap.org/en-us/advocacy-and-policy/aap -health-initiatives/Screening
- ▶ CDC Act Early: www.cdc.gov/ncbddd/actearly
- ▶ Early intervention resources by state: www.parentcenterhub.org/find-your-center
- ▶ National Center for Learning Disabilities (NCLD): www.ncld.org
- ▶ National Alliance on Mental Illness (NAMI): www.nami.org
- ▶ National Society for the Gifted and Talented (NSGT): www.nsgt.org

Understanding Daily Needs

Kayden is pounding on a Batá drum. Rachel and Cecilia are whacking the djembes. They are jumping and laughing, listening to the sounds, and enjoying one another's antics. Malek and Tomas begin running in circles around the other children. Ms. Evelyn prompts, "Let's make room so we all can dance. Can we wave our hands up high? Can we touch the floor down low?" The children move seamlessly from running to dancing. They imitate Ms. Evelyn's motions.

Ms. Evelyn recognizes the moment when happy play begins to escalate. She steps in before anyone bumps into a drum or topples another child. She diverts the children's energy into constructive dance. The children are happy to go along with the fun. They have no idea that Ms. Evelyn has saved them from potential harm. To the children, this thumping and dancing is the best part of their afternoon.

TEACHER TIP

Getting Out Energy

When we see there is a lot of physical energy, we set aside our plans and take the children outside to run and play. They love the riding toys, and the exercise and fresh air also help them sleep better after lunch.

Toddlers are developing fast, with new skills often emerging daily. What they could not do yesterday they do confidently today. Once they master a skill, they move to the next challenge.

With fast-moving toddlers in a group, safety is a top priority. Scan the room to anticipate problems. Are too many children gathering in one place? Are there enough materials for everyone to participate? Do you notice signs of fatigue or frustration? Are children wandering? Is energy high and in need of calming with an alternate activity? Your constant attention is critical.

STRATEGIES FOR SUCCESS

Planning Ahead

Planning ahead can help you monitor a group of toddlers effectively while focusing on individual needs. This will help you minimize common issues and maximize success. The following strategies will help you anticipate and prepare for children's needs.

Arrive early. Coming in twenty minutes earlier can help you ensure that your materials and plans for the day are ready. Set aside paperwork and other tasks. Do them when children are napping or after they leave.

Avoid overstimulation. Toddlers can handle intense stimulation only for a limited time. Watch for signs of high excitement, flailing arms or legs, or pulling away. Knowing how much stimulation toddlers can handle is as important as giving them enough physical and mental challenge and activity. Toddlers need a gentle and caring adult nearby to step in and provide an off-ramp when necessary.

Anticipate needs. Toddlers require constant supervision. You must note what is happening in the moment and use that information to anticipate what children will need. Following are examples of balancing responsive interaction with anticipation:

► *Draw children's attention to their surroundings.* "Use your eyes to see if there is space for us to roll."

► *Tell children what comes next.* "We will have a snack when we come inside." "We will read one more book before naptime."

► *Ask what a child needs.* "Would you like to wear your sweater or coat?" "Do you need a drink?"

► *Give guidance for practical needs.* "Your pants are getting in the way. Let's roll them up." "Your milk is near the edge. Can you push it away?"

► *Promote productive engagement by asking guiding questions.* "Can you fit the animals in the dump truck?" "Do you think all the blocks will balance on the bucket?"

Remember that fatigue, thirst, earlier frustrations, or a changed home schedule strongly affect a toddler's ability to handle each moment. What children can handle one day they may not be able to manage the next. You are the only one capable of monitoring stimulation and helping children make needed adjustments. Toddlers depend on your sensitive assistance.

Strength-Based Practice

Mattiya and Simone use wooden blocks as microphones. They sway as they sing "Twinkle, Twinkle Little Star" loudly. Talley joins them, and they sit on the bench. "I'm calling Mommy," says Talley. They hold the blocks to their ears as cell phones to call their mothers. They sing into the phones, "I'm bringing home a baby bumblebee. Won't my mommy be so proud of me!" Ms. Chloe chimes in and helps them finish the song. She asks, "Did you sing to your mommy on the phone? What did you tell her?" "I told her we were singing," Mattiya says. Simone asks, "Where was my mommy? My mommy wasn't there." "I think your mom had to go and help your baby brother," Ms. Chloe says.

Ms. Chloe knows the girls love to sing. She follows their lead. Since the girls remember only the beginnings of the songs, Ms. Chloe joins in to help them sing. She wants to encourage their initiative in "calling" their mothers.

Strength-based practice requires a commitment to communicating plans and ideas in affirming ways. It means talking about what you and the children *can* do instead of what you cannot do. With strength-based practice, you and families work together to find, encourage, and build children's strengths.

SEEING FROM THE CHILD'S POINT OF VIEW

Honor My Way of Being

Honor my way of being. I have my own strengths.
Support my growing skills. I am learning fast.
Build my competence. I want to be successful.
Cheer for me. I want you to know I am here.
Build on my cultural gifts. I am proud of who I am.
Nurture my confidence. I am creative and strong.
Treat me with honor and kindness.
I will live up to the words you say about me.

STRATEGIES FOR SUCCESS

Encouraging Children

The following strategies can keep toddlers from unnecessary frustration and help them experience success:

▶ **Reinforce what is going well.** Frame experiences in a positive way when you talk with coteachers. Say, "I am so proud of Tanya," instead of, "It has taken me two weeks to get Tanya to put her things away." Children are listening, and they will grow into the positive words they hear said about them.

▶ **Use the children's own words.** A young toddler often said when he was upset, "I want to snuggle." When he was sad after naptime, his teacher responded, "I want to snuggle." He looked surprised but immediately calmed down and came to her. Children learn their way of talking from their families, so using family words is comforting.

▶ **Create consistent rituals and routines.** When toddlers know what to expect, they experience less stress. Sing a favorite mealtime song daily, play the same lullaby at naptime, and keep the same order of events before going outside.

▶ **Honor children's requests.** If a toddler says "stop" or "no," honor these words and stop. Say, "Thank you for using words to tell me what you need. Do you want to put on your shoes by yourself?" Unless safety is a concern, honor a child's request.

▶ **Actively include all children.** When a child goes to a quiet area and chooses to lie down with a book, this action demonstrates an active choice. However, if a child is simply standing alone doing nothing, check in. Engage the child in personal conversation and an activity.

▶ **Avoid distractions.** Put away phones on the playground and in the classroom. Hold yourself and others accountable. Both indoors and outdoors, remain fully tuned in. Toddlers' safety and well-being require your full attention.

Understanding Your Influence

"Let's stick the apples onto the cart." Ms. Carin sticks bits of tape on the children's arms. They add their tape to paper apples and stick them to the side of a large box. She talks as they play. "Do you need another piece?" "Here is a long piece. Do we have enough apples on our cart?" She lifts up Joshua as he tries to climb in. "Here you go, Joshua apple. Let's put you inside the apple cart." She picks up Eli and says, "Okay, Eli apple—up you go into the apple cart." Miley sits on the floor next to the box and quietly sticks pieces of tape onto her pant leg. Ms. Carin adds five new pieces of tape to Miley's arm. Miley smiles, picks the tape bits one by one, and sticks them onto her pants.

Ms. Carin knows her children love to play with tape. She hands out little pieces as long as the children remain interested. One of the parents has donated several large boxes. Ms. Carin has made an apple train by hooking the boxes together with a piece of thick rope. She sits on the floor with the children and plays apple train with them.

While this seems like simple play, a lot of learning is going on. Ms. Carin helps the children practice fine-motor skills as they pick tape off their arms. She knows they are practicing social skills as they wait to get tape and make room for one another around the box. She observes the children's persistence and focus as they concentrate on picking up and sticking the tape. She sees they are learning cause and effect as the tape sticks the paper apples onto the box. Most importantly, the children are enjoying a close relationship with Ms. Carin as she touches them gently, picks them up, and encourages them.

To work with toddlers, what characteristics are needed? Your cheerful greeting begins the day for families. They respond to your empathy and kindness. Your personal care for each unique child creates an experience of safety. Flexibility and patience help you be kind and reassuring. Your creativity can turn a morning of box-and-tape play into a rich toddler learning experience. These characteristics are a good fit for toddler teachers.

Your approach to caring for toddlers—whether you are strict about cleanliness or let children get dirty, how much you expect them to help, how you comfort them, how you support independence—comes from your personal beliefs about child rearing. Exploration of professional guidelines can ensure that your practices are aligned with what is best for child development and learning.

The National Association for the Education of Young Children (NAEYC) code of ethics describes a standard of practice that ensures fair and equitable interactions with all families and children. This position statement (NAEYC 2011) focuses on essential characteristics of teachers, including knowledge of child development; understanding of children in the context of family, culture, community, and society; and respecting the dignity, worth, and uniqueness of each individual. It helps teachers recognize that children achieve their full potential in the context of relationships based on trust and respect.

FAST FACTS: WHY THIS WORKS

Recognizing the Impact of Early Care

Your work as a toddler teacher is very important. High-quality care gives toddlers an early and lasting advantage in learning and life (Gloeckler and La Paro 2015). Your interactions with toddlers can impact the following outcomes:

▶ Cognitive and language gaps by twenty-four months are well documented for children from families in higher and lower socio-economic settings (Ferguson 2016).

▶ Children's language skills from age one to two years predict their preliteracy skills at age five (Kuhl 2011).

▶ The majority of toddler settings in the United States are of poor to mediocre quality, with only 10 percent of toddler classrooms rated high-quality in a national study (Child Care Aware 2016; Laughlin 2013).

▶ Across the United States, quality of care is so low that it can harm children's development (Barnett and Hustedt 2011).

▶ Access to high-quality care is limited. When child care services are available, they are often of low and mediocre quality for children from low-income families (Nores and Barnett 2014).

▶ For both center-based and home care environments, the interactions between caregivers and children do not have a sufficient level of social, language, and cognitive stimulation to advance children's academic and social outcomes (Fuller, Gasko, and Anguiano 2010).

Early care settings are not neutral in their impact on child development, especially in the critical months between infancy and the pre-K years (Vandell et al. 2010). Low quality in a toddler's relational and learning environment can harm the child's development. Low-quality programs have the greatest negative impact on vulnerable children (Fraga, Dobbins, and McCready 2015). Disadvantaged children disproportionately attend programs with less-educated teachers and lower relational and instructional quality (Goldhaber, Krieg, and Theobald 2014; USDOE 2015). Of toddlers who receive federal aid (Child Care and Development Block Grants), 70 percent are more likely to be in lower-quality center-based care (Matthews and Reeves 2014). Because of these concerns, professionals and policy makers are embracing the need for change.

When you consider daily experiences through the eyes of children, you can understand how they are completely dependent on you. They cannot control what happens at home. They cannot change what happens when they come to your classroom. You are the one who sets the emotional tone. You are the one who can notice when a child needs extra support. As a teacher of toddlers, you are a protector, advocate, teacher, and nurturer. You have the ability to make a lasting positive difference in the lives of children and their families.

———

Quick question: As long as children are safe, why do they need enrichment before pre-K? I thought preparation for kindergarten starts when children are four years old.

Simple solution: Birth to three is the most critical time for rapid brain growth. The language, learning, and social skills needed in pre-K are dependent on earlier experiences. For more information on toddler brain development, see the following resources:

- "Baby's Brain Begins Now: Conception to Age 3"
  www.urbanchildinstitute.org/why-0-3/baby-and-brain

- "Brain Development"
  www.zerotothree.org/early-learning/brain-development

- "InBrief: The Science of Early Childhood Development"
  https://developingchild.harvard.edu/resources/inbrief-science-of-ecd/

———

Quick question: How can I possibly talk to all the children enough? I am constantly distracted by everything that needs to be done.

Simple solution: To increase opportunities for conversation, assign a primary teacher to a smaller number of children. This will support personal and responsive interaction during play. The primary teacher should be consistent in attending to self-care needs. She is the one who will comfort these children during napping and help them during lunch. Over time these children will respond by seeking their primary teacher for comfort and assistance.

2

Preparing the Environment for Play

Carefully chosen and well-organized materials can help you create experiences that meet the unique needs of rapidly developing toddlers. This chapter will introduce easy-to-use tips and strategies to prepare a high-quality environment for play. A bit of planning and creativity will make a difference in children's behavior and engagement. By observing how children respond, you can adapt materials and spaces to create an inviting setting for imaginative play and learning. As you explore this chapter, you will discover a rich variety of activities and materials that will engage and delight the bodies and minds of active toddlers.

Understanding the Impact of Space and Materials

"Here we go round the mulberry bush, the mulberry bush, the mulberry bush. Here we go round the mulberry bush, early in the morning," Ms. Kelly sings cheerfully. The children wave green streamers as they run around the table. Amie and Jack run to the center of the room. Michael rolls under the table, happily waving his arms.

When the song ends, Ms. Kelly reaches for a basket on the table and holds a banana in each hand. "I ate one of these for breakfast. What is it?" Michael peeks out from under the table to see and shouts, "Banana!" Ms. Kelly holds up an apple and says, "I ate one of these for lunch. What is it?" Josiah and Mimi shout, "Apple!" "Yes. These are bananas, and this is an apple. We are going to eat fruit for our snack today." Then Ms. Kelly sings, "Go bananas. Go, go bananas." The children run around the table again, waving their green streamers.

Ms. Kelly knows these toddlers need plenty of movement every morning. She also knows how to foster active movement when space is limited. She pulls out a table, calls it a mulberry bush, and shows the children how to wave streamers as they run around it.

Ms. Kelly layers the children's learning. She uses the space for jumping, running, marching, and practicing following directions. She uses the fruit to teach the children about the food they eat. For the children, this activity feels like play. To Ms. Kelly, it is an activity carefully planned to support the children's physical, cognitive, and social development.

Ms. Kelly doesn't mind Michael rolling under the table or Amie and Jack running away. She knows they will come back on their own. She is glad the children shout the fruit names, because she loves that they feel safe to express their joy. She knows exuberant play is perfect for toddlers. There will be time for quiet play in a few minutes.

Whether your space is small or large, you should evaluate it carefully to plan the best layout. How you plan and manage your space will affect how well you support your group of active children.

Modeling your room on the photos you see in early learning furniture and toy displays or catalogs may be tempting. But remember that carpets are manufactured to fit on standardized looms, and companies want to highlight items to entice buyers. Often photos show spaces best suited for preschoolers. These settings and materials may not be appropriate for younger children.

While you can buy child-size equipment and high-quality learning materials, you can also take many small steps with your current materials and space to yield great improvements. Your space, equipment, and materials need to be safe and well suited to the developmental needs of toddlers. The following tips can help ensure happy and engaged children.

STRATEGIES FOR SUCCESS

Planning Space for Toddlers

Plan adequate space. Toddlers tend to play next to peers rather than with them. They are just beginning to regulate their bodies and emotions in the context of others. A small space invites conflict. Ample space allows freedom of movement and minimizes frustration.

Modify your space for the children in your care. Adapt the suggestions in this book safely to your unique situation. If a child has a visual impairment, spaces and furnishings in set locations are important for navigation. If a child has limited mobility, make sure all materials and activities are accessible. Evaluate and adjust your space as needed so all children have equal access and opportunity to engage with spaces, materials, and activities.

Consider children's perspectives. Where would you go first if you were a toddler entering the room in the morning? What materials would draw your attention and inspire your imagination? Invite children in with child-safe, carefully prepared materials and interesting activities.

Keep a toddler mind-set. Between eighteen months and three years, children need enough stimulation for active play. They need to move freely and run up to fifteen minutes per hour, which adds up to three hours per day (Pate and O'Neill 2012). Each child and group of children depends on your responsiveness to balance active and quiet play.

Explore dual and portable uses for furniture and materials. Larger items, such as lofts, risers, and attached shelves, are secure and stationary, but you can use other spaces flexibly. Tabletops are useful for individual or group activities, while the space underneath serves as a cozy den with pillows or cushions. By using baskets, bins, and containers to carry materials from shelves to an open space, children will have easy access to materials and ample space to play.

Choose multiuse items. Select materials that can be used in open-ended ways. For example, a tub of interlocking bricks can be used as blocks, cars, or pretend food. Flexible toys, such as sponges and small containers, can be used for many purposes.

Shift directions as needed. High-quality teaching depends on your sensitivity and flexibility in response to the moment-by-moment needs of each child. If you notice something works well, note that and use the approach again. When something does not work well, quickly revise your approach to meet the concentration levels, activity needs, and play patterns of each child.

TEACHER TIP

Shifting Your Mind-Set about Space

After struggling for several years with our limited space, we decided to make a radical change. We placed our tables on one end of the room, where we could push them back to make space for movement. We decided our carpet wasn't big enough for our energetic toddlers, so we moved our circle time to the center of the room, where everyone had plenty of space. We began using the space above, below, and around tables for activities. The payoff has been terrific.

Making Small Changes for Big Results

Maggie and Davis roll into the corner of the block area. Maggie pushes herself away with a cloth block grasped firmly in her hands. Davis shrieks and then wiggles away. Ms. Faye is watching carefully. "Good for you, Davis. You needed some space, and you rolled away. Thank you, Maggie, for being gentle. You are good friends. I have a bag of balls. Can you both help me pull them out?" They pull the bag over to an open area. Maggie and Davis pull and tug until the balls roll out.

While the children are napping, Ms. Faye and her coteacher slide back the shelves in the block area to make more room. They place the smaller cloth blocks into a container that can be lifted out onto the rug. They learned from watching the children that they need to increase the space near the shelves.

Ms. Faye has learned how to respond to the challenges her children face. Today she shifts the children into a new activity—pulling balls from a bag. However, she realizes that the confined block area presents another challenge. She knows a minor adjustment can make a world of difference.

A fresh look at available space can revolutionize the way children respond. Sometimes a minor adjustment, such as moving a shelf back a few inches or regrouping a table and chairs, creates a lot more room.

Many teachers store cots underneath a climbing platform without realizing it is a preferred play space for toddlers. The covered area can inspire meaningful play. With a bright awning, the space can become a restaurant. With picnic baskets and stuffed animals, it can become a cave. The following tips will help you make the most of the space you have:

- **Brainstorm with coteachers.** Discuss what works well and what you could tweak for better results. Open collaboration can bring new insights and creative solutions. If needed, call in extra hands to help you make physical changes.

- **Tame the need for storage.** The storage needs of adults often compete with the space needs of active toddlers. Use well-labeled clear bins on higher shelves for your belongings. Store desk accessories away from curious hands in a toolbox or caddy. Tame clutter and keep organized with a to-do basket. Stay a few extra minutes after children leave to organize materials and paperwork.

- **Consider unused spaces.** Make the most of what you have. With colored netting draped over one end of a table, flashlights and pillows provide a cozy area for looking at picture books. Two linked tables can be used as a gas station. A carpet and bright pillows in front of an unused cupboard invite quiet play. The materials can invite imaginative play and be tucked away after use.

- **Modify traffic patterns.** Many classrooms are divided into tiny spaces designed to separate children but that instead increase toddler frustration. Creating a well-designed traffic-flow pattern can maximize a small space and allow freedom of movement.

TEACHER TIP

Making the Most of a Traffic Pattern

I moved the piano, shelves, and puzzle table to the center of the room. The impact was instant. The circular space around the center allows the children to race their cars and push their doll buggies freely. During our active circle time, we waddle like ducks and swing our trunks like elephants as we walk around that center island. I wish I had thought of it sooner.

Creating Indoor Space for Big-Body Play

Harrison balances on a large cube with his arms spread. He jumps off with a loud "Ta-da!" He climbs back up and jumps again and again. Two children come over to watch. Ms. Lee says, "You are jumping so high! Here's a cube for Josie and one for Aerie." She lays the blocks several feet apart. As other children approach, she pulls out a low plastic strip and says, "Here is a balance beam." She laughs as the children step carefully over it. "You look like circus performers!"

Toddlers love to climb, roll, scramble, and jump. They are driven to test their balance and strength. Ms. Lee sees that other children are interested in Harrison's physical play. She quickly intervenes to provide more equipment. The children spend several minutes jumping and balancing before moving on to rolling on mats.

Toddlers need enough space for their bodies to move freely. They are constantly in motion—running, inverting, and balancing on anything they think will hold them. Active play gives children the opportunity to work on coordination, develop sensory integration, and gain confidence that they can control their bodies to accomplish what they need and want to do.

FAST FACTS: WHY THIS WORKS

Understanding Sensory Integration and Movement

Sensory integration is the brain's ability to organize and interpret information received through the senses to use the body effectively within the environment (Bull 2015).

Toddlers touch, see, hear, taste, and smell in order to learn and understand how objects and experiences work (Parks 2014).

Two other senses provide important input for active children. The vestibular sense is how the brain integrates balance, posture, coordination, and equilibrium as children use their muscles and body systems to move. Proprioception is a child's perception and awareness of where the body is in space (Bagdi, Vacca, and Waninger 2007). Author Jan White (2013) suggests that children need active play to learn to move their bodies in just the right way to achieve *what* they want to do in the *way* they want to do it. This gives them control over themselves and increases their confidence in navigating the environment.

Teachers can attest to the level of energy possible in a room of toddlers. Researchers in Great Britain found that an average toddler expends the same caloric energy in a day as an adult who does 250 minutes of boxing, runs thirty miles, or cycles eighty-two miles at twelve to fourteen miles per hour! Researcher Carrie Ruxton (2012) found that a toddler's daily energy is equivalent to six hours of hurdling, six hours of rowing, or eight hours of singles tennis. Toddlers need safe outlets for this energy.

A prepared space allows children to do what is natural—roll, climb, explore, or lie quietly, as they desire. Toddlers need a healthy outlet for their energy. At home, children may climb on the couch, roll on pillows, or crawl under a coffee table to entertain themselves. In a group setting, they need space for their lively play, with riding toys, tunnels, and indoor climbing equipment. Toddlers also need a soft, cozy area for quiet recovery. Children need secure physical boundaries with safe materials—and within these spaces, freedom to play and relax as they choose.

Whether your program has a designated room and time for gross-motor play or you are confined to a single area, you can encourage movement in creative ways. Include the following:

- **Ball play:** Fill woven or plastic baskets with balls of varying textures and sizes. Indoors, children can toss balls into the baskets or roll them back and forth with an adult. Include multipurpose and textured balls, so some bounce and others roll. Include tennis balls, beach balls (deflated for storage), and balls with bumps and ridges on the surface. Balled socks, yarn balls, and beanbags work, too. (*Choking hazard warning: For children under the age of three, avoid any object that fits completely into a choke test tube 2¼ inches long by 1¼ inches wide, which approximates the fully expanded throat of a child under three.*)

- **Empty-space play:** An empty space invites imaginations to bloom. Without props, children may roll, dance, bend over onto their heads, or balance on one leg. In a sunny space, children can chase their shadows or make hand shadows on the walls. Self-guided play may include lying down quietly, sitting against a wall, or whatever suits the physical and emotional needs of children in the moment.

- **Fabric play:** Children can wave, wear, or throw parachutes, ribbon streamers, colored scarves, feather boas, or capes. These experiences invite group interaction, free movement, whole-body expression, focus, and coordination.

- **Riding and climbing play:** A variety of push-bikes, scooters, trucks, and vehicles invites imaginative play and practice for coordination of movement and balance during speed. Push-pull carts and wagons, as well as riding toys, may double as walking supports. Indoor climbing equipment can include a slide with steps and ramp or pillows of different sizes. These activities support balance and whole-body movement.

- **Balance play:** Foam floor tiles invite stepping, jumping, and balancing practice for one or more children. Blocks; low, sturdy containers; plastic strips; or a commercial beam bring pleasure and fun. Children can push or pull child-size vacuum cleaners, brooms, mops, and lawn mowers to coordinate balance and motion. Baskets and plastic containers also serve many purposes, as children climb in, hide under, or use the side as a support for walking and pushing.

- **Soft-mat play:** Indoor mats, soft climbers, soft block sets, ball pits, climbing pads, and large pillows provide variety and safety as children explore the limits of their strength and balance through somersaults and rolling. A soft area with cushions, beanbags, or a plush carpet can provide a break and relaxation.

From one to three years, children add skills almost daily. The equipment and materials you provide in September may not be suitable in January. Over time you will need to keep pace with toddlers' needs for increasing challenge and ongoing support.

Inspiring Engagement and Imagination

The lights are dimmed as the children gather under the palm trees. The trunks are twisted brown butcher paper that climbs up the wall like vines. Large green leaves overhang the children. Mr. Patrick reads the book *I Can Help* by David

Hyde Costello. He makes a high-pitched voice for the duck and a silly voice for the monkey. The children laugh at the giraffe stretching up for the tree, and they all say "awwww" together when the monkey gets a sliver. Mr. Patrick passes out stuffed animals—ducks, monkeys, giraffes, and a gorilla—and the children hug them tight. He plays the song "Circle of Life" from *The Lion King*. Ms. Grace takes the hands of two children who want to dance.

Mr. Patrick and Ms. Grace know how to combine materials and music to engage toddlers in a multisensory experience. The overhanging tree branches and dimmed lights set the scene for engagement. Mr. Patrick shares a short book that demonstrates helping in a way toddlers understand. After reading he responds to their need for movement by offering an opportunity to dance. By integrating all the senses, these two teachers capture the children's attention and light up their imagination.

STRATEGIES FOR SUCCESS

Making Playtime Work

The following ideas will help playtimes go more smoothly for toddlers:

▶ **Demonstrate new materials.** Model how to fit a puppet over your hand and make it talk. Show how a ball rolls down a spiral ramp. Model several ways to feed a doll. Don't limit how children can play, but show appropriate boundaries and safe use.

▶ **Provide multiples.** Keep ample materials and multiples of favorite items so each child can participate. This will minimize frustration and ensure fun for everyone.

▶ **Follow children's lead.** Remember that toddlers have short attention spans. Monitor and facilitate play. When you see that a child wants to move on, assist in shifting to another activity.

▶ **Step in, step back.** There is a balance between anticipating children's needs and giving them time to figure things out. Let children work through momentary frustrations. Evaluate whether the challenge is matched by capability. If a challenge is more than a child can handle independently, step in to give support. Learning to monitor and guide play requires patience and practice.

The following materials and resources represent appropriate, enjoyable play for toddlers. To captivate curious minds and keep active bodies happily exploring, highlight several new activities each week. Observe what works well and note possible modifications to items or spaces. If something is not working, move on to another activity. Consider how you might add to well-loved activities and experiences to extend learning.

Loose Parts

Loose parts are open-ended objects used in imaginative play. Children can manipulate them in multiple ways. Loose parts invite toddlers to explore textures, compare similarities, spot differences, and play in experimental ways. Toddlers may enjoy simply touching the objects. They may line up or stack some parts. They may take objects out and put them back into a container. They may sniff, roll, or look at items through a magnifying glass. A child's curiosity will lead this play.

How can you store loose parts? Attractive trays, wooden bowls, and other individual containers invite children to lift and move materials independently. Woven fabric baskets with handles or traditional baskets are beautiful and invite children to explore. Unusual pouches, pots, and bins engage play as much as the materials held inside do.

Children should have a designated space in which to explore loose parts, such as a low table or a special mat. Light tables encourage toddlers to explore the colors, patterns, and designs of objects. Empty picture frames of various sizes placed on a low table invite toddlers to design shapes with natural objects.

As you collect loose parts, be sure to follow safety precautions. Avoid small buttons and other choking hazards. Never offer batteries or magnetic materials, such as beads or connectors, that can be swallowed. Supervise activities at all times. See the choking hazard warning on page 32 and inspect materials before and after children play with them.

When children are presented with loose parts for quiet play, they tend to play with them safely and respectfully. Even children who are normally rambunctious are captivated by the beauty and textures of the materials. Introduce the following types of collections, and model how to interact with them:

- **tools of all kinds:** tongs, small measuring tapes, wood tools, child-safe lengths of plastic pipe and connectors, latches, buckles, wooden pegs, measuring cups and spoons, small kitchen gadgets

- **natural objects:** twigs, cut branches, pieces of bark, seedpods, cinnamon sticks, spice pods, pebbles, driftwood, leaves, feathers, bits of rope, cork, shells, pinecones, living flowers, dried flowers and herbs, rock and mineral specimens, seashells, fossils, magnifying glasses for visual exploration

- **empty containers and material bits:** spools, old-fashioned clothespins (to place on container edges), muffin tins, small toolboxes with collections of keys on safety chains, lids and disks of various sizes

- **paper and fabric:** cardboard tubes, small boxes, bits of netting and various textures of fabric, ribbons, decorative sewing notions, colorful and beautiful papers for ripping, balling, and rolling

- **sensory tools and materials:** hair and nail brushes, pastry brushes, massage balls, sandpaper, silk scarves, pastry rollers

You can store loose parts on a low, open shelf so children have independent access to them. Model how to transport the items so children can do so independently. You may prefer to provide a loose parts table every day, rotating the available objects. Children will be curious to discover what is new and explore the different materials. Provide responsive support and supervision as they play.

Cardboard Boxes

You can construct individual play spaces, vehicles, and buildings with boxes of various sizes. You will need duct tape, paint or markers, and a play theme such as trains, tunnels, boats, spaceships, castles, houses, tree houses, garages, or farms. Boxes can become tubes for crawling or repair stations for parking vehicles. Toddlers are also happy with a plain, empty cardboard box. They will sit in it or turn it on its side to create a space for playing with cars, tools, or dolls. The possibilities are endless.

Construction Activities

Construction materials help toddlers practice hand-eye coordination and dexterity. In the process, children learn new vocabulary about math and spatial relationships. They begin to add to their understanding of location and size words, such as *up, down, under, above, below, between, around, more, less, top, bottom, tall,* and *short.* Through construction play, toddlers learn how objects move, balance, and fit together.

Keep materials in clear tubs or containers on low shelving, and place them on the floor or low tables for active play. Make construction activities available daily, as they present a variety of challenges and purposes. With new materials, you can model beginning ways to play, and over time encourage the children to discover new ways to use the materials. Construction materials include the following:

- **wooden blocks:** unit blocks of various sizes and shapes

- **classic toys:** Uncle Goose classic alphabet blocks, Froebel block sets, Montessori block and dexterity activities, Waldorf tree blocks, Pratt unit blocks

- **magnetic sets:** toddler-safe magnetic geometric shapes, Magna-Tiles, magnetic wood blocks

- **commercial brick and peg sets:** large interlocking bricks such as Legos, peg-and-board sets, bristle blocks, interlocking plastic shapes, snap beads, stacking peg sets, gears

- **rod and tube sets:** construction tubes, flexible interlocking squishy shapes, pop beads

- **large cardboard, hollow, and fabric blocks**

Ramps and Tubes

Tubes and ramps of various lengths and types make terrific inclines for balls, cars, and other objects that roll and slide. Toddlers learn to solve problems as they experiment with rolling and sliding objects. Their understanding of physics begins to grow with words like *fast, slow, heavy, high,* and *low.* Commercial ramps and spiral towers for balls and cars are available for toddlers. You can buy such ramps and tubes or make them with the following materials:

- Wrapping paper tubes, packing tubes, and paper towel tubes can be joined with duct tape or used independently.

- PVC pipe and other plastic tubing can be cut at one-, two-, and three-foot lengths.

- Wooden cove molding can be cut in various lengths.

- Swimming noodles can be cut lengthwise in half.

- Use sponges, small boxes, or tall boxes to anchor the upper end of ramps.

- Balls, plastic eggs, cardboard cylinders, cars, small blocks, and random objects of various sizes will roll and slide.

Fine-Motor and Logic Play

Toddlers enjoy supervised fine-motor play in brief periods as they increase their hand strength and dexterity. Not yet ready for the challenges of preschoolers, they enjoy pushing pipe cleaners through colander holes or holes punched in plastic container lids. They can press pom-poms through holes into containers. They flip on-and-off switches and fasten buckles attached to a pegboard. Toddlers can begin to use shape sorters independently. My favorite fine-motor and logic play materials include the following:

- **Stacking activities:** Provide stacking and nesting cups, rings, blocks, plastic containers, and Matryoshka dolls for taking apart and fitting together.

- **Logic and fine-motor play:** Toddlers can tuck large rubber bands around pegs on a geoboard to make their own designs. They can match lids to plastic containers. Mr. Potato Head and similar toys encourage children to arrange pieces without one correct form or solution.

- **Magnetic building materials:** Appropriate materials include blocks, sticks, geometric shapes, and train cars that attach. (Check all magnetic materials for safety. All objects must be safe in size and contain no small or loose parts, such as marbles or small magnets, that can be swallowed.)

- **Puzzles:** Include wooden puzzles with pegs for children to lift each piece. Make puzzles with photos of animals, children's families, children, and familiar objects. Laminate and cut each photo into two pieces that children can match.

- **Mixed-materials play:** Toddlers enjoy pushing lengths of drinking straws into playdough. They like playing with pom-poms inside shoe boxes. Funnels, tubes, and kitchen utensils make water and sand play enticing. Children combine objects and play materials creatively.

- **Paper, fat pencils, markers, paint boxes, and child-safe scissors:** Toddlers seek experiences with materials they see adults use. At eighteen months to two years, toddlers may become obsessed with pencils, paint, and markers. By about thirty months, children show interest in child-safe scissors. They will begin to cut using two hands if you hold a paper or ribbon for them.

The materials and objects in this section illustrate the types of activities that can be available on a regular basis. Begin with materials you have on hand and gradually add to them. When you offer at least three highlighted choices each day in addition to regular materials, you will see the engagement level increase. When you present materials attractively, they become favorite activities for eager hands and minds.

Along with featured materials, a range of fine-motor materials should be available on shelves easily accessed by toddlers. Consider what children can handle independently. Keep notes on what children enjoy. Talk with your coteacher daily to review what goes well and what can be improved. Match materials and spaces to the needs of the children in your care.

In addition to having easy access to materials, children need enough physical space to play independently. For example, you should have floor space for block play so children can spread out and build without worry that another child will interfere. You should also have open space on tables and mats for children to play with construction materials. The key here is your own daily responsiveness. Adjust space, shelf materials, and table materials so children are actively—and happily—engaged.

Keep written notes on what works well and what you want to change next time. You will notice when children strengthen skills, use new words, and add to their play choices. As you tune in to how and when children are engaging, you will become more sensitive to what they are feeling and enjoying.

STRATEGIES FOR SUCCESS

Reflecting on Play Support

Increasing quality means reflecting on the best use of spaces and materials. Your reflection will be well worth the effort. The following steps can encourage the most effective use of spaces and materials for play:

▶ **Supervise for safety at all times.** All toddlers need an adult close by, scanning for safety and anticipating what will help them play successfully. Careful observation is essential to avoiding problems and ensuring success.

▶ **Protect space for independent play.** Children need to be able to play independently as desired. Provide individual tubs, floor mats (like yoga mats), or place mats to give children protected space.

▶ **Vary placement of books.** In addition to a book area, place baskets with themed picture books (animals, trucks, careers) near similar objects. For example, place truck books above the trucks shelf.

▶ **Brainstorm with coworkers.** Ask, "How do you think this is going? How can we support play better? What do you think is missing?" Daily reflection creates a spirit of shared learning and makes teaching more effective.

▶ **Look for donations.** Ask families and friends to donate needed items. Visit a thrift store for scarves, bowls, tubes, containers, small baby blankets, loose parts, sewing scraps, children's magazines, and books. Ask local businesses for play and learning items (chef hats, toothbrushes, boxes, and art materials).

▶ **Ask families to share skills.** What interests and experiences do your families want to share with the children? Perhaps parents have professional or work skills they could demonstrate. Families love to share favorite songs, dances, games, and stories.

▶ **Be a constant learner.** Be a keen observer, always learning about each child through daily experiences. Keep a notebook to record observations. Make changes as soon as you see the need to match the developing skills, special abilities, and unique characteristics of each child.

Supporting Socio-Dramatic Play

"Old man rain," says Terrance over and over. "Old man rain." He seems to want something. "Yes, it is raining!" responds Ms. Kristin, pointing to the windows. "We need to use our rain boots." "Old man rain," Terrance repeats. "Oh! You mean, 'It's raining, it's pouring, the old man is snoring!'" Terrance laughs. Ms. Kristin and Ms. Carla laugh, too, and sing the song together. They hold pretend umbrellas. All the children run over. Everyone stomps in a pretend puddle and holds up a pretend umbrella.

Ms. Kristin and Ms. Carla stay tuned in to Terrance. They keep watching and listening until they understand what he wants. He is delighted when they understand that he is asking for a well-loved song and umbrella play. The teachers' empathy and care helps them share in Terrance's delight.

Through play toddlers practice practical life skills and imitate the people they love. They act out the roles and actions they observe. A toddler who watches an adult change a lightbulb or fix furniture becomes obsessed with tools. After a parade, toddlers are captivated by fire trucks and marching bands. After an umbrella walk in the rain, children quickly adapt their play. They watch their family members cook, do laundry, and sweep—and want to be like them.

You can inspire and support socio-dramatic play with objects that are familiar to toddlers. The materials and scenarios you prepare should reflect the experiences, cultures, and abilities of the people in your families and community.

Community and Career Play

Toddlers reenact what they see in their daily lives. They see what happens when their pets go to the vet or when they visit the doctor. Veterinary items, like a bench, short leash, pet bowls, and stethoscope, will inspire pet care. A small wagon, purses, reusable market bags, and small empty food boxes will inspire shopping. Firefighter hats, boots, and miniature water hoses (cut from inexpensive clear tubing) will delight little rescuers. While commercial costumes are fine, a few trips to a thrift store can yield items for costume play.

To encourage community and career play, read picture books about going to the doctor or vet, visiting the market, riding the bus or train, or building a house. Choose stories that depict the life experiences of your toddlers. Children will act out what they see with related props in dramatic play.

Cooking and Homemaking

Daily home life skills are the heart of toddler play. Children enjoy opportunities to imitate their family members and to develop self-responsibility. They may choose an apple and use an apple press, set the table with a mat and dishes, or practice pouring a cup of water. Watering plants, putting away groceries, and arranging spoons in a drawer organizer are activities that build daily life skills.

Kitchen tools are toddler favorites. Small skillets and pans, colanders, sifters, and utensils will be well used. Well-loved utensils include whisks, eggbeaters, measuring cups and spoons, spatulas, plastic garlic presses, small wooden mortar and pestle sets, wooden spoons, spider strainers, and basting brushes. Be sure to include objects that represent the food cultures of your children, such as woks, coffee strainers, and tea sets.

Food containers can include bowls of different sizes, plastic cups and plates, and mugs. While there are plenty of commercial play foods for toddlers, open-ended items invite more creativity. Knitted, crocheted, or felt "foods"—even a bowl of blocks—can invite hours of happy "cooking." Toddlers love to play with oven mitts, dishwashing gloves, aprons, eyeglasses, purses, wallets, and keys. Place keys on appropriate key rings for safety. These represent items children find in their own kitchens at home.

Tools, tool benches, belts, work boots, and work gloves are part of home play. Pastry rollers double as paint rollers as children pretend to paint the baby's room. Mops, brooms, and rags will be favorite choices as well, as children act out cleaning they have seen. Cleaning and work tools can be stored in bins or baskets for children to retrieve independently.

Toddlers act out laundry activities over and over. A hole cut into a cardboard box makes an impromptu clothes washer and dryer. Children will pull clothes out and place them into a basket, dump them out, and wash them again. Laundry play gives children practice in sorting and matching.

You can foster gardening play with gardening gloves, small plastic trowels and rakes, buckets, sunglasses and sun hats, and dirt tubs. This makes terrific outdoor play—or indoors on a low table covered with plastic or paper. Include bits of bark, leaves, small twigs and seedpods, and picture books about gardening.

Dolls and Nurturing Play

Toddlers act out their own self-care skills by washing their dolls' faces and hands and by dressing or rocking them. Include doll bottles, blankets, rocking chairs, strollers, beds, pacifiers, high chairs, and small bowls and spoons. Cut simple blankets from flannel fabric. Represent a variety of ethnicities in dolls and accessories. Add picture books for toddlers to "read" to their babies or stuffed animals.

Dress-Up Clothing

Boots, shoes, hats, scarves, vests, and work-related items like tool belts, work vests, aprons, dresses, and coats all inspire play. Place clothing on small coat racks and low hooks for easy access and cleanup. Install a Plexiglas mirror at children's level so they can see themselves as they dress. Let families and friends know you are collecting hats, shoes, and other items.

Themed Buildings and Accessories

Toddlers begin to "make it talk" as they make sounds and conversations for toy animals and little people. They enjoy boats, pirate ships, dollhouses with furniture and dolls, firehouses with trucks, barns or zoos with animals, train stations with trains, or buses that hold people. You can make buildings for these activities from small shipping boxes or shoe boxes.

Cars and Trucks and Things That Go

With accompanying beeps and roaring sounds, children will find many ways to play with vehicles. Create a simple parking garage out of shoe boxes for cars, and make train station tracks and trains with permanent marker on a yoga mat. Draw roads on file folders and laminate them for independent use with three or four small cars. Of course, commercial sets or train tables are fine, but children are just as happy to play with homemade materials.

Cultural and Local Tradition Play

Community resources expose toddlers to unique cultural and seasonal experiences, and they reenact these in play. In cold climates, indoor snow play can involve dressing a snowman with scarves, hat, and mittens. A farmers' market can involve sorting real vegetables into tubs or making flower bouquets in vases. Reflect regional and ethnic practices in foods and cooking tools, games, music, dances, instruments, artwork, and seasonal traditions. Children may imitate birthday parties and other special events. These may feature piñatas, flowers and fruit, special foods, wreaths, or decorations.

Indoor Science and Nature Play

Living plants, science toys, picture books that show realistic images of everyday animals and plants, magnifying glasses, bug collections, and other natural collections invite curious toddlers to look more closely at the details of living things. Children can add items they have collected outdoors, including shells, pinecones, and other natural objects. Explorer hats, aprons, crayons, and small pads of paper can invite toddlers to participate in play.

Sensory Play

Children use their senses to satisfy their curiosity. Sharing delight with a caregiver over blowing dandelion fluff into the breeze or feeling the crunch of a seedpod bursting in the fingers lights up the brain with both emotions and understanding about how the world works. The list below can inspire you to think in new ways about materials for sensory play:

- **Molding materials:** Toddlers enjoy flattening nontoxic molding dough with a spatula or rolling pin, and pressing marks and patterns with spoons, forks, plastic animals, cars, brushes, combs, cookie cutters, and other small kitchen utensils.

- **Texture play:** Fill small baskets with squares of textured fabric, tiny stuffed animals, teething rings, or beanbags.

- **Scents:** Fill scent bags with lemons, oranges, popcorn, cinnamon sticks, lavender, or other available fruits, herbs, spices, and flowers. Children can help fill the bags and then describe the ingredients inside.

- **Foam:** Use nontoxic washable paint for individual fingerpainting on a cookie sheet.

- **Container sand play:** Individual or group sand containers inspire play with scoops, cups, tubes, sifters, shakers, tongs, spoons, and pans. Hide themed play items in the sand for a treasure hunt.

- **Water tables and individual water tubs:** Water tables and tubs serve multiple purposes for open-ended play. Provide waterwheels, funnels, cups, bowls, sifters, paddles, tubes, boats, cooking items, sponges, and small toys that sink or float. For individual tubs, add bubbles, cars, plastic dishes, dolls, or doll clothing for washing. Rinsing and hanging doll clothing over a line is a favorite activity. Water play with accessories helps children coordinate their fine-motor skills.

- **Helping activities:** Toddlers are eager helpers. They can wash tables with a small pan of plain water or plain water in a squirt bottle, and small brush or paper towel. They also enjoy sweeping, mopping, and dusting. These are pretend play activities that children imitate and take pride in accomplishing.

- **Art materials:** Alternative painting materials such as combs, brushes, pinecones, leaves, straws, wooden stamps, torn paper, crepe paper, soft wire, and pipe cleaners are wonderful sensory materials.

Promoting High-Quality Learning through Play

Abby and Gianna stand on their tiptoes, peeking out the window at the bird feeder. "Red bird, red bird!" Abby chants. Ms. Valeria moves the bench so the girls can sit and watch. "Yes. The red bird is a cardinal. There is another one. Hold still so the yellow finches will come back, too. Look! There are the finches. After lunch we can fill the feeders with seeds." The girls make pecking sounds and giggle. Ms. Valeria drapes feather boas over their shoulders and says, "You can be birds and fly over to your house." She wraps a boa over her own shoulders and "flies" over to get the birdhouse. She retrieves the birdhouse and sets it on the bench for the girls to play.

While the other children are busy at play, Ms. Valeria notices that Abby and Gianna are captivated by the bird feeder. She teaches them the birds' names and introduces bird play with the feather boas. Ms. Valeria knows that the real birds and the pretend birds are all part of the same experience for the children. The girls quickly join in as Ms. Valeria models how to fly with the feather boa.

The materials and space of a toddler room are simply objects that invite play. They become part of high-quality learning experiences when you introduce and connect them to children's interests and needs. Your supportive interaction draws children more deeply into the wonderful world of guided play.

While a curriculum or topic plan can provide a basic framework for themes and activities, your most important role is to follow children's interests and choices. Toddlers achieve new milestones daily. What objects and activities engage their attention? What emerging skills need support? Your role is to evaluate and adapt the spaces and materials indoors and outdoors to meet the children's needs.

As you plan activities, you will continue to design experiences that match your children's expanding developmental needs. Younger toddlers imitate real life in their play. They are focused on their own goals and may not sustain play for more than a few minutes. They don't intentionally interact and coordinate their play with other children. Instead, they work or explore next to each other—sometimes laughing at each other's antics or copying one another—but primarily intent on their own activity.

FAST FACTS: WHY THIS WORKS

Exploring a Framework for Play

Mildred Parten (1932) provided a framework for play that is still used today. Parten's stages of play can help you think meaningfully about what children are doing when they play and evaluate how they interact with others socially (Bernstorf 2012). While theorists do not think these stages are sequential, the following descriptions help you evaluate children's play and provide essential support:

▶ In **unoccupied play**, children observe what others are doing, but do so simply out of momentary interest. They have no particular desire to know about or do what others are doing.

▶ In **onlooker play**, children position themselves purposefully to see or hear everything that is happening. They actively want to know what others are doing and may interact to find out.

▶ In **solitary or independent play**, children are fully focused on figuring out their own play. They have items or toys different from those of other children and do not watch what others are doing.

▶ In **parallel play**, children play separately from but nearby each other. They may mimic actions they see or play with similar toys or participate in similar activities at the same time. But they play independently and are not interested in changing what they are doing to coordinate with others.

▶ In **associative play**, children interact and pay attention to what others are doing. However, the play is not organized or coordinated purposefully. Two children may play next to each other with food items in a housekeeping area, and the social interactions are more central than in parallel play.

▶ In **cooperative play**, children play together in a purposeful way. They work together to organize an activity, and each child may have an assigned role. This level of play requires more advanced language and social skills to sustain.

STRATEGIES FOR SUCCESS

Honoring What Children Need

The following are great strategies to honor the needs of children while helping them create satisfying play experiences:

▶ **Build awareness of others.** Drawing attention to others during play is an important first step in awareness. "You and Karissa both have baby dolls. Are you taking them for a walk outside?" "Tobias, you baked a chocolate cake. Max, you made a vanilla cake." These prompts help children understand that others are playing near and sharing similar experiences.

▶ **Redirect verbal energy.** Rather than suppress loud voices, introduce a question-and-answer activity, such as "What does an elephant say?" ("Ahroooo!") "What does a lion say?" ("Roar!") Alternately, introduce a fingerplay song, such as "The Itsy Bitsy Spider."

▶ **Repurpose physical energy.** Toddlers need a great deal of active playtime. Multiple toddlers together may chase each other, fall on one another, or roll together on the floor. Be sure to provide an open space for them to be active, with plenty of time outdoors for them to run and move. Use music to channel energy for jumping, spinning, and hopping.

▶ **Refocus creative energy.** When children are unfocused and acting silly (blowing bubbles, sticking out their tongues, rolling around and laughing), give them something creative to do that will engage their imagination. Pass out aprons, spoons, and bowls for cooking to make pancakes. Read *Curious George Makes Pancakes* by Margret and H. A. Rey. Dress up as dancers and dance in front of a large mirror. Read *Giraffes Can't Dance* by Giles Andreae.

▶ **Introduce new materials during play.** Introduce new objects in the context of imaginative play. "Let's take a picnic lunch to Grandma's. What can we put in the knapsack?"

RESOURCES FOR GROWTH

Evaluating the Purpose of Play

You can evaluate your activities by considering how each experience directly influences children's development. Think of an activity you have planned. Discuss each of the following questions with your coteacher.

1. **Does this interaction build cognitive understanding and language skill?** Are children learning specific words and new concepts? Do children learn more about how things work or relate?

2. **Is this activity or material interesting or motivating?** Does this experience influence children's motivation to learn or try something new? Does it engage children in personally interesting and meaningful exploration?

3. **Does this activity respect and build physical development?** Will this plan allow for a flexible balance of active play and ongoing opportunities for children to rest and relax?

4. **Is this play, routine, or expectation emotionally safe and enjoyable to each child?** Is this activity going to bring delight, satisfaction, and fun? Will this activity be effective for multiple children to do near one another? Is there enough adult support and interaction to ensure competence and success?

———

Quick question: Are there ever too many choices of materials?

Simple solution: You will know you have presented too many materials when toddlers appear aimless and unable to choose and engage in an activity. Too much stimulation results in overexcitement. You will know you don't have enough materials when children become fussy or bored, or want what other children have. Materials should support dramatic play, sand and water play, nature and science, fine motor, music and movement, art, sensory and physical play, and construction and block activities. Rotate items and introduce increasing levels of challenge to keep pace with children's emerging skills.

———

Quick question: I have a limited budget. What should I buy for my toddlers?

Simple solution: Multicultural dolls, wagons, strollers, fine-motor and construction materials, blocks, and riding and climbing equipment need to be purchased commercially. Make a list of the objects you want most, and buy them as you are able. Add alternative homemade toys like the following:

- A set of unit blocks is fabulous, but substitutes can work just as well. Empty cereal and macaroni boxes that are secured shut; clean, empty cylindrical plastic containers with lids from protein powders; and milk or juice cartons that have been washed and taped shut all form fantastic blocks for play.

- Collect and clean safe dress-up clothing and hats from thrift stores. Buy bolt ends of fabrics for scarves and doll blankets at fabric stores for pennies.

- Collect items for play, such as cardboard tubes, plastic containers, large and small empty boxes, and other loose parts. Make the most of creative substitutes and homemade items for dramatic play.

3

Boosting Learning through Guided Play

The key features of a nurturing, play-based environment are shared conversation and mutual enjoyment among caregivers and children. This chapter introduces the elements of guided play that increase children's engagement and extend their learning. Play themes and age-appropriate music, art, and nature activities meet the creative needs of toddlers. Caring, positive interactions support and enrich learning and are essential to high-quality care. By observing, guiding, and participating in play, you can provide needed stimulation for children's social, language, physical, and cognitive development.

Honoring the Child's Way of Being

It is a hot day. After coming in from the playground, the children drop to the floor and pant. They have had drinks of water, but several children are whining. Ms. Cara pulls out a basket of soft blankets and pillows. She pats the floor next to her. "Time for snuggles!" The children spread their bodies over the cool blankets and pillows. As Ms. Lin begins to read Mercer Mayer's *All by Myself*, Ms. Cara moves closer to the children who need extra support and rubs their arms.

Ms. Cara notices that the children need a nurturing, quiet activity after playing outside. She and Ms. Lin had planned a period of indoor free play. But they can see that the children need a calming activity. Ms. Cara uses the blankets and pillows to aid relaxation and joins the children on the floor.

The book's familiar pictures and words draw the children's attention. Ms. Lin talks about tasks the children like to do by themselves. The children like her simple questions: "Can you brush your hair all by yourself?" The children are quickly absorbed in the reading.

It isn't enough to decorate a colorful room or prepare an interesting theme. Tuning in to the moment-by-moment needs of children requires flexibility. Ms. Cara and Ms. Lin make a decision that best serves the physical and emotional needs of the children in the moment. Their sensitivity to children's cues is rewarded by an enjoyable reading time.

As a toddler teacher, you have taken on a big task with enormous returns. A great deal depends on your moment-by-moment decisions. When you are patient with children's needs, they learn how to be patient with themselves and others. They develop positive feelings about their worth and capability. Considering children's perspectives and imagining how they feel is helpful.

SEEING FROM THE CHILD'S POINT OF VIEW

Depending on You

When someone is waiting for me, I feel valued.
When there is a lap with a hug, I feel loved.
When things are predictable, I feel secure.
When someone reads to me, I feel happy.
When I can move and spin, I feel free.
When I have a place to snuggle, I feel calm.
When I figure it out by myself, I feel competent.
When you cheer me on, I feel confident.

Toddlers are completely vulnerable. They depend on adults to guide their day. They are often woken before their bodies want to wake. They are asked to go to a caregiver when they would rather curl up at home with their family. They are expected to conform to an adult's schedule and plans.

Just when toddlers are gaining control over their bodies, they are often asked to ignore what they want and do what others want. Just when children need predictability to function well, a topsy-turvy plan, a crisis, or a time crunch may interrupt their day. Busy adults may overlook or ignore toddlers' needs. Adults must recognize how their choices influence the way children respond.

Toddlers are wired for a one-on-one relationship with a caregiver. They don't yet have all the skills needed to navigate the social demands of a group setting. When they join a group with other toddlers, they depend on your emotional presence to comfort and help as needed. Establishing your classroom's spaces, materials, and interactions to foster children's success is up to you.

Although toddlers reach predictable milestones, their consistency varies day to day. They may be exuberant one day but clingy the next. They may demonstrate a skill independently one day yet ask for help the next. Toddlers vary greatly in speech and language development. A task one child can ask for and manage, another child cannot. You must remain sensitive and responsive to meet toddlers' daily needs.

Toddlers benefit from an environment designed to minimize frustrations. They have short attention spans and are absorbed in their immediate experiences and sensations, so you will need to apply your understanding of typical ranges of development. These dynamics are important during play as toddlers discover new experiences, learn to get along with others, and attempt new skills. Individual children will need differing challenges and levels of support.

FAST FACTS: WHY THIS WORKS

Exploring the Roots of Interdependence

Developmental psychologist Erik Erikson suggested that toddlers need to navigate a balance of dependence and emerging independence (Erikson 1993). Sometimes they stay within the boundaries of complete security with a caregiver. Sometimes they step outside this protection to take risks and try new experiences. They venture from the security of their caregiver to test their growing competence. This cycle of exploration and reassurance is important to children's growing understanding about their world. As they know and do more, they may need more reassurance. They may fall and get hurt, be frightened by a loud noise, or experience frustration. They will return for a hug and encouragement when they need comfort or safety.

With nurturing and consistent care over these months of rapid development, toddlers develop positive self-esteem and healthy autonomy. They find a balance between taking risks and exercising caution. Toddlers stretch their limits to meet expanding challenges. At the same time, they gain skills to navigate healthy and interdependent relationships with peers and adults.

Boosting Learning with Purposeful Conversation

Aria concentrates to put words together: "Baby. Park." Ms. Jacquie is watching her play. "You are pushing the baby buggy. Are you going to the park?" Aria responds, "Buggy." Ms. Jacquie smiles. "Are you walking your baby in the buggy to the park?" Aria repeats, "Park." Ms. Jacquie adds, "Yes. Your baby is going to the park with you. Does your baby need a blanket to stay warm? Here is a blanket for your baby." Aria tucks the blanket around her doll and says, "Blanket. Baby." Ms. Jacquie gives the doll a kiss and says, "You wrapped your baby with a warm blanket. You and baby can go to the park and play on the swings."

Ms. Jacquie enjoys watching the children's play to see what they are doing and thinking. She knows that children imitate in play what they do at home. She also understands that asking questions and introducing ideas can increase toddlers' understanding. By describing what Aria does and introducing new ways to care for the doll, Ms. Jacquie is guiding Aria's play with a purpose. Aria is just beginning to put words together. Ms. Jacquie is preparing her for an explosion of new language that is just ahead.

A play-based environment requires you and the children to be active partners. Children are free to choose activities, but it is essential that you scaffold their learning. First you observe how children play. You prepare the materials and activities in a way that provides stimulation and engages their interest. As they play, you introduce vocabulary and demonstrate new ways to use the materials. You provide individualized attention and support.

As you share laughter and happy conversation, your interactions may look effortless. But boosting toddlers' language requires deep understanding and practice. Play is how toddlers learn. The following strategies will help you foster learning and boost vocabulary as you interact with children during play:

- **Narrate the child's actions.** Describe what you see. "Your car is rolling down the ramp. Did you push it?" Children may not respond verbally but will do so over time. "How did the car go up the ramp?" Preverbal children and those just beginning to use words will show you how the car got to the top—and how it rolled down. Watching and listening can provide insight on children's understanding. Narration focuses a child's attention on what just happened. It highlights thinking strategies and choices that lead to success. "You put the round block in the hole." "You put the big block on the bottom. You balanced the small block on top." "You walked around Mya's truck." "You threw the paper into the trash." "You worked hard to slide the puzzle into the tray."

- **Describe your own actions.** Language-rich conversation strengthens understanding of cause and effect. "I am opening the blinds so we can see outside." "I put the crayons inside the box so we can find them later." "I am hungry. I will get our snack ready." "I am putting on my scarf because it is cold." "When I put the food in the refrigerator, it stays cold." Describing your thoughts and actions makes your feelings, reasoning, and planning visible to children.

- **Ask questions.** Questions support language and cognitive growth. "Where does the square block fit?" Watch and listen for the response. "In here!" Before a child has the verbal ability to answer fully, you can fill in the answer. "Look. The round block fits in the round hole." As children develop increasing language skill, continue to ask questions. "Where is the monkey climbing? Is it going up the tree?" "Where is your puppy hiding? Is it under the blanket?" "Where are you driving your car? Is it going into the tunnel?" Some toddlers will be able to respond, "The car is driving in the tunnel." Others will say, "Car going in tunnel." Children's responses show you what they understand and can do.

- **Describe the world.** Your interest in the world guides children's attention. Describe cloud shapes and car colors. Stop and listen when an airplane flies overhead. "Do you hear the airplane roaring?" "I hear the *chop, chop, chop* of the helicopter. Can you point to it in the sky?" "Do you hear the *cheer, cheer* of the cardinal? Where is the cardinal hiding?"

- **Talk about feelings.** During play, toddlers learn to understand, recognize, and express emotions. Emotion talk gives toddlers the words to express their own feelings. During housekeeping activities, you can say, "Dolly is crying. She wants a hug from her mommy." "Say good-bye to big brother! Tell him to have a happy day." During boat play, you might say, "Sailor is excited! He is jumping up and down. He gets to drive the red motorboat." At lunch you might say, "Sofia is happy. You gave her a yellow napkin. It matches her shirt."

TEACHER TIP

Getting Materials Ready

It is hard to express what it means to be a responsive teacher. Each of my toddlers is so different. I watch the children play. I pay attention to how they use the toys, and I introduce new words that increase their understanding. Sometimes I need to add new toys or materials. I can plan ahead, but being responsive means I match what I prepare and how I interact to the children's needs.

When you know how to use rich language interactions, you can intensify and enrich children's experiences. You can use beautiful words to draw attention to the sights, sounds, and smells you notice around you. You can lead children into deeper levels of engagement. Your conversations throughout the day are critical anchors for language development and ongoing learning.

Exploring the Impact of Language-Rich Interactions

Responsive, rich language experiences result in greater rates of social, cognitive, and linguistic development for young children (Landry et al. 2014). During the preschool years, teachers can enhance learning by helping children plan and take on roles within play (Prairie 2013). But for toddlers, play functions primarily as a means to practice skills and imitate the ways they see objects used (Shrimpi, Akhtar, and Moore 2013). Toddlers depend on joint attention and positive shared emotions during conversations to boost vocabulary and learn new concepts (Shin 2012). Joint attention includes coordinated engagement as partners interact, communicate mutual feelings, and follow each other's visual focus on an object or event.

Researchers show that that joint attention also includes nonverbal ways of communicating, such as listening and manipulating objects together (Akhtar and Gernsbacher 2007). During play the ongoing mutual activity of joint attention, shared activity, enjoyable emotion, and language positively affects children's immediate experience. This partnered support during play also has a lasting effect on children's engagement, understanding, and language development.

Using Observation to Understand, Document, and Support Learning

Jaden lines up all the square tiles and drives a car across them. He makes car sounds and stays focused even when the other children play nearby. Jaden brings over a shoe box and places all his cars inside, saying, "This is the gas station. I help Daddy put gas in the car." Mr. Tim asks, "Do you go to the gas station with your daddy?" Jaden responds, "Daddy puts gas in the lawn mower." "Oh, he gets gas for the car and the lawn mower. Then does he mow the lawn?" "Yes. He makes a big noise." Mr. Tim takes a card from his pocket and writes down what Jaden says.

Keen observation skills are essential for working with toddlers. Mr. Tim keeps cards with him throughout the day. His coteacher keeps a clipboard nearby. They learn as much as possible about each child and take notes to share with families. They also use the notes as a record of children's progress.

Informal observation is an ongoing, daily priority. You will become a keen child watcher, continually seeking to understand children by watching and listening. Then you will reflect on the behaviors you observe. Your documentation is objective evidence you can share with coteachers and families.

Observation is intentional and purposeful. It gives you the information you need to nurture, teach, and empower each child. Observation includes a focus on each area of development. Taking objective and detailed notes helps you remember important moments. You can document the following areas of growth in a child's observational record:

- descriptions of each child's personality, characteristics, and emotional sensitivities

- unique strengths, preferences, enjoyed activities, and special interests

- accomplishments and milestones

- developmental changes, including new vocabulary and growth in physical dexterity, social skills, and independence

- examples of play and conversations that show what a child understands and can do

- learning that takes place, such as a child remembering an event, expressing ideas, or asking questions

- how a child responds to experiences, the environment, materials, and peers

- special and funny moments

- conversations that reveal a child's unique perspective

- areas of development that need support

Informal records help you identify strengths you want to build and skills that need your attention. As you keep records over time, you become more keenly attuned to small changes. Your notes help you recognize sooner when a child needs more stimulation, challenge, or intervention. They help you evaluate how your current level of support—through words, physical assistance, materials, and activities—is working to build children's strengths. You can reflect on each child's progress and plan adjustments in your approach.

Observation can also be formal, meaning that you set aside a regular, specific time to observe play and document children's development, understanding, and abilities. Formal documentation may include the elements listed above, as well as the following:

- **Anecdotal records:** You can record objective notes that document your observations on a specific date. "Sonja saw that Mia was crying and brought the doll to her. Sonja pushed the doll into Mia's arms. Sonja patted the doll after giving it and stood nearby as Ms. Bixby helped Mia. Sonja's empathy was evident by the concern on her face." In anecdotal records, you can describe what led up to an incident, what happened during the event, and how it turned out.

- **Checklists:** Checklists can capture details about growth over time and be used with developmental milestones to document children's progress in each domain. They are used along with anecdotal notes, photos, and records to capture a child's experience. You can also create a checklist that captures the completion of an activity, or types of activities that are accomplished independently (using the potty, holding a cup, standing on one foot, holding a book without assistance).

- **Formal and informal assessments:** Specific screenings and inventories are available for toddlers that help professionals identify developmental concerns or delays. Ongoing observation, record keeping, and documentation can help you understand children's current abilities and plan or adjust your approaches to boost their skills.

- **Work samples:** With toddlers, you can capture play events and social interactions by writing what children say, taking photos and video of children's activities, and saving materials (paintings, photos of playdough creations, and so on). These documents can both capture what is happening currently and help you compare changes over time.

As you interact with children throughout the day and stay near to observe, document, and encourage their learning through play, you, too, will benefit. You will become more sensitive to children. You will more quickly recognize and better understand what they need from you. As you focus on children's daily progress, you will be able to share their joy and celebrate their achievements.

FAST FACTS: WHY THIS WORKS

Examining the Impact of Media and Technology

Significant risks are associated with media use by young children. The American Academy of Pediatrics (AAP) states that "for children younger than 2 years, evidence for benefits of media is still limited, adult interaction with the child during media use is crucial, and there continues to be evidence of harm from excessive digital media use" (AAP 2016, 2).

The following research illustrates why limiting media for toddlers is important for their development:

▶ E-books decrease child comprehension of content and reduce the important back-and-forth interactions with adults needed to boost language and learning (Reich, Yau, and Warschauer 2016).

▶ Exposure to a television, computer, or mobile device prior to sleeping interferes with sleep duration and is associated with suppression of endogenous melatonin by blue light emitted from screens (Parent, Sanders, and Forehand 2016; Shochat 2012).

▶ Earlier age of media use onset, greater cumulative hours, and noneducational content are significant and independent predictors of poor executive functioning in preschoolers (Nathanson et al. 2014).

▶ Increased media use is associated with lower language skills (Chonchaiya and Pruksananonda 2008).

▶ Increased viewing of physical aggression or media violence—even by toys—is associated with greater frequency of aggressive behaviors (Daly and Perez 2009).

▶ Background TV noise is associated with reduced playtime and reduced child focus during play (Schmidt et al. 2008).

▶ Media viewing for toddlers is related to lower attention function at age seven (American College of Pediatricians 2016).

Restricted use of media in childcare settings is an important indicator of high quality. Technology limitations are essential in toddler settings. The United States Department of Agriculture provider handbook includes the following restrictions (USDA 2016):

▶ for children under age two, no screen time, including TV, video, and DVD viewing or computer use

▶ for children over two years old, only thirty minutes total of screen time *per week* in a child care setting

▶ computer use in increments of no more than fifteen minutes

▶ for all ages, no screen time during meals or snacks

▶ inform families if screen media are used in child care programs

▶ screen time used only for educational or physical activity programs

▶ commercial-free screen time

In addition the joint position statement of NAEYC and the Fred Rogers Center for Early Learning and Children's Media at Saint Vincent College (2012) says that passive technology use and any type of screen media are inappropriate replacements for active play, engagement with other children, and interactions with adults. The report urges that teachers and caregivers prohibit passive use of television, videos, DVDs, and other noninteractive technologies and media in early childhood programs for children younger than two and discourage passive and noninteractive uses with children ages two through five.

Expanding Concepts with Themed Boxes

When Ms. Carin approaches, Ian slides down into his cardboard canoe and waits. He holds the cushion over his face. In a moment, he pops out for a hearty peekaboo and laughs. Ms. Carin laughs, too. "Hi there, Mr. Boatman. I see you are paddling your canoe down the river. Where are you going?" "I am going on a picnic." "Are you bringing your lunch?" "I have a cookie," says Ian. "Here is a banana," says Ms. Carin. She hands Ian the banana, and he slides back down into the canoe.

During play, toddlers test their mastery over their actions. They practice beginning self-regulation skills as they hold still or concentrate to look at a picture book. Ian knows he is in control and that Ms. Carin is waiting until he peeks out of his canoe. He laughs with delight at controlling the timing of his peekaboo and at the look on his teacher's face when he pops out. Having recently ridden in a boat and seen a canoe for the first time, Ian is excited to re-create that experience through play.

Thematic play gives toddlers the opportunity to interact meaningfully with familiar objects. They enjoy acting out remembered experiences. The following four themes can help you assemble props, materials, costumes, and books to make play come alive for toddlers. Most children will enjoy these examples, but the options are endless.

Going to the Beach

The sight of ocean waves, the smell of salty air, and the sound of seagulls mesmerize children. For this play theme, use an ocean sounds recording to calm and soothe. Include brightly striped beach towels or colorful flannel, sunglasses, sun hats and visors, shovels and pails, flippers, and swim goggles. In the pails, place shells and plastic or laminated paper fish. Include a sunshade or umbrella. Children can "swim" around cardboard box "boats" while listening to the soothing sounds of ocean waves. Place individual dish tubs with sand and hidden shells on a plastic shower curtain for more beach fun.

Here are some suggested children's books:

- *At the Beach* by Salina Yoon

- *Beach Day* by Karen Roosa

- *A Day at the Seashore* by Kathryn Jackson

- *Good Night Beach* by Adam Gamble

- *Sea, Sand, Me!* by Patricia Hubbell

Going on a Camping Trip

Toddlers catch on quickly to the fun of camping. For this theme, nature sounds can set the mood for a hike. Prepare backpacks with small child-safe flashlights, camp hats, toilet paper tubes linked like binoculars, and magnifying glasses. Put tree branch sections and four- to six-inch twigs in a basket for making a pretend fire. Create cardboard box canoes and kayaks with cardboard paddles. Books in a basket inside an open play tent will inspire reading by flashlight. Don't forget to sing campfire songs.

Here are some suggested children's books:

- *Baby's Animal Friends* by Phoebe Dunn
- *The Bug Book* by Sue Fliess
- *Bugs* by Andrews McMeel Publishing
- *Curious George Goes Camping* by Margret and H. A. Rey
- *Eyelike Nature: Sticks, Stones, Leaves, Seasons,* and *Snow* by PlayBac
- *Good Night Lake* by Adam Gamble
- *Hands Can* by Cheryl Willis Hudson
- *I Went Walking* by Sue Williams
- *The Listening Walk* by Paul Showers
- *Max Goes Fishing* by Rosemary Wells
- *Wonders of Nature* by Jane Werner Watson

Enjoying Snuggles

Toddlers ask for and receive lots of snuggles and comfort at home. Children in group care settings, too, need many snuggling opportunities. For this theme, use soft Celtic music or gentle guitar, harp, or recorder music to soothe and calm. Provide beanbag chairs, cardboard boxes, or a play tent. Tuck in teddy bears or stuffed animals with blankets, doll-size baby bottles, soft brushes, and picture books about cuddling and love.

Here are some suggested children's books:

- *Carry Me* by StarBright Books
- *Cuddle* by Elizabeth Verdick
- *Eating the Rainbow* by Star Bright Books

- *Families* by Star Bright Books

- *Global Babies* by the Global Fund for Children

- *Global Baby Bedtimes* by Maya Ajmera

- *Hugs and Kisses* by Roberta Grobel Intrater

- *Lots of Feelings* by Shelly Rotner

Traveling

Children enjoy hearing the sounds and music of different cultures. For this theme, try the Putumayo Kids CDs, such as *Dreamland: World Lullabies and Soothing Songs*; *Asian Dreamland*; or *WorldPlayground*, depending on the mood you want to set. Include small travel cases or purses with travel clothing, hats from different cultures, maps (cut a large map into smaller pieces), and wallets with pretend credit cards. Toddlers absolutely love to pack their bags and have money like adults do. Provide multiple travel bags or purses with similar materials for full participation. Cut pictures from travel magazines to illustrate animals and sights children might see in their travels. Provide stuffed animals that match the travel location.

Here are some suggested children's books:

- *Airplanes: Soaring! Diving! Turning!* by Patricia Hubbell

- *Amazing Airplanes* by Tony Mitton

- *Boats: Speeding! Sailing! Cruising!* by Patricia Hubbell

- *Cars: Rushing! Honking! Zooming!* by Patricia Hubbell

- *Chugga-Chugga Choo-Choo* by Kevin Lewis

- *A Day at the Airport* by Richard Scarry

- *I'm Taking a Trip on My Train* by Shirley Neitzel

- *Things That Go* by Sterling Publishing

- *Trains: Steaming! Pulling! Huffing!* by Patricia Hubbell

Peekaboo Caterpillar Tunnel

Connect the flaps of empty cardboard boxes and cut holes in the sides and tops. Toddlers can scoot caterpillar-style through the "cocoon" and pop out to say hello. For this theme, nature sounds can provide a soft background setting for wiggles and wings. Toddlers love to be butterflies with tutus, feather boas, and caps or antennae. Add colorful scarves for dancing and flying.

Here are some suggested children's books:

- *Are You a Butterfly?* by Judy Allen

- *Peek-a-Boo!* by Roberta Grobel Intrater

- *Peek-a-WHO?* by Nina Laden

- *Pop Goes the Weasel: A Silly Song Book* by Annie Auerbach

- *Ten Little Caterpillars* by Bill Martin Jr.

- *The Very Hungry Caterpillar* by Eric Carle

- *Waiting for Wings* by Lois Ehlert

- *Where Butterflies Grow* by Joanne Ryder

Toddlers are just beginning to expand the ways they play. They need the close proximity, support, and encouragement of adults. Sometimes you will want to sit near and watch, and sometimes you will participate in play. Observe carefully and keep a written record describing what children do and say. You can take pictures and videos that document what you see and share these with families. As you plan play themes with your coteachers, you can discuss how individual children have responded to materials. Then you can decide what to add or change to promote needed learning and skill development.

You can maintain play themes for as long as the children find them engaging. When you change themes, prepare the children by reading a book and modeling how to use the materials. Store your old materials in a clear container so you can reuse them easily.

As you think about play themes your toddlers will enjoy, consider materials and books you already have. You may find that families enjoy contributing play props and ideas. Most themes that are workable indoors can work outdoors, too. These themes and materials can add creativity and fun to outdoor time. You will find that imaginative play themes inspire joy and benefit your interactions with children.

FAST FACTS: WHY THIS WORKS

Understanding the Need for Guided Play

For toddlers, play is motivated by the satisfaction of mastering objects and actions and the delight in sharing pleasure with others (Honig 2006). Developmental psychologist Jean Piaget (1951) suggested that through play, children construct their understanding of the environment around them. Researchers Susan Recchia and Jeesun Jung (2013) explain that adults enrich children's understanding by suggesting new ideas, linking play to past events, and making connections between toys. Adults are active participants as they observe and adjust materials to meet children's increasing cognitive and social needs.

Through play, children make mental relationships. "When I push this peg hard, it slides through the workbench hole." "When I let go of the car, it goes around the chute and rolls out on the floor." "When I stack the blocks straight, my tower stays upright." Adults lift children's understanding through cognitive scaffolding, which includes efforts to enhance a child's cognitive development in ways that match the child's needs (Kwon et al. 2013). Scaffolding may take the form of assisting when needed, making connections, asking questions, and extending learning by describing, explaining, and modeling.

Researchers Elena Bodrova and Deborah Leong (2007) suggest that toddlers are limited by their existing knowledge and skills. Their growing language mastery, developing self-concept, and increasing understanding of how objects work mean that play itself changes as rapidly as the child's development. Through play, toddlers practice needed social, emotional, and self-regulation skills.

Engaging Children in Music and Movement

Greyson sits on a pot and bangs on an overturned dishpan with wooden spoons. He makes a lot of noise! Ms. Liz waits, knowing he won't keep it up very long. As soon as Greyson finishes banging, he uses one of the plastic coffee tins as a hat. Izzy and Elle join the fun and hold plastic lids on their heads. Ms. Liz begins to pat the dishpan with her hand in a steady beat and chants, "Let's have a hat parade. Let's have a hat parade." After she has the children's attention, she sings, "I am wearing a big red hat, a big red hat, a big red hat. I am wearing a big red hat, tra la la la la." The children march and laugh.

Music and movement are cornerstones of toddler play. Exploring musical instruments, making sounds, dancing freely, and tapping rhythms are important parts of learning. The following materials allow children to explore making music, sounds, and patterns:

- **Music station materials:** Store hand percussion instruments, such as drums, castanets, egg shakers, finger cymbals, maracas, and rhythm sticks, in a clear container for easy access. Melody instruments, such as hand-bells, song flutes, ukuleles, xylophones, and small keyboards, are perfect for toddlers. Dance equipment, such as dance slippers, tutus, costumes, hula-hoops, culturally diverse dance dresses, hats, and scarves, all inspire movement. Secure a Plexiglas mirror at the children's eye level so they can see their costumes and watch themselves dance and play.

- **Soothing sound makers:** Unique sound makers such as rain sticks, wind chimes, and singing bowls fascinate toddlers. Small bells, gongs, chime trees, bell chimes, and tubular bells struck or stroked with a small mallet make quiet, magical tones that toddlers love.

- **CD collections:** A CD player with a collection of toddler-friendly songs can jump-start group singing and dancing, as well as fingerplays that combine songs and poems with hand and finger motions. Most high-quality bookstores and online sources offer a wonderful selection of folk songs and simple toddler songs. Following is a list of CDs enjoyed by many toddler teachers:

Birds, Beasts, Bugs, and Fishes: Little and Big by Pete Seeger

A Child's World of Lullabies: Multicultural Songs for Quiet Times by Hap Palmer

Dr. Jean and Friends by Dr. Jean

Dr. Jean Sings Silly Songs by Dr. Jean

Return to Pooh Corner by Kenny Loggins

Singable Songs for the Very Young by Raffi

Wee Sing Children's Songs and Fingerplays by Pamela Conn Beall and Susan Hagen Nipp

Wee Sing Nursery Rhymes and Lullabies by Pamela Conn Beall and Susan Hagen Nipp

World's Best Kids Songs by Juice Music

You Are My Little Bird by Elizabeth Mitchell

Music provides an opportunity for exercise, social fun, self-expression, and developing coordination. The following tips will help you engage toddlers in music throughout the day:

- Enjoy interpretive dance to music. Wave your arms like a tree in the wind. Wiggle like a snake. Scratch your ribs like a monkey. Children will do as you do.

- Make up a tune for your actions. "This is the way we wash our hands." Sing with different voices. "Let's sing like a daddy (down low)." "Let's sing like a baby (up high)."

- Play soft classical music during transitions, an art activity, or naptime.

- Omit the last word of any song you sing daily so children can fill in familiar words: "Ee-i-ee-i . . ." (Children will fill in the "o.")

- Use fingerplays and short rhyming songs throughout the day.

- Wear a hat or costume that matches a play theme when you dance.

- Pass out stuffed animals or finger puppets for toddlers to hold while they sing and dance.

- Pass out lightweight scarves and wave them in the air to the beat of music.

- Make or buy shakers to play with music.

- Pass out song flutes, pennywhistles, drums, and cymbals. (Wash flutes after use.) Lead a marching band.

Promoting Art Appreciation

Ms. Ramona and Ms. Madalyn are on their knees next to a white canvas drop cloth on the playground. The children kneel, stand, or crouch next to the fabric. They dip cars into flat containers of brightly colored paint and roll the cars onto the fabric. "We are making roads for our cars today," Ms. Madalyn says. Next to her, Joshua buzzes, "*Brmmm brmmm*," as he roles his car through the paint and onto the canvas. Ms. Ramona says, "Our road workers are painting roads for their cars to drive on." When they are finished, the children dip their hands in pans of clear water and dry off with paper towels. They remove their smocks and run off to play.

Ms. Ramona and Ms. Madalyn are helping the children create their own play mat. They have two parent helpers who assist the children as they dip their cars into the paint. When the paint dries, Ms. Ramona will take the canvas home and seal it to protect the paint, let it dry, and return it to school. The wheel tracks will become roads for the children's toy cars. Ms. Madalyn knows the children will remember the sunny day when they made the play mat.

As the teachers help children create car tracks, they smile and laugh, sharing their own joy. They draw toddlers into the pleasure of self-expression and the fun of activities designed for them. The children's delighted shrieks and giggles show that this experience is just right for them.

If you are currently doing art activities, consider adding new approaches or expanding your materials and tools. If you are adding art for the first time, this list can help you plan activities that are perfect for eager, high-energy toddlers:

- **Plan group projects.** Group projects can provide a happy, supportive experience. Communal art gives children a sense of pride and a memory of a happy playtime. Murals, mats, large pieces of butcher paper, and bedsheets allow for using many media, including paint, markers, and dot and puff paints. The children should choose their tools and colors.

- **Enjoy splatter art.** Lay a white sheet over a shower curtain to protect the floor indoors, or work outdoors on grass. With adults sitting next to children or holding children on laps, the children dip clean flyswatters in flat, square containers of liquid watercolor. They splatter the color wherever they like on the fabric. The children enjoy the physical activity and the painting.

- **Prepare alternate spaces for painting.** In addition to using paper and paints at a table, toddlers love to wear a smock and stand at an easel or wall. Hang fabric from a clothesline outdoors and provide spray bottles and large brushes to apply color. Attach paper to outdoor easels for happy fresh-air painting. The children should determine their own colors and style.

- **Use a variety of sensory materials.** Include many textures of paper, materials, and paint, including three-dimensional materials. Use mixed media: foam paint, dot paint, puff paint, watercolor, fingerpaint, and tempera with sand.

- **Include textured surfaces.** Use markers, pastels, and watercolors on fabrics, T-shirts, drop cloths, egg cartons, tubes, wavy papers, textured cardboard, sandpaper, and boxes.

- **Include fine-motor play through printing, stamping, and painting.** Cut up fruits and vegetables to make prints on paper. Use feathers, leaves, pine branches, pinecones, or sticks to roll, press, or brush paint onto paper or fabric. The children can press cookie cutters, pebbles, and shapes into playdough or molding materials.

- **Create collages.** With glue in child-size squirt bottles, experiment with collage using color, textured paper, leaves, fabric strips, and torn paper. Offer tissue paper cut in circles, squares, and triangles to press onto a gluey surface.

- **Make mobiles.** Toddlers enjoy crumpling tissue paper, which you can hang with ribbons or string in front of the window to catch the light.

- **Increase self-awareness.** Provide hand mirrors. Print black-and-white photos of children's families and provide watercolors for children to paint with fingers over family members.

- **Try body art.** Use large butcher paper to trace hands, feet, full body, or shoes. Press handprints or footprints in clay; make handprint wreaths or thumbprint bugs and butterflies.

- **Paint with alternative materials.** Offer sponges, sticks, feathers, combs, large brushes, toothbrushes, hairbrushes, or cotton balls.

Art materials should be available daily and enjoyed in displays. Each art piece should be unique and reflect the child's choices. Family volunteers are a wonderful source of ideas, support, and energy. Extra hands and lots of patience can plant the seeds for a lifetime of art appreciation.

Activating Nature and Outdoor Experiences

Ms. Alondra tiptoes across the grass with the children. "Look. I see a bunny." The bunny disappears into the bushes. "Where bunny go?" asks Nedra. "Where did bunny go? Bunny hopped away to look for some food. Let's bring our shovels to the garden." The children gather around the garden and squat to dig with their plastic tools. Ms. Alondra says, "We are getting our garden ready to plant seeds. Let's look for worms." "A worm!" Ms. Alondra stretches it out on her hand, and the children gather around to touch it.

On a sunny day, the children help Ms. Alondra in the garden. They drop stones into a large plastic bucket. They help Ms. Alondra carry pails, watering cans, and plastic tiles over to the fence. They are going to plant lettuce. Today they are digging in the dirt and looking for worms. Ms. Alondra knows the children feel important helping her.

Nature exploration and gardening play a major role in young children's learning. Many educational philosophies prioritize outdoor time for children with gardening, climbing, and exploring. Children like to look for bugs, watch butterflies, and spot animals. They like to carry a bench and sweep a sidewalk. They like to collect dandelions and place them in containers. They love to run and catch the wind in their hands. Give children ample opportunities and time to play in the fresh air and to interact with living things in natural settings.

Toddlers enjoy living things. They want to help fill bird feeders. They enjoy listening to bird calls. They can learn the names of familiar birds: cardinal, sparrow, robin, chickadee, and finch. They enjoy watering lettuce, caring for individual flowerpots, and helping in garden beds. They eagerly dig with a trowel and love to hold a bag or basket to collect cut herbs, lettuce, or flowers. Children enjoy caring for a classroom pet, such as a fish, bird, or gerbil.

Pot and container gardens are great places to start planting and growing projects. Read books with pictures of familiar plants and gardening activities. If safe spaces are available, a walk outside or to a local park can give children an opportunity to explore and play with objects they find, such as leaves, sticks, pebbles, flowers, and bark. Provide children with plastic pails or containers to store their treasures.

The benefits of fresh air and hearty exercise can inspire your planning. Outdoor play increases toddlers' natural motivation and their joy of discovery. The following equipment and materials can help you foster rich outdoor experiences:

- **Outdoor equipment:** To encourage active play, outdoor areas for toddlers can include swings, slopes, steps, slides, and a range of surfaces. Rocking, climbing, and balancing equipment should be toddler-safe and well kept. Adults must remain close by to assist and encourage. Opportunities to jump and run freely and to pull on bars and ropes or spin around a pole invite active participation.

- **Outdoor safety:** All outdoor equipment must meet all federal and state guidelines for safety, including separate areas for children of specific ages. The American Society for Testing and Materials (ASTM) provides standards that are part of state child care licensing and require adequate cushioning and fall zones on surfaces, as well as appropriate height and maintenance of equipment. Following the detailed regulations helps ensure the safety of young children during equipment use. In addition to ensuring equipment, surface, and boundary safety, you must carefully supervise children at all times.

- **Outdoor materials:** Outdoor spaces allow flexible use of play materials. Outdoor water and sand tables can contain scoops, trowels, sifters, colanders, cups, waterwheels, and floating toys. Sandboxes should provide a variety of digging, stacking, and molding tools. Other outdoor projects are water buckets with paintbrushes for use on outside walls, sidewalk chalk, and nontoxic bubbles. Riding vehicles, scooters, and wagons can be present for active physical play, along with a variety of hoops and balls.

STRATEGIES FOR SUCCESS

Following Children's Lead

As you consider how hands-on themed play, music, art, and nature play can inspire engagement, the following steps can help you make the most of your time:

▶ **Stay at children's eye level.** As you interact with children, consider their perspective. Get on their level to listen and talk. Positive emotional connections are as important as learning interactions.

▶ **Follow children's interests.** If a child is fascinated by insects, add a bug catcher and a magnifying glass to outdoor play. Encourage the interest with a picture book about bugs, and look together for bugs under rocks and on trees.

▶ **Enjoy real-life experiences.** Toddlers' play reflects their life experiences. Building a simple bird feeder platform suspended from a wire can help children understand how tools work. Watching a dog groomer brush a pet will inspire stuffed animal play for weeks to come. A walk to collect leaves creates meaning when the children later play with those leaves.

▶ **Join in the fun.** Toddlers like and need to interact with caring adults. Enjoy the fun of rolling a ball, throwing beanbags, and playing ring toss.

Toddlers learn in the context of their own lively exploration and enthusiastic activity. Your job is to enrich their art, music, nature, and language experiences to delight their senses and let them feel the joy of discovery. The quality of materials and your modeling, support, and conversation matter.

Over time you will learn how to step back and notice the details of children's play. What interests them? Are they smelling or touching? Are they curious about how something works? What unique understanding do they bring to their experience? Most importantly, how is this playtime encouraging children's confidence and pride in their accomplishments?

Guided play fosters child-centered choice and discovery. You stay nearby at all times to supervise safety and to enhance learning. Your close proximity to children also opens a world of learning for you. You will discover increasingly effective ways to help toddlers grow and learn through play.

RESOURCES FOR GROWTH

Creating a Learning Plan

A daily learning plan will help you prepare high-quality experiences. You can use the plan to prepare adaptations for children with special needs and support for dual-language learners (see chapter 7). Include a purpose, plan, and materials list for the following:

▶ dramatic play themes

▶ music, movement, puppets, and fingerplays

▶ social and emotional learning

▶ age-appropriate circle activities

▶ tabletop activities and themed play

▶ books for child exploration and interactive reading

▶ math, science, and nature play; fine- and gross-motor activities; creative arts and sensory exploration; sand and water play; and outdoor learning

It is not the presence of materials alone, but how you encourage and support children's engagement that brings learning to life. A detailed plan will help you prepare for a successful teaching experience.

———

Quick question: Is it too early to teach STEM (Science, Technology, Engineering, and Math) to my two-year-olds?

Simple solution: While toddlers are too young for formal STEM training, they love to feel the textures and sizes of container lids or use them to smooth foam or sand onto a tray. They see the designs take shape and begin to put words to them: "round and round," "smooth," and "soft." Exploration builds understanding about how things work. Counting familiar objects, fingers, children, and play materials, and talking about numbers and number words (*more, less, bigger, smaller*) during activities builds children's math understanding. Toddlers love to roll balls down a slide or ramp. By providing a variety of experiences with loose parts, ramps, blocks, fine-motor play, and art materials, everyday activities bring STEM concepts to life.

———

Quick question: We can't seem to coordinate what the children do outdoors, and it ends up feeling like wasted time instead of an opportunity to connect. How can we use our outdoor time more constructively?

Simple solution: Outdoor time is as important as indoor time for interaction and learning. Give your full attention to the children and encourage what they enjoy. Many activities can enrich outdoor play:

- Organize a circle game or dance together.

- Introduce strollers and dolls and "take the babies for a walk."

- Create opportunities to "go camping" with a tipi, open tent, or fort by anchoring a blanket on a tree and securing it to the ground with pegs.

- Create an obstacle course with cones or boxes. Model how to run around them, and children will quickly follow.

- Show children how to jump in and out of a hula-hoop lying on the ground.

- Play modified field hockey with paper towel tubes as sticks and soft balls provided for each child.

- Play "fetch." Throw balled socks for the "puppies" (children) to bring back to you.

4

Setting Positive Routines and Expectations

Predictable routines and expectations can influence toddlers' experiences throughout the day. This chapter introduces effective strategies for morning routines, dressing and diapering, toilet training, mealtimes, and napping. Your sensitivity and caring during daily self-care routines and activities foster toddlers' positive self-concept and growing competence. Your consistent daily patterns and interactions create warm relationships and trust.

Ensuring Positive Morning Routines

Tyisha's dad carries her into the room on one hip. Teddy bear, blanket, and backpack spill from his other arm. He smiles at Ms. Rachel and says, "Bear helped us bring Momma to the train this morning." Ms. Rachel reaches for the blanket and backpack to lighten his load. She smiles at Tyisha and tickles Bear on the head. "Are Daddy and Bear going to read with you?" Tyisha's dad responds, "We'll read until Daddy says good-bye." They read for a few minutes before hugging good-bye and blowing kisses.

During this morning routine, greetings and hugs are exchanged. Ms. Rachel makes eyes contact and connects personally with each child. She helps with coats, shoes, and belongings. These moments teach one of the most important lessons of the day. Feeling loved and secure during drop-off routines helps children feel safe as they make the transition from home to a group setting.

A positive morning routine has significant benefits. Children feel confident that adults are tuned in and ensuring their safety. Family members feel valued as partners in the care of their children. Teachers feel authentic affection and regard. A positive morning routine creates an essential relational bridge.

The word *family* is similar to the word *familiar*. In the safety of familiar others at home, children learn what intimacy feels like. They form deep roots of identity. The way children are treated and the words they hear build their understanding about how relationships work. In the same way, a secure morning welcome builds trust between families and teachers and helps children feel at home.

The first fifteen minutes of the day offer a golden opportunity to connect with and nurture children. A seamless transition from home to group setting requires commitment and planning. The following approaches will help you provide the essentials of nurturing care:

- **Smile.** Children watch for your recognition and joy when you see them. Research shows that this positive emotional connection relaxes and comforts children (McCrory, De Brito, and Viding 2010).

- **Make it personal.** Make eye contact, get on the child's level, and give your complete attention. "I have been waiting for you to come. I have a special book about camping for you today." "I cut out a beautiful photo of a horse last night for you. I know you love the horse book, and I have it here for you to read."

- **Notice the details.** "I love your purple bunny. Is she having breakfast with you today?" "I like your firefighter sweater. Are you a firefighter today?"

- **Invite families in.** "Maddie would love to read a book with you." "The nature and science area has new seedpods that we gathered outdoors yesterday. George can show them to you." "Would you like to put together the new giraffe puzzle with Ethan?"

- **Demonstrate that you value families' input.** "Would it work best for me to call you during naptime?" "Would you like us to leave Hannah's sweater on while she sleeps?" "Would it work best to keep the papers until you come back?" Let families know in small ways that you want to make things "best" for them.

- **Strengthen the relationship between families and children.** "Shoshana is lucky to have you as her mom. She can't wait to see you and spend time with you this afternoon." "I notice that Andrew laughs just like you. I love how his face lights up when you come." "Joelle is your little shadow. She says, 'Here, honey!' just like you do when she hands me things."

- **Say a cheerful good-bye.** "Have a happy day!" is a wonderful phrase that toddlers quickly pick up. They will join you in saying, "Have a happy day!" to their family members. Words matter. A positive send-off creates lasting reassurance that children are happy, too.

When play activities are ready and waiting, families can see the planning and care that you have invested. They learn about the kind of day their child will enjoy. Children are drawn to activities that invite them to explore. This is a time to engage children's brains and bodies and to set the tone for the day. The following activities are perfect to jump-start a fabulous day for toddler exploration and learning:

- **Engage through learning themes.** If you are teaching children about owls, prepare a table with picture books about owls. Include wooden bowls with feathers, a stuffed owl, owl photos, beautiful colored images, crayons, and paper.

- **Promote sensory awareness.** Offer a variety of tactile experiences, such as multisensory balls, squishy fidget toys, or foam play. Prepare a smelling table with bowls of bright citrus fruits and cinnamon sticks. Offer bubble play with soap bubble jars and bubble tubs. Introduce beautiful textile pieces, such as lace, satin, velvet, and textured fabric, with small leather or silk pouches. Prepare a bowl of fluffy powder puffs, soft powder brushes, and satin ribbons, and talk with children about the textures. "The silk is smooth and shiny." "The brush is soft and fluffy."

- **Provide a daily art table and easels.** Toddlers love to start the day painting with a family member.

- **Prepare enticing tabletop activities.** Provide multiple learning games and fine-motor materials. Curious hands can explore playdough with rollers, cookie cutters, and molds. Sorting activities with animals, shapes, and designs activate thinking. Activity boards with large zippers, Velcro tabs, and buckles invite daily life practice for little hands.

- **Refresh the items in your sand and water table.** Prepare new items daily, with objects to sort and utensils that pour and sift. Rotate themes for sand and water play to match your teaching. For example, shift from fish, seashells, shovels, and other beach items to cooking utensils, worms and insects, or tool play.

- **Offer special activities that families can do with children.** Family members may want to join children at a puzzle table or a sorting activity. Special projects that involve families can include tracing children's hands or feet, stringing beads, creating a collage, or printing with natural objects (potatoes, vegetables, pinecones, or leaves).

Planning a Predictable Schedule

"We are making a parade," sings Mr. Tony. "Around the park we go." Toby pulls the telephone by its string and walks backward. Maggy pulls a long tape measure behind her like a puppy. Kamile pulls a tiny green dinosaur on wheels by a leash. Only Diyari has a traditional toddler push wagon—with two dolls inserted into the handles. Mr. Tony picks up his feet and marches deliberately. The children copy him without prompting. "We are marching to the zoo to see the lions roaring. What other animals will we see? We will see a giraffe eating leaves. We will see a walrus swimming."

Across the room, Ms. Lacey has taped large pieces of colored paper to the floor. Several children are rubbing chalk onto the paper. Ms. Lacey sits next to them and points out Mr. Tony's parade. "Diyari is walking her babies. Do you see?" "I think Mr. Tony is taking everyone to the zoo. We can draw zoo animals with chalk."

Mr. Tony and Ms. Lacey have moved their outdoor time indoors because it is raining. They have planned this time well. The children shriek and laugh as Mr. Tony quickly switches directions. After the parade, Mr. Tony reads a zoo book under a tent, which is a camouflage-patterned sheet held up by hooks on the wall. Several children choose to sit with him, while others jump over hoops and roll over large soft blocks on a mat. The children enjoy plenty of active play. Then they take a break to draw with the chalk.

If you were to visit twenty toddler settings, no two would have the same written schedule. Programs may start or end earlier or later. Programs in different climates adjust indoor and outdoor activities to the weather. A block schedule can provide a more homelike daily experience while meeting children's need for appropriate learning challenges, language stimulation, and individual attention. You should plan your schedule with a flexible mind-set that prioritizes minimizing transitions and responding to your children's unique needs.

Your schedule may include the following elements:

7:00–8:00 a.m.: *Morning drop-off routines and enrichment activities.*

8:00–8:30 a.m.: *Breakfast.* Mealtime will vary depending on your situation, but it should happen within an hour of children's arrival.

8:30–9:00 a.m.: *Flexible group activity or free-choice play.* For older toddlers, an age-appropriate greeting, dancing, and brief story with puppet and fingerplay activity can jump-start the day. Alternatively, you may use this time for individualized free-choice play.

9:00–10:00 a.m.: *Outdoor gross-motor play.* Fresh air and active play boost children's well-being. Substitute indoor active play when weather prohibits outdoor play.

10:00 a.m.–12:00 p.m.: *Free-choice guided play.* During a well-supervised and purposeful time, children participate in self-chosen activities. Activities include dramatic play, art, music and movement, block play, nature and science, fine-motor and gross-motor activities, sand and water tables, and home and nurturing play. A soft, cozy area for privacy and a book area should always be accessible.

12:00–12:30 p.m.: *Lunch.* Lunch is time to build relationships, foster active conversation, and encourage children's well-being.

12:30–1:00 p.m.: *Quiet time for reading, soft music, and transition to nap activities.* Set out prepared baskets on a carpeted area with large pillows. The children may enjoy "reading" to their stuffed animals before naptime.

1:00–3:00 p.m.: *Nap routine and sleep.*

3:00–4:00 p.m.: *Afternoon transition time for guided group and individual play.* Offer puzzles, playdough, one-on-one time, and small-group reading to meet the needs of your children. Flexible snacktime, bathroom needs, and hand washing are part of this important time of day.

4:00–5:00 p.m.: *Outdoor or gross-motor play.* Afternoon active play is essential for toddlers' bodies and minds. In warm climates, families may pick up children from an outdoor playtime. Teachers prepare for, participate in, and encourage creative movement and big-body play.

5:00–6:00: *Transition to home.* Should the day continue longer, children may return indoors for hand washing and additional play activities. This time can include group book reading, puppets, fingerplays, and personalized interaction.

Toddlers feel comfortable in a homelike setting where other children are engaged in reading, play, or a guided group activity while one or two children at a time are supervised in hand washing or toileting. If you currently use dedicated time for hand washing and toileting, consider ways to individualize self-care routines that don't require other children to wait.

The goal is to create a predictable day yet ensure that you are responsive to children's needs. If the children are all leaning over their lunches, rubbing their eyes, and looking listless, but naptime is thirty minutes away, go ahead and prepare the children for napping. When children are happily engaged in play, give them a few extra minutes. Sensitivity to children will help you make the most of your day.

Toddlers feel most capable and secure when daily routines are consistent. The routines for hand washing, mealtimes, circle times, activities, and diapering must be so familiar that children know exactly what to expect. Predictable and positive routines reduce children's anxiety and increase their confidence.

Keeping Track of Activities

We use a monthly calendar to keep track of our daily activities and support our lesson planning. For each day, we list in detail three tabletop activities. We include an art project; a fine-motor table with sorting, lacing, and puzzle activities; and a sensory table that challenges children's thinking and imagination. For example, we cover a table with bubble wrap, and the children drive cars over the top. They say, "It's a bumpy road." We focus on descriptive words like *fast, slow, around, under, over, across, next to,* and *between.* Our tabletop activities calendar keeps us accountable. The children can't wait to see what is waiting each day when they arrive.

Meeting Individual Needs

Amani is hard at work pulling the doll's shoes off. After several attempts, he succeeds and tries to put the shoes on his own feet. He says, "The doll shoes are too small." "You are right," replies Ms. Isabel. "The small shoes fit the doll's feet. The big shoes fit your feet. Can you put your shoes on?" Amani pulls out the sock wedged between his toes. Ms. Isabel says, "I can see you have on one red sock and one orange sock." Amani laughs. "That's funny!" He keeps working at his shoes until the Velcro is fastened. "I put on my shoes by myself." Ms. Isabel smiles. "You noticed they were on the wrong feet and switched them. Good for you!"

Amani knows the colors of his socks. He has a keen sense of humor and advanced language skills. Ms. Isabel knows that Amani's ability to express himself is not typical. He celebrated his second birthday just two months ago and usually plays with the children who are almost three. Ms. Isabel is committed to supporting his skills. She knows the children in her classroom have a wide range of abilities and need individualized support.

When children are more advanced in development, they may seem to be able to play independently and may look at books alone for a long time. In the same way, children who are quiet or who speak another language may not call for attention. It is up to you to consider the needs of every child and to provide stimulation for growth.

With a twenty-one-month age span, toddlers vary in development depending on their age and experiences. Meeting the needs of all children in a toddler classroom is a priority. The following strategies can help you understand and connect meaningfully with each child:

- **Keep track.** Keep a written record when you see new skills emerge so you can introduce appropriate challenges when needed. Some teachers keep a clipboard, notebook, or note cards. Others use digital apps such as Tot Tracker and Kidfolio.

- **Ask personal questions.** Whether you are sharing a meal, talking outdoors, or reading to children, make your questions personal. When you set the table, ask, "Do you help your daddy sort the silverware?" A child may say, "Yes, I put the spoons in the drawer," or "I help Daddy put the plates on the table." In this way, you learn details about children's experiences.

- **Ask children about their play.** "What is your worker doing?" A child may respond, "I am using my chain saw. I am cutting wood." "I am mowing the lawn." A child may ask to put on gloves. You can ask, "Do you wear gloves to mow the lawn?"

- **Build on individual interests.** Toddlers become obsessed with certain types of play. Provide toys that reflect their interests and expand their knowledge. For example, when a child enjoys tools, provide puzzles with pictures of tools and books that show how tools are used. "The man is using a screwdriver to fix the squeaky door. He needs to squeeze some oil in the hinge. Can you use a screwdriver to fix the kitchen door?"

- **Notice children's level of engagement.** When children become aimless or overexcited, this is a sign that they need a different kind of engagement. Demonstrate new ways to use soothing materials or introduce a more challenging shape sorter or puzzle.

- **Give personal support during transitions.** Successful transitions depend on predictability and personal support. A bundle-up song will keep children focused and remind them of needed steps to prepare for going outside. One-on-one attention is needed when one activity shifts to another. With months of predictable repetition, children will begin to follow automatic routines. However, with still-developing fine-motor skills and emotional regulation, children will need your ongoing direct supervision and assistance.

SEEING FROM THE CHILD'S POINT OF VIEW

Knowing What I Need

I wish I could stay with my mom. My stomach aches. I wonder if she will come back. I am cold, but someone is telling me to take off my coat. I am not hungry, but someone is telling me to eat. I want to be by myself, but someone is telling me to play with other children. Everyone is talking, and it is loud in here. I just want a pillow, my blanket, and a sippy cup. I want a lap and someone to read a book to me. I need a familiar face and arms to give me a hug and help me feel secure.

Nurturing Effective Self-Care Routines

"We got a polka-dot nose and polka-dot toes," says Ms. Heather while changing Jayla's diaper. "We are just a polka-dot pooka-beara girl today, aren't we?" Ms. Heather coos to Jayla, who giggles. Ms. Heather says, "I saw your mommy brought the blue blanket for you today." "Blue blanket today," repeats Jayla. "You are going to have a happy naptime with your blue blanket that Momma brought," says Ms. Heather. Jayla giggles again. "Here you go, sweetie pie. We have your snap snapped and your sweater buttoned. You are all ready to get down." She helps Jayla sit up and guides her down onto the floor. Jayla runs over to the sink, and Ms. Heather helps her wash her hands. "You are all clean! Do you want to go back to play with your bear?" Jayla wiggles down and runs to play, leaning over the wagon and picking up her bear.

Positive self-care routines build positive habits. This diapering and handwashing routine is a sweet time for Ms. Heather and Jayla to enjoy each other's company. Ms. Heather sings a made-up rhyme designed to make Jayla feel special and loved. Jayla knows the routine and runs directly to the sink for hand washing. A combination of predictable sequence and personal connection has created a happy self-care routine.

Toddlers are highly invested in consistent routines. Even small changes can cause concern or emotional upset. When children see you vary a routine, they will correct you. "The cup goes in there." "My shoes go here." "I want my blanket." The daily routines help children feel safe.

To promote self-awareness of the body, you should respect thirst, hunger, and toileting as individual needs. Instead of carrying out routines in a mandated or restricted way, respond personally throughout the day. The following steps can help you support children's bodily needs:

- **Tune in to physical cues.** Notice when children rub their eyes or seem listless or tired. Listen carefully to hear when a child's tone of voice changes. You will become an expert at intervening early to meet children's needs.

- **Narrate what you see.** Narration helps children recognize and describe their needs. "I hear your voice is frustrated. Do you need help fitting the book into the box?" "I see you pushing away Seth with your hand. Is he too close to your body?"

- **Honor nonverbal cues.** When a child pulls away, say, "I see you don't want to be touched now. That's okay. Can you pull off your own sock?" If you are holding a child's arm gently while talking, and the child pulls away, offer reassurance. "It's okay. I don't have to touch your arm." When you honor children's space, belongings, and bodies, they learn to honor themselves and others.

When you are gentle, kind, and responsive to children's physical needs, they learn to be gentle, kind, and caring about their own needs. Caregiving routines are incredibly influential in the way children feel about their worth and dignity. Children who are honored during meals, diapering, nose blowing, dressing, shoe tying, and cleaning up feel loved and safe. So much of their life is involved in being wiped up, cleaned up, and "gotten ready" for the next event. These caregiving routines are the real moments of connection, where personal words, caring conversations, and gentle assurance can make all the difference in a child's adjustment to a group setting.

Connecting during Dressing and Diapering

Ms. Debbie whispers to Daria, "Ready for diaper change?" Daria takes her teacher's hand and follows her to the changing table. Ms. Debbie pulls out the steps, and Daria climbs up, still holding Ms. Debbie's hand. "You have a new shirt. How soft and cozy." Daria responds, "I got a fox on it." Ms. Debbie says, "Yes, it is a red fox. Is he snuggling on your tummy?" Daria answers, "Mr. Fox needs his diaper changed." Ms. Debbie laughs and says, "I will change your diaper and Mr. Fox's diaper."

Ms. Debbie enjoys diapering times because she can connect personally and make each child feel special. She knows her eye contact and personal connection is an important emotional and physical experience for Daria.

Children's bodies are sensitive. Diaper changing, toileting, and nose blowing can represent physical discomfort to children. In addition these are private needs and require physical contact with a caregiver. During physical care routines, children will watch your face for reassurance. They will trust you when you use caring words. The following strategies will help you meet children's physical and emotional needs:

- **Be private.** Ask if you may check a diaper or assist with bathroom needs. Talk softly or whisper in a child's ear.

- **Honor the child's words and nonverbal cues.** Ask, "May I check your diaper now?" If the child says "no," say, "Okay. I'll be back in a few minutes, when you are ready." A child who comes willingly is practicing choice and cooperation.

- **Let children choose their diapers.** This teaches children responsibility for their own toileting needs.

- **When you change a diaper, talk softly and personally.** "I loved your drawing. Shall we give it to your momma?" "Your eyes are so blue, just like your daddy's. Where are your eyes? Can you blink your eyes?" This is a good time to teach body parts. "Let's pull your feet through your pants. Here is one leg. Here is your other leg."

- **Reassure children.** Children may associate diaper changing with irritation. Fear of irritation may cause resistance. When wiping a bottom that is chapped or sore, say, "I will be gentle. I will use some cool cream." Ask families what they say when using diaper cream and use the same words, like *bottom cream* or *goop*. You may need to reassure a child when you first offer a diaper change. "Time for a diaper change. I will be very gentle. Are you ready?"

- **Talk with families.** Find out how they soothe and reassure their child. Use the same songs, games, or routines used at home. Ask family members to demonstrate how they look at, talk with, and comfort their child.

TEACHER TIP

Making Self-Care Fun

Imagine how toddlers feel when someone like a giant gorilla swoops down, picks them up from behind, and carries them over to a changing table. How much better it is to make a child feel special. In our classroom, we say, "Let's go together and change your diaper. Ready to come up?" During diapering, we play peekaboo and ask the children to show us their eyes, nose, and other body parts. We sing a cute bubble song while washing hands. We make self-care fun, and our children love to come with us.

FAST FACTS: WHY THIS WORKS

Understanding the Science of Hand Washing

Hand washing is essential for you and the children in your care. The CDC places hand washing at the top of its list of disease prevention measures. Hand washing is especially important for toddlers, who often put hands and objects in their mouths. Wash hands before and after meals, after outdoor play, after diapering or toileting, and after nose blowing, coughing, or sneezing.

Here are the steps: Wet hands and apply soap. Lather the fronts, backs, and insides of hands, as well as between fingers. Rub hands together for at least twenty seconds, or long enough to sing "Happy Birthday" twice. Rinse hands well under running water. Dry hands using a paper towel and turn off the faucet with the towel. Check out the science behind hand washing at the CDC website: www.cdc.gov/handwashing/when-how -handwashing.html.

Standard health precautions for staff include wearing latex or nonlatex gloves during contact with body fluids, including nose blowing, diapering, toileting, and before giving any first aid for cuts, scratches, bloody noses, and so on. Even when you wear gloves, careful hand washing is required afterward. Carefully remove gloves and dispose of them. Hand washing follows glove removal.

Supporting Sensitive Toilet Training

"Very good, my big boy. Hold up your shirt. There you go." Ms. Elaine helps Thomas gently as he uses the toilet. "I can hold up my squirrel shirt," says Thomas. "Good job, Mr. Squirrel. Good job, Thomas. I can help you snap your pants." Thomas says, "I have a bear on my big-boy pants." "Yes, you do," responds Ms. Elaine. "Mr. Squirrel and Mr. Bear did a great job today."

Ms. Elaine grins. She high-fives Thomas and helps him adjust his clothes. Their positive conversation makes the interaction fun. Training success depends on calm support and encouragement with each child.

Toilet learning happens differently for each child. Readiness depends on more than physical size. It requires maturity of the bladder's nerves. It also involves children's feelings about being wet or soiled and their ability to sense when they need to "go."

"Going to the potty" is complicated! It involves noticing the urge soon enough, getting to the bathroom on time, getting undressed, sitting on the potty, and relaxing the muscles that allow "going." These are the same muscles that a minute earlier, the child used to "hold it." This multistep recognition and ability to control one's body is a big developmental milestone.

Children must experience stress-free potty time. They need you to be respectful and gentle. Toddlers may have emotional concerns. They may worry when they see their poop disappear down a big toilet. In addition loud toilet flushing is startling and scary. It should not take place when children are learning to use the potty. Some children want to cover their ears. Others prefer to leave the room before you flush. Be sensitive and responsive to their cues.

What should you do when a child wants to use the bathroom but is already wet or soiled? Say, "I'm so proud of you for coming to the bathroom. You are making progress. Soon you will be able to go to the potty by yourself." Perhaps a child uses the bathroom but "misses" and gets clothing or the floor wet. Your response should be, "You are making wonderful progress. I am so proud of you for going to the bathroom. Let me help you change." Always point out a child's efforts and progress.

Toileting should never involve disappointment, frustration, impatience, or anger. Never hurry children to go or to wipe, scold them for using too much toilet paper, or express concern about their progress. Gentle support, kindness, and caring interactions are essential. It helps to remember that children are doing their best. They need you to be encouraging, positive, and matter-of-fact.

TEACHER TIP

Cheering Children's Success

Sometimes the younger toddlers show interest because they see their friends using the potty. We let them come in and sit on the potty when they want to. We hug them and treat them just like their friends. We make it fun and make a big deal of their interest. I know some teachers give stickers for children who "go," but we do the potty dance over their successes. The children just love it.

Signs of readiness include staying dry for longer periods of time and showing interest in using the potty. In a group setting, you will find that children often come to the bathroom when they see others come. Stay realistic and patient. Inconsistency is natural. Focus on progress and celebrate success.

Like all aspects of self-care, successful toileting depends on your positive relationships with children. They will enjoy coming to the bathroom when you make it a happy time together. There are terrific resources to encourage toddlers, including books, songs, and pictures—but nothing works better than your consistency, respect, and pride in children's growing maturity.

TEACHER TIP

Tuning In to Physical Cues

Families ask us how we get their children to use the potty. They think maybe we just put them on every two hours or so, but that's not the case at all. We become good child readers. We can see that they need to go when they hold their pants, get squirmy, or just get "that look" on their face. Working with toddlers has taught me to stay super tuned in to their physical cues. When we see that they need to go, we go with them and make it fun.

Taking Care of Nose Blowing

Children may associate nose blowing with discomfort or difficulty breathing. Perhaps someone has squeezed their nostrils too hard or they have experienced pain during nose blowing. Children don't know how long nose blowing will last, and this can cause anxiety. Always offer verbal reassurance. "I can see you need help with your nose. We will be very gentle. We will blow out and count one, two, three, and it will be all done." If the child needs to blow again, stop for a moment and notice physical cues. Before the second blow, say, "Here we go again. I will count one, two, three, and then you will be finished."

Plastic gloves may worry children. During nose blowing (and diapering), tell children, "I am going to wear gloves to stay clean." Ask children if they want to feel the gloves on your hands. Say, "The gloves are soft. They keep my hands clean."

When children need their noses blown, here are the steps:

1. Say, "I see you have a runny nose. Let's blow your nose together."

2. Offer the child the tissue box. Let the child pull out a tissue. This is an important step for teaching independent nose blowing in the future, and children love to do it.

3. With family permission, offer a warm, damp tissue or use a hypoallergenic wipe when a child has a sore nose. Say, "I made the tissue warm so it will feel nice on your nose." Or say, "Your mom says the wipe will feel soothing."

4. Use the same words each time. "We will blow gently, count one, two, three, and it will be all done."

5. Follow with eye contact and reassurance. "Do you want to blow again, or are you okay?" Some children will say, "Again." Others will say, "Okay." This tells children they are in charge of how much help they need. It prepares them to be responsible for their own self-care in the future.

6. Together, you can wash hands and make bubbles to wash the germs down the drain. "Let's wash our hands before we go back to play." When you do this every time, children associate nose blowing with hand washing.

Making Mealtimes Happy

"I got a bulldozer." Mateo pushes the piece of chicken into the potatoes with his finger. Ms. Julia says, "Yes, you have a chicken bulldozer. Is your tummy hungry for chicken?" Mateo persists, "I got a bulldozer." Ms. Julia follows his lead. "Can you help the bulldozer put the chicken into your mouth?" Mateo pops a piece of chicken into his mouth, chews, and smiles. He points to his throat and says proudly, "Down my throat and into my tummy!"

During infancy, feeding is a time for rocking, snuggling, touching, and reassuring. This need for connection and nurturing remains a priority during toddlers' feeding times. Between twelve and eighteen months, toddlers focus on learning to feed themselves and holding a cup independently. They take on greater responsibility as they watch and then participate in simple food preparation, like placing finger foods on a plate. Between two and three years old, they want to help set the table and clean up. These tasks should be a positive and enjoyable part of mealtimes.

Children need a balanced variety of nutritious meal and snack options. Encourage them to decide what and how much to eat—and respect these choices. Toddlers are exploring food textures and may make a mess or refuse to eat. Stay calm and let children own their food choices. Day-to-day variations in children's appetites and preferences are perfectly normal.

Your own food values and preferences may become evident during mealtimes. You may feel the need to control what a child eats or make suggestions to prevent a mess. However, experts warn against any situation in which a caregiver takes control and pressures a child to eat. Adults must honor children's internal hunger and eating cues and support their choices (Pérez-Escamilla et al. 2017). Nonresponsive feeding is linked to poor lifelong dietary habits and increased childhood obesity (AAP, APHA, and NRC 2011). Responsive feeding, by contrast, is a way of responding to the child's cues for hunger, support, and fullness, and remaining sensitive to honor the child's needs and choices (Hodges et al. 2013; McNally et al. 2016).

Positive mealtime experiences can influence children's long-term relationship with food and healthy lifestyle decisions. Mealtime is an important time to show children warmth and acceptance. It has a powerful impact on a child's developing sense of security.

FAST FACTS: WHY THIS WORK

Using Positive Strategies at Mealtime

In a large twin study of 1,921 families, researchers found that genetics was responsible for 46 percent of instances of food fussiness and 58 percent of refusals to try new food (Smith et al. 2017). This suggests that children's food preferences are wired partly through heredity. Most young children show food preferences, and these are likely to continue into adulthood.

The study also found that the most important impact on children was positive adult modeling of healthy food behaviors. When children see caregivers enjoying foods over time, they adopt similar positive attitudes and choices. The authors note that natural aversions may remain, such as dislike of certain flavors or textures.

In a group setting, toddlers may feel anxious at mealtime. They may miss their mothers or others who feed them at home. The smell and presentation of the food, the meal routine, and your words and gestures may not feel as comforting and familiar as those at home. When there are cultural differences, the spices and flavors may seem odd. Unable to explain how or why they feel uncomfortable, toddlers may cry, and you may not understand why. For these reasons, communication with families and sensitivity to children is essential.

One child ate snacks, often choosing a muffin or piece of fruit, but refused to eat lunch for weeks. The teachers assumed the child wasn't hungry. Until the teachers talked with the family, they didn't realize that in the family's home culture, parents feed young children by hand. The child never used a fork or spoon at home. Understanding family mealtime practices can help you better support children.

Share your observations in nonemotional words with the child's family. "I notice that Amie will take a few bites at snack but does not participate in lunch." "I notice that Ronin does not eat beans." A parent can provide useful information. "Yes, at home we sit next to Amie and spoon-feed her." "Ronin likes beans only when they are cut into tiny pieces." Family insights can help bridge the home and group setting and help you make sense of experiences toddlers can't explain.

Providing Support for Napping

Shawna is struggling with her shoes. The laces are double knotted. It takes Mr. Tucker a few minutes to untie them. Shawna says she is hot. The buttons on her sweater stick. Finally, the shoes are off and the sweater is replaced with a blanket tucked around Shawna on the cot. Mr Tucker says, "Now you are ready for sleep.

Do you want me to draw a cookie on your arm or your back?" Shawna smiles, "On my back." Mr. Tucker makes two circles on her back, decorates them with raisins by tapping gently, and tells her, "Time to lie still so the cookies can bake in the oven."

Successful daily naptimes are possible. The nap routine is one of the most important times of day for toddlers. Soothing music, a darkened room, a quiet book, and physical support make this a special time for children to connect one on one with you.

Naptime reminds children of their families and can make children feel lonely. This emotional vulnerability may happen daily or may surface when a child is over-tired or feeling unwell. Remember children's deep need for reassurance, and focus on providing predictability. When naptime routines are consistent, children feel secure and fall asleep more easily because they know what will happen next.

In all self-care routines, understanding what families do with children at home helps. Sometimes toddlers associate napping with snuggling and a bottle or nursing. Sometimes toddlers fall asleep by rocking or sleeping in their parents' bed. Even with different naptime routines in a group setting, children can be successful.

Over time your calming presence, a tucking-in routine, and back patting signal that it is time to fall asleep. When you begin this routine with a quiet reading time, often children fall asleep immediately. When toddlers associate naps with soft music, endearments, and comfort, naptime becomes a time of relaxation instead of worry.

Following are some tried-and-true approaches to get a room full of toddlers to sleep. These skills are not a magic formula. A consistent calming routine creates the best possible conditions for sleeping. Use some or all of these suggestions until you find a combination that works for your children:

- **Book reading:** An after-lunch routine of book reading can serve as an effective transition. Many toddler teachers read a book or tell a story while children are on their cots, and then follow with a back patting routine.

- **Naptime puppet:** A naptime puppet can read a story and say good-night, then visit each cot and kiss the children's cheeks and whisper, "Night-night."

- **Soothing music:** Soft music can serve as a cue for children's sleep. Whether it is the "House at Pooh Corner," a soft lullaby, or another favorite recording, your specific music should be reserved for naptime.

- **Sound machine:** The soft sound of ocean waves or rain can be comforting to young children. Alternatively, nature sounds combined with soft music may become well loved for sleeping.

- **Individual attention:** With a few minutes of focused attention, a child will quickly relax. You can whisper to each child and spend a few minutes with each one. While some children fall asleep almost instantly, others need assistance to transition from awake to asleep in a group setting. Children will anticipate and enjoy this soothing time.

- **Personal comfort items:** Some children want to bring a soft blanket or stuffed animal from home for sleeping time. With family permission, pacifiers are okay for younger toddlers if used for sleeping at home.

- **Laminated family pictures:** Many teachers provide a laminated photo of each child's family to hold during naptime. Children love to take their families to bed.

- **Physical touch:** Gentle physical soothing helps children transition from wake to sleep. Touch releases oxytocin, which acts as a hormone and brain neurotransmitter to help children feel safe and comforted and aids in relaxation.

- **Special good-night words:** Whispered good-night words share your personal care. They are special and meaningful to a child. Whatever words you choose, use the same ones every time. "Good-night, Miss Mary Muffin." "Sleep tight, dreamy delight." "Happy sleeping, happy Noah."

Healthy sleep habits are an important part of toddlers' physical and emotional development and well-being. Be sure your routine is comforting, consistent, and positive. Naptimes will become sweet times of day for children and for you.

STRATEGIES FOR SUCCESS

Patting Backs at Naptime

For each of the following patting techniques, ask the child, "Would you like me to pat your back?" Take into account verbal and nonverbal responses. A child who nods "yes" but wiggles away from your touch has nonverbally said "no." Always honor the child's comfort and permission.

▶ **Hand rest:** Some children fall asleep easily with a hand pressing gently between the shoulder blades—just a bit of weight to help the child feel secure.

▶ **Back pat:** Pat gently between the shoulder blades. Let your hand's weight fall gently into the pat.

▶ **Back rub:** Place your palm between the shoulder blades. Rub with a gentle up and down motion. Alternatively, press gently and rub in a light circle between the shoulder blades.

▶ **Stationary circle:** Place your palm between the shoulder blades. Without lifting your hand, make a small, quick circular motion. The result is a slight body jiggle, like the calming motion a child feels while riding in a car.

▶ **Creative cookie:** "Sprinkle flour" by drumming your fingers lightly between the shoulder blades, "roll out the dough" by pressing and pulling your hand up and down, and decorate the cookie by pressing in "raisins" and outlining the cookie with "icing."

▶ **Paintbrush:** Use your fingers like a paintbrush. Stroke with your fingertips in an up and down motion. Tell the children you are painting their backs with sleepy dust.

Here are some troubleshooting tips for naptime:

▶ **Children can't settle down.** When you notice children struggling to calm down for sleep, increase the frequency and intensity of exercise and outdoor time. With enough exercise earlier in the day, naptime will be a natural part of rest and recovery.

▶ **Music doesn't help.** To boost brainpower, add a classical spin. The rhythms and melodies of soft classical music can aid the transition to napping. Many soft classical mixes and nature sound mixes are available for toddlers.

▶ **A child doesn't go to sleep independently at home.** When a child is used to being rocked at home, sit next to the child's cot or offer a brief lap cuddle before transferring the child to the cot.

▶ **Children need to transfer to one afternoon nap.** Younger toddlers are often sleepy in the morning. Communication with families is essential to ensure a consistent schedule, especially for toddlers who are just consolidating a morning and afternoon nap into one afternoon nap. Try to begin younger children's sleep routines thirty minutes earlier. They will be the first to fall asleep.

▶ **Children want a pacifier.** When younger toddlers use a pacifier to sleep at home, and if families agree, it is important to let children use a pacifier to sleep away from home. Over time children become less dependent on sucking to self-soothe.

TEACHER TIP

Knowing What to Do about Pacifiers

We follow families' desires for children's pacifier use. We offer cold teething rings for children who want to chew. We find that most children give up pacifiers easily when they arrive in the morning, since they know they can have them again at naptime. When families allow a pacifier at naptime, multiples are kept with the children's belongings in their cubby.

Choosing Books to Share for Napping

While toddlers love to have any of their favorite books read to them, books about sleep can set the scene and quiet the mood. Sleepy tots enjoy the following books:

- *Big Bed for Giraffe* by Michael Dahl
- *Goodnight Baby Bear* by Michael Shoulders
- *The Good Night Book* by Amy Beckman
- *Goodnight, Goodnight, Construction Site* by Sherri Duskey Rinker
- *Goodnight Moon* by Margaret Wise Brown
- *The Goodnight Train* by June Sobel
- *Go to Sleep, Little Farm* by Mary Lyn Ray
- *The Napping House* by Audrey Wood
- *Sleepy Time* by Gyo Fujikawa
- *Snuggle the Baby* by Sarah Gillingham
- *Steam Train, Dream Train* by Sherri Duskey Rinker

Using Snuggle Routines for Waking

Jabari wakes up before the other children and brings his bunny with him to Mr. Pacy. He takes a box from the table and crawls onto a big square pillow. "What is in your box?" Mr. Pacy asks. Jabari pulls the lid off and takes out a small board book of *The Little Train* by Lois Lenski. One by one, he lifts out four little train cars. Mr. Pacy sits next to Jabari and helps him connect the cars. He sings softy, "Can your train go up the hill, up the hill, up the hill? Can your train go up the hill and down the hill again?" He and Jabari read the book together. "Where is the train going? The train goes over the bridge, and across the tracks. The cars stop to let the train go by. Who is watching the train go by?" Jabari points to the cow. "Yes, the cow is watching. Who else is watching?" Jabari points to the horse. "Yes, the horse is watching, too."

To engage children when they wake up, Mr. Pacy has put each of the Lois Lenski books *Cowboy Small, Policeman Small, The Little Train, The Little Fire Engine, The Little Airplane*, and *The Little Sailboat* in a box with small matching toys. With the fire engine book are small fire engines and people. With the airplane book are goggles and small airplanes. The children love to see what will be waiting for them in the boxes after naptime.

Still groggy upon waking up, toddlers may not know where they are and may want to be with their families. One child woke crying every day. After a few days, the teachers talked with his mother. She explained that at home, she snuggled with him and gave him a bottle after naps. The teacher offered him a sippy cup and lap reading after naptime.

Many teachers anticipate challenges when toddlers go to sleep but may not recognize the important transition that happens when children wake up. Having planned activities waiting for children as they wake can ease the transition. Some teachers prepare snack so that as children wake up, they can come and sit with a teacher to eat and talk quietly. Time for closeness with caregivers conveys important messages.

Minimizing Transitions

Ms. Ana notices that several children have dumped their dolls into a basket and are looking for something to do. She starts the music for Leroy Anderson's "Sleigh Ride" and takes a colorful streamer from a box on the floor. She holds the streamer like a horse's reins as she gallops around the carpet in time to the music. This is all the invitation the children need. Six children run to get streamers. When the music stops, Ms. Ana plays "Caballito Blanco" ("Little White Horse") on the Autoharp. She shows the children how to tap the castanets so they sound like little horses' feet.

Across the room, Juan and Martin are "cooking" with Ms. Ibbie. They stir small blocks in the toy pans and dump them in big scoops onto Ms. Ibbie's plate. She pretends to eat *huevos fritos vuelta y vuelta* (fried eggs over easy), much to the children's delight. Ms. Ibbie says, "Good breakfast, Martin and Juan. Now should we ride horses with Ms. Ana?" The boys run over to play, still wearing their aprons. Ms. Ibbie stays with Dani, who wants to sit on her lap.

Rather than make all of the children come to a circle time, restrict their movement, or ignore their desire to finish up other activities, Ms. Ana and Ms. Ibbie follow the children's choices about when and where to participate. Their goal over time is to bring children together and to gradually extend the amount of shared activity time. The teachers know that with familiar and inviting routines, toddlers often join in by choice.

Circle time is different for toddlers than for preschoolers. Young toddlers may be able to sit for only a few minutes and need to be supported on or near a teacher's lap. Likewise, two-year-olds need active movement. Children become absorbed in activities that don't fit in a highly structured schedule. As a result, a toddler group time should have open borders.

An important goal of toddler teaching is to shorten or eliminate waiting time. Sitting with nothing to do and waiting for other children are invitations for boredom and frustration. Hand washing, preparing meals, diapering, and organizing children into activities are typical waiting times. The following are age-appropriate strategies to minimize waiting during transitions:

- **Use actions instead of words.** Sing a song, start a dance, or introduce new materials to shift children's attention and energy quickly.

- **Adapt cleanup times to toddlers' needs.** Rather than cleaning up as a group, assist a small group of children to finish an activity. Then transition two children at a time to hand washing or diapering.

- **Prepare snack as a choice during playtime.** In this way, teachers can help small groups of children wash hands while others play. Fewer children will need to transition at the same time (Hemmeter et al. 2008).

- **Overlap activities.** Plan free play, dance, creative and tabletop activities that children can continue to enjoy while others begin washing hands for a snack or meal. Don't leave children alone at the table after their hands are washed. Stagger the beginning of eating so those who are ready to eat can begin with an adult present. Children may leave the table when they are ready, rather than sitting and waiting for others to finish.

Making the Most of Songs and Games

Songs and games are a natural part of daily life with toddlers. Mr. Tony leads a parade after the children finish breakfast. The children push and pull anything they like, and Mr. Tony makes up a parade theme to match the children's energy level and the books they have been reading. Today they are zoo animals.

Music inspires engagement. A box of instruments—xylophones, bells, cymbals, song flutes, drums, shakers, and tambourines—along with streamers can spark musical play. Encourage children to express themselves through dance: swaying, jumping, twirling, and turning.

In addition to more traditional songs and fingerplays, musical play can become an essential part of your daily routines:

- Sing for fun while changing diapers and hand washing.

- Use a specific recording of soft music to introduce naptime, lunch, or another daily routine.

- Use simple, familiar melodies to sing action songs for transitions, such as when children are picking up toys, putting on jackets, or going outside. "This is the way we go outside." Try singing to the tune of "Wheels on the Bus" or "Mary Had a Little Lamb." Make up songs whenever you need them.

- Use poems with rhythm, such as "The Bear Went over the Mountain," "One, Two, Buckle My Shoe," and other Mother Goose rhymes, for marching.

- Read rhyming books, such as *Brown Bear, Brown Bear, What Do You See?* by Bill Martin Jr. and Eric Carle, *Pretend You're a Cat* by Jean Marzollo, or *Where Is the Green Sheep?* by Mem Fox.

- Link music to learning. Use action and description words while you dance. "Let's run fast. Let's march slow." "Shake the rattle up high. Shake it down low."

- Demonstrate music sounds with handbells, rain sticks, shakers, and drums. Make these available for children during play.

- Listen to classical, jazz, folk, ethnic, multicultural, instrumental, solo vocal, and children's choral music, and songs from different eras, such as 1940s big band or swing music.

- Incorporate multicultural music. Introduce folk songs in English, Spanish, French, or Latin. Include songs representing children's home languages.

- Introduce American folk songs, such as "A Tisket, a Tasket," "Little Sally Saucer," "She'll Be Coming around the Mountain," "Old MacDonald," "Twinkle, Twinkle, Little Star," and "I've Been Working on the Railroad."

- Toddlers love the sound of the human voice. Listen to barbershop quartets, a cappella singing (no instruments), and children's choir music.

- Use drums to keep rhythm. You can create drums from all kinds of containers: dishpans turned upside down, coffee cans, oatmeal tins, yogurt containers, bowls, or pots.

- Make shakers with clear plastic bottles of various sizes. Fill them with rice, beans, and other small objects. Superglue or duct-tape them shut to ensure safety. Introduce shakers during dance time.

- Play classical music in the dress-up area. Be sure the children have a wall mirror and dance costumes.

Music gives children many opportunities to practice self-regulation. When toddlers march or play an instrument, they make their bodies do as their brains say. Toddlers follow directions when they play follow-the-leader games or copy you.

When they dance, toddlers recognize where they are in space and practice coordinating all their body parts to get where they want to go.

For children experiencing stress, music allows a release of emotions and soothes the body. It lets all children participate equally, without restrictions. Absorbing and responding to the emotions in music can be therapeutic, especially within a caring and safe setting.

FAST FACTS: WHY THIS WORKS

Using Music to Boost Self-Regulation

Music is an essential part of daily activities in a toddler classroom. It offers unique benefits to young children:

▶ A musical childhood activates a love of music and singing that can enhance emotional well-being for life (Bock 2016).

▶ Listening and responding to music increases children's emotional regulation (Foran 2009).

▶ Music gives children complex, creative, multisensory, and whole-body experiences that positively impact memory, language acquisition, executive function, and brain plasticity (Winter 2014).

▶ Repeated experiences with music and play with musical instruments give children the opportunity to plan, monitor, and guide their behavior. They learn to stop and go, move fast and slow, and control soft and loud—all activities that help them practice behavior regulation (Winsler, Ducenne, and Koury 2011).

▶ Children have the opportunity to practice leadership and self-regulation when they engage with others in musical activities, especially with teacher support (Rauduvaitė and Virganavičienė 2015).

▶ Music activities increase executive function, including memory, language acquisition, and brain plasticity (Collins 2014).

▶ Music training improves cognitive abilities of children, including memory and verbal fluency, and brain activation (Zuk et al. 2014).

▶ Music experiences help children calm down, keep concentrated and interested, express and enhance happiness and energy level, and fantasize through mental imagery. It is a safe and joyful means of nonverbal emotion expression (Saarikallio, 2009).

▶ Music promotes development in all domains, as it integrates the body, brain, and emotions, especially in self-regulation and soothing (Parlakain and Lerner 2010).

———

Quick question: I would like my coteacher and I to create a much more child-centered and creative classroom. Right now we get stuck in the daily routines of trying to take care of physical needs. What is the first thing we should do?

Simple solution: Making changes requires open communication between you and your coteacher. Set aside time to talk about what you would like to do. Pick two items from your list as a starting point. Perhaps you want to reduce waiting time. Arrange your schedule for reading or dancing time while your coteacher attends to hand-washing needs. Prepare reading baskets and creative activity tables that one of you can support while the other helps with bathroom needs. Check out the many suggestions in chapters 2 and 3 to help you prepare creative table activities. When these toddler-centered materials are available along with well-prepared interest areas, children will remain engaged through their own choice and effort for increasing periods of time.

———

Quick question: We are looking for books to help children understand self-care routines. What do you suggest?

Simple solution: Children love to see their own self-care routines depicted through children's books. In addition take photos of children washing their hands and eating a meal. For diapering and potty topics, cut pictures from parenting magazines or print a color photo from the web. You can create a notebook with these photos to talk about with your children. Here are some self-care books that are terrific for toddlers:

- *All by Myself!* by Aliki
- *All by Myself* by Mercer Mayer
- *Froggy Gets Dressed* by Jonathan London
- *Henry Helps Clean His Room* by Beth Bracken
- *I'm Growing!* by Aliki

5

Strengthening
Social Skills

The emotional world of a toddler is a quickly changing landscape, with calm moments of happiness that can shift to tears. Children must rebound from separation, navigate close proximity with peers, and handle the brief stress of transitions. They are learning to recognize and express their emotions using words rather than acting out their feelings. This is a tall order for a two-year-old in a rapid and dynamic stage of social development. This chapter will address the development of social skills. You will discover practical strategies that assist toddlers in managing feelings and participating in caring and cooperative behaviors. Toddlers take their cues from adults and depend on their calm consistency and patient support of emerging social skills and emotional competence.

Exploring Emotional Competence

Rosa says, "I can do it. I can do it." She pulls on the doll in Shiloh's hands. Shiloh hangs on tight. Ms. Maeve intervenes, saying, "Rosa, Shiloh's baby is cold. Can you find a sweater for the baby?" "Baby needs a sweater," says Shiloh. Ms. Maeve encourages the girls to choose a sweater. She asks, "Are the babies going for a walk? Do you want to share the double stroller or push your own?" "Double!" says Shiloh. "Where will you take your babies?" asks Ms. Maeve. "We go to the park," says Rosa. "You are taking your babies to the park," says Ms. Maeve.

Rosa and Shiloh are figuring out their play goals and their emotions at the same time. Ms. Maeve helps the girls resolve their conflict by introducing a task they can achieve together. Rather than lecture about sharing or taking turns, she uses the play scenario to teach important skills. Ms. Maeve helps Rosa consider Shiloh's need. She also encourages Shiloh to express her need verbally: "Baby needs a sweater." The girls' ability to put their needs and feelings into words is part of emotional competence.

Emotional competence includes a child's ability to recognize, express, and manage emotions (Eisenberg, Spinrad, and Eggum 2010). The journey toward competence begins in infancy, with adult attentiveness during bonding and feeding times. Infants make mental connections among their caregiver's facial expressions, the sequence of events, and the activities around them. Noticing and interpreting facial cues is a first step toward emotion recognition.

At first, infants regulate their emotions when caregivers respond to needs. Infants regulate—or match their breathing, muscle tone, and body rhythms—to adults. When caregivers respond immediately and consistently to cries of hunger or wet diapers, infants begin to anticipate what will happen next. They will stop crying and wait because they know a dry diaper is on its way. However, when infants experience inconsistency, they may continue to cry because they aren't sure their needs will be met. A pattern of security with caregivers provides an anchor for emotional regulation.

Emotional competence depends on language skills. Toddlers are still learning to identify their feelings and link emotions with word labels. Their emotions can be reactive and immediate. The gap in language skill can cause frustration when children want to communicate their needs. With increasing vocabulary, toddlers can ask for what they need rather than act out their feelings.

By age two, children begin to use words to identify basic emotions, such as happy, sad, or mad (Warren, Denham, and Bassett 2008). They more quickly identify that a certain situation makes them feel anxious, upset, or happy. They also are quick to show their affection and express empathy and concern for others (Knafo et al. 2008). While toddlers are gaining some control, they still depend on your assistance —your coregulation—to manage emotions.

Toddlers don't have the background knowledge to make sense of what they see happening, unless you tell them. "Mommy is leaving now for work. After naptime she will drive the car back and get you. She will be excited to give you a big hug." "Mr. Jacks is happy to bring the food to our classroom. Then he will take food to the children in Ms. White's room." Explanations help children feel reassured.

Toddlers depend on physical assistance. Children on riding toys may get stuck in the corner and not be able to turn around. They may struggle with other children who are too close, because they can't figure out how to make enough space for themselves. They rely on you to show them how to turn around or find more suitable space. Over time toddlers will gain the physical skill and knowledge to handle these challenges. But for now they depend on you to help them solve the issues that bring frustration.

Toddlers rely on your emotional support to calm down. When children are upset, you can hold their hands gently and say, "Let's breathe together." Maybe you will get on a child's eye level and say, "Let's get a drink of water together." With repeated practice over time, they will learn "When I am upset, I can calm myself." "When I am overexcited, I can walk away and choose another activity." Your ability to tune in and intervene early helps them manage emotions.

TEACHER TIP

Keeping Fair Expectations

There are times when I just want toddlers not to be toddlers! I want them to calm down and be patient. Then I remember that I myself have a hard time staying calm when I am upset. In my personal life, I sometimes fly off the handle when I don't get my way. I realize how unrealistic my expectations for toddlers have been. Reflecting on my own emotions has helped me be more patient and helpful with the children.

Capturing the Immediacy of Toddlers' Feelings

Gavin sits inside the low wooden block wagon and propels it with his feet. He leans forward and places his palms on the floor. Then he peers upward from his crouching position and says to Ms. Jeri, "Salty." Ms. Jeri understands. "You are Salty the Turtle!" At the same time, Kayla climbs over a beanbag chair and bumps into Gavin, who bursts into tears. Ms. Jeri checks on Kayla to be sure she's okay. Next she hugs Gavin and helps him push his wagon away from the beanbag. "I'm sorry, Salty! Can you come over to your turtle nest? We can find your turtle eggs."

For toddlers, feelings are intense. Gavin is delighted with his ability to move the wagon by himself, excited to tell his teacher about Salty, and startled by Kayla. He shifts from smiling to crying within seconds. With Ms. Jeri's help, he calms quickly and returns to playing near another beanbag chair.

Because Ms. Jeri treats Gavin and Kayla kindly, they learn the following:

- Regardless of the problem, someone loving and kind can help me.

- When I feel out of control, someone will help me without getting mad.

- Other people always deserve respect.

- When someone is struggling, they need support and care.

- Frustration is never a reason to treat someone unkindly.

When children experience kindness and patience in response to their emotions, it affects how they feel about themselves. When they feel accepted, children see themselves as emotionally and socially capable. The following realizations are important for children's mental health and for sustaining strong and healthy relationships throughout life:

- I am worthy of love and respect.

- I can be patient with myself and others.

- It is okay to be imperfect.

- Even when I make mistakes, I am still learning.

- I can handle a situation better next time.

- When I feel bad, I can always choose how I respond.

- I can show compassion for my needs and others'.

Toddlers are completely absorbed in the moment. They can't yet evaluate an experience in the context of other events. Will their families come back? They aren't sure. Will they recover from distressing feelings? They don't know. When you consider emotions from a toddler's perspective, their drama and intensity make sense.

Not only do toddlers have limited perspective, but their emotions depend on multiple factors, such as stress, fatigue, and hunger. They can be clingy one moment and happy the next. Daily life with toddlers can go quickly from fun to frustrating, so you will need a toolbox of positive strategies. Fortunately, toddlers can recover quickly from upsetting or unpleasant experiences with your support.

Adding to the emotional intensity is toddlers' egocentric nature. They are focused on their own immediate needs. At the same time, their desire for independence drives them to take charge of challenges. Toddlers like to do things for themselves when they physically can. This combination of inward focus and outward drive can make for an emotional roller coaster.

Take time to think about toddlers' perspective. What do you look and sound like to them? What lessons do you teach them about emotions? Children learn from you how to show empathy. They notice how you tend to others' needs. As you observe carefully, you will see how much influence you have on children's responses. You can gain greater insight when you consider their perspective.

Quiet Doesn't Mean Good

Don't overlook me when I am quiet. Look at me carefully. I am standing apart from the group. Maybe I don't have the right words to say. Maybe I am missing my family. Come and talk to me. Help me feel comfortable joining you and the other children. Being quiet isn't being good. It is my way of telling you I need you.

Knowing What You Believe

In a 2015 Zero to Three national survey, researchers found that about half of parents underestimated how early and deeply babies and toddlers responded to other people's intentions and feelings. Fifty-nine percent did not know that young infants could experience feelings like sadness and fear. Twenty-four percent said they thought children as young as one year could control emotions, such as not having a tantrum when frustrated. Forty-three percent thought children could share and take turns before the age of two, when this skill does not develop until between ages three and four. Fifty-six percent thought that children have the ability to resist the desire to do something forbidden before the age of three, yet most children cannot begin to do this until almost four. Children's abilities to manage emotions and regulate behavior continue to develop from age three through the preschool years (Zero to Three 2016; Moilanen et al. 2010).

The CDC–Kaiser Permanente Adverse Childhood Experiences Study (ACES) surveyed more than seventeen thousand adults about their childhood experiences. It found that traumatic emotional experiences affected long-term mental and physical health just as much as harmful physical experiences. Safe, stable, nurturing relationships and environments for all children can affect mental and physical health positively for years to come (CDC 2016).

Fostering Emotion Recognition and Expression

"Ooh! It is *freezing* cold out here!" Ms. Piper shivers in an exaggerated way. She hugs her arms to her chest and knocks her knees together. "Let's do a happy dance to keep warm." She skips around in a circle and waves her arms up high. The children copy her and laugh. Then Ms. Piper says, "Let's do a silly dance!" She waves her arms down low and stomps her feet. The children laugh and do the same. Then they run off toward the swings.

Ms. Piper helps the children understand what the body feels like when it is cold, silly, and happy. Her playground game encourages the children to channel their energy and learn at the same time. The exaggerated movements are fun and focus children's attention on their bodies and feelings.

The steps of emotion recognition are complex. Children must first identify what they feel and then label the emotion. They need to be able to calm themselves and ask for help.

When a caregiver becomes upset, the child feels anxiety, fear, or stress as a result. The child feels more out of control. However, when a child yells, "Help!" and a caregiver remains calm and assists with the need, the child sees that using words brings positive results. Toddlers need to know that using words will bring needed relief.

Emotional learning occurs throughout each day. During diapering, feeding, and soothing, toddlers experience empathy and closeness. As you feed the fish together, they feel pride in taking responsibility. When they use words to get what they need, they gain competence. They feel a sense of belonging as they eat together with you and their friends. They gain a sense of social identity, empathy, and belonging while talking about their families, caring for their dolls, and playing with stuffed animals (Paul 2014).

Here are some ways to help children recognize their feelings:

- **Describe your own emotions in toddler-friendly ways.** "When Tasha is sick and has to stay home, I feel sad." "When I try to pull on my boots and they get stuck, I feel frustrated."

- **Model expression of feelings.** "I am feeling cranky. Let's put on happy music and dance to help us feel cheerful." "I feel frustrated. I can't find my slippers. I will look under the desk for them."

- **Make word pictures.** "I feel so happy, I could hop like a bunny!" "I am so tired, I could crawl into bed like a bear going to sleep for the winter." "I am so content, I could purr like a happy kitten." "When I go outside to run, my feet are jumpy little puppies."

- **Expand emotional vocabulary.** Introduce rich vocabulary to toddlers. Along with *sad*, *mad*, and *glad*, introduce *miserable*, *furious*, and *delighted*. "It's raining. I feel miserable because we can't go outside to play."

- **Tune in.** Watch children carefully for cues that they are tired or overexcited. Don't wait until the child is out of control. Step in and describe the feelings you see. "You look tired. Would you like to read with me for a few minutes?"

- **Play with mirrors.** "Ooh, I see you smiling. That's a happy face." "I am making a silly face. I see a funny face." "I am making a sad face."

Here are some strategies to help children use words to express their feelings:

- **Describe the child's feelings.** "I see you are disappointed. Let's find another hat to wear." "Mia is sad. She wants her grandma to stay and play."

- **Validate what the child is feeling.** "I know you feel sad saying good-bye to your dad. We will give him a big hug this afternoon."

- **Give options.** "I know you are excited. Let's come over here to jump." "I know you are mad. You can squeeze the pillow."

- **Read picture books.** Choose or make books with pictures of children's facial expressions. "The girl feels sad. Her friend went home." "The boy is laughing. The dog is funny!" "The puppy is excited. Daddy is home." Ask questions. "What does the girl feel?" "Why is the boy happy?"

- **Talk about feelings during children's play.** "Your doll is sad. She fell down and got hurt. Let's give her a bandage." "Puppy is happy. He is running outside with his mommy."

- **Make stories personal.** Take photos of children playing and laminate them. Place the photos in a basket. Invite toddlers to choose pictures of themselves and other children. Say, "Look at you! What are you doing in this picture?" Let the child answer. Say, "You look (happy, sad, excited) in the picture."

- **Play with your face.** In this game, the child copies the adult. "Where is my happy face?" Smile. "Where is your happy face?" Child smiles. "Where is my sad face?" Make an exaggerated sad face. "Where is your sad face?" Child makes a sad face. You can also play this game while looking in a mirror.

- **Link frustrations to solutions.** "I know you are mad. You can squeeze your hands together when you feel frustrated." "I know you are upset. We can talk together until you are okay." "I see you are sad. I'm going to sit quietly next to you and keep you company."

When you talk about emotions, focus on the present. Toddlers relate to what is happening in the moment. They don't typically speculate or imagine how they might feel if something happens in the future, which is a more abstract idea. Toddlers respond to questions about immediate events. "The dog is jumping. It is excited because Bobby came home." This focus on the present will open many opportunities to talk about feelings.

For children to respect others, they must first know what respect looks and feels like. Respect for emotions is at the heart of a child's personal identity and sense of security and worth. An environment of safety and respect for toddlers will instill a lifelong awareness of and respect for others and themselves.

Holding Realistic Expectations

Emma laughs. She throws back her head and waves her arms. She watches Jasper bump the ball with his forehead and snort. Each time Jasper snorts, the children who are watching laugh harder. Emma reaches for the ball, but Jasper pulls it away. She bursts into tears and wails, "My ball. I want the ball!" Ms. Paloma says reassuringly, "There are balls for both of you." Jasper lets out another loud snort, and they both laugh, even though tears are still falling from Emma's eyes. "Let's all kick a ball and run after it," Ms. Paloma says.

Ms. Paloma has been laughing with the children over Jasper's antics. She quickly tunes into and validates Emma's feelings. She knows that helping children develop social skills is one of her most important responsibilities.

When a toddler is upset, crying, or needs help, it can provoke intense emotions in you. Perhaps when you were young, you remember when someone said, "Stop crying," or "Why are you crying?" Maybe when you were sad, someone said, "You'll be okay." Perhaps you fell down and someone said, "You're not hurt. Get up." These dismissive remarks can leave a lasting impression.

You may wonder about the best way to respond to toddlers' experiences and emotions. You may recognize that when toddlers are hurt, they can't think their way out of their feelings. Yet you may worry that validating their feelings may "baby" or spoil toddlers. It can be helpful to think of yourself as an emotion coach.

Emotion coaching uses teachable moments to foster helpful, socially positive behaviors. Coaching uses children's immediate experiences to instill understanding. To be an effective emotion coach, you must first notice what children are feeling. The next step is to validate and help children label their emotions. The third step is to find a solution to meet children's needs (Gus, Rose, and Gilbert 2015).

Emotion coaching conveys important beliefs and values, including the impressions you received about emotions as a child, both positive and negative. Take time to evaluate your responses and be sure you communicate positive messages. Your goal in emotion coaching is to affirm that emotions are part of everyone's daily experience. You show children that they can manage and use their emotions in positive ways. You help children accept and honor their own and others' feelings.

Emotions can be scary to a toddler who feels out of control. When children are angry, sad, or fearful, they need an adult to be emotionally solid and calm. This response creates a safe and reassuring space for toddlers. When adults get upset, children learn that their emotions have the power to shake up the grown-ups! That can be scary. It threatens children's need for consistency and security. Instead of simply managing their own upset, they now have to manage the additional fear they experience because of adults' anger. Clear emotional boundaries and calm respect are essential for healthy relationships.

An adult's ability to remain logical and calm accomplishes these important goals:

- It allows the adult to think about the child's needs.

- It allows the adult to validate the child's emotion. "I can see you are upset." "I know you are sad." "I feel sorry that you got hurt."

- It allows the adult to focus on a solution. "Let's spend some time together." "Let's read a book, and I can tickle your arm." "Would you like to come and get a hug and a drink of water with me?"

- It allows the adult to remain near to be physically reassuring. "I will stay here and keep you company while you feel sad." "I will help you figure out what to do." "We can do this together."

Knowing that adults will remain calm allows children to express feelings without fear. It helps children separate their emotions from adults' emotions and reframe their experiences more quickly. "I got hurt for a few moments, but the hurt went away." "I felt sad, but I now feel comforted." "I felt angry, but I moved on to play with something else." Successful resolution builds needed competence.

Viewing emotion and behavior as separate can be helpful. This is challenging when a child is having a tantrum or lying on the floor refusing to get up. However, most so-called misbehavior is simply a child's way to express a need.

Emotional expression is not misbehavior. When children show strong emotion, this is simply communication. In the best way they can, children are telling you what they feel. When they use words, say, "Thank you for telling me what you feel." When they show you their feeling by jumping up and down, stomping feet, falling down, or refusing to move, you can say, "Your body is telling me that you feel (excited, mad, disappointed)." Once you identify the emotion, you can help children find a strategy to address the need.

Crying or having a tantrum is not misbehavior. When children cry, they need to know that this is a way their bodies show their feelings. You can reassure the child. "It is okay to be sad and cry. I am going to make sure you are okay." "When you are ready, we can talk together." These responses invite the child to connect and find comfort.

Feeling angry is not misbehavior. If a child hits in anger, you can say, "It is okay to be angry, but you cannot hit. I need you to be safe." Offer alternatives. Say, "We use our hands to be gentle" or "Let's solve the problem together."

Frustration is not misbehavior. Toddlers want to be able to zip a coat, fit a toy car inside a garage, eat what they see adults eating, or ride with a seat belt instead of a car seat. The difference between what they know is possible and what they can actually do brings frustration. Be reassuring. "Soon you will be able to do it by yourself." "When you get bigger, your seat belt will look just like my seat belt." A simple statement will help the child stay calm.

Using Stories and Puppets to Teach Emotions

Miss Mimi puppet says, "Alex, it's time to take a nap." Alex puppet responds, "But I want a drink of wahhhh-ter." The toddlers giggle. Miss Mimi puppet says, "Alex, it's time to go to sleep." Alex puppet says, "But I want a muhhhhh-fin!" The children laugh louder. Miss Mimi puppet says, "Alex, you have to take a nap right now." Alex puppet squeaks, "I'm soooo tiiiired. Okay, I will go to sleep now."

Ms. Leslie's children have had trouble shifting to naptime. She uses puppets to act out the children's struggles. Ms. Leslie knows that toddlers don't yet reflect on their own behavior. But they can see and understand the message when puppets act it out. Today she brings Miss Mimi and Alex to the naptime routine and has Mimi tuck in Alex.

If you haven't used puppets before, you may feel silly making up stories or voices. However, once you try it, you will be amazed at how quickly your children are captivated. Your puppet can read a storybook, sing a song, or lead a fingerplay. It can act out a situation that relates to the daily lives or challenges of your children. As long as the puppet time is brief and holds children's attention, it can be a daily activity. Puppets bring stories and lessons to life.

Children relate to emotions acted out by puppets. Make-believe characters can say, "Good-bye, Momma," and feel sad. Another character can say, "Come and play with me." By seeing puppets act out children's experiences, children can see and experience happy resolutions to their own feelings. Children will look at and talk to a puppet as if it is a real person. You will be able to capture children's imaginations and calm them through quiet puppet play.

Understanding the Role of Stress

Ms. Debbie tells her director, "Jessie came on Monday with his babysitter. He cried all day. Different relatives picked him up over the next few days, and I didn't see his mom the entire time. By Friday he was inconsolable. He kept saying, 'Where

Mommy is? I want Mommy.' He protested when his babysitter came to get him. When his mom came back the next week, she looked awful. She said she had been involved in a domestic dispute. This situation was unbearable for Jessie."

Sometimes, the stress and trauma children experience is evident. You may recognize family stress, or families may tell you about their struggles. However, even when children look perfectly fine—with tidy clothing and clean hair—they may be experiencing stress at home.

Toddler teachers need to understand the role of stress on development, learning, and behavior. Often what seems like a behavior issue is a result of stress. Toddlers cannot always tell you in words what they feel, so you need to communicate frequently with families and watch for signs of stress in children's behavior. Whether you work in an urban center, a rural setting, or a suburban neighborhood, you may notice that children and families today are experiencing unprecedented stress (Kuo et al. 2012; Schwartz-Henderson 2016).

Experts explain that while all children experience stress at times, they recover quickly with the support of a nurturing adult (National Scientific Council on the Developing Child 2005/2014). However, toxic stress occurs when there is frequent, strong, or prolonged adversity without the buffering protection of adult caregivers (Shonkoff 2016). Toxic stress is especially detrimental during the toddler years, when children's brains and bodies are vulnerable. This kind of stress can affect children's ability to regulate emotions and behavior.

FAST FACTS: WHY THIS WORKS

Exploring the Impact of Stress

For toddlers ages sixteen to thirty-six months, having a family, school, and community that provide stability and safety is essential to healthy development. Children birth to age five are at high risk for exposure to traumatic events because they are completely dependent on adults (Buss, Warren, and Horton 2015). More than half of young children experience a severe stressor (Zero to Six Collaborative Group 2010). Early childhood stress may have the following effects:

▶ Early adversity, especially poverty-related stress, is physiologically stressful for families, and this in turn is detrimental to children's development (Blair et al. 2015).

▶ Exposure to traumatic events can cause a range of social, emotional, and behavioral problems. Ongoing stress compromises healthy development and puts children at risk of persistent, serious psychological problems later in childhood and adulthood (Mongillo et al. 2009).

▶ Traumatic events causing risk to children's development and adjustment include poverty, parental stress during toddler years, marital stress, family violence, and

> maternal depression. The temperament of a child and health issues can magnify the impact of other stress factors. These early influences are reciprocal, meaning that they interact with one another and continue to affect development over time (Mänty-maa et al. 2012).
>
> ▶ High rates of community violence, high unemployment, family conflict, quality of parenting, availability of social support, parental depression, and single parenthood together impact toddlers' adjustment and behavior (Heberle et al. 2014).

There is a concern in toddler classrooms, as studies have found atypical increases in cortisol level in children (Lisonbee et al. 2008). Cortisol is a stress hormone. Even in adequate care, young children have an increase in cortisol that is not present when children are at home (Gunnar et al. 2010, Watamura et al. 2011). Becoming well educated about the importance of monitoring stress in the family, community, and classroom is a critical issue for toddler teachers.

The good news is that you can make a difference. The research shows that both parents and children benefit from a sensitive relationship with a primary caregiver who knows them well. You can build a responsive, supportive relationship that increases children's resilience. Your trusting bond and shared intimate knowledge of caregiving can provide needed support for families and improve outcomes for children (Margetts 2005).

As an early childhood professional, you are a mandated child abuse reporter. This means that when you observe active signs of child abuse or ongoing neglect, the law requires that you contact your state's child protection services. While discovering, hearing about, or reporting abuse can be emotionally difficult, you have a legal obligation to actively protect children's physical and emotional well-being.

The Child Welfare Information Gateway, part of the US Department of Health and Human Services Administration for Children and Families, provides specific information about how to report suspected child maltreatment. This website defines abuse and neglect, explains the reporting process, and provides contact information for each state: www.childwelfare.gov/topics/responding/reporting/how.

A predictable schedule and routines help children feel safe and secure when other parts of their lives are unpredictable. The following strategies provide practical ways to provide a healthy emotional setting:

- **Provide a safe physical and emotional environment.** Be sure activities are predictable, soothing, and calm. Make sure all adults speak, act, and respond in a positive and caring way with children.

- **Monitor your own responses.** Notice and take responsibility for your own stress. If your stress feels unmanageable, or if you struggle with anger or frustration over a prolonged period of time, seek professional counseling.

- **Use responsive comforting.** A blanket, a teddy bear, hugs, or a few minutes of lap time are important aspects of emotional management. "When you feel upset, you can cuddle the teddy bear." "When you are sad, you can get a hug."

- **Encourage active physical play.** Games and vigorous dance are linked to overall well-being. Adequate active movement calms children's bodies and helps them focus and self-regulate (Becker et al. 2014).

- **Provide items from home and have conversations that keep children connected to their families** (Yeary 2013). This may be a T-shirt, a laminated photo, a child-safe photo book, a recording of a family member singing, or happy conversation about families. "We are going to paint a picture and give it to Mommy when she comes." "After we play and take a nap, Daddy and you are going to go to the park."

When children know they can turn to you for help and support, they will do so when needed. Once they know what a safe and caring relationship feels like, they will ask for comfort when they need to feel close, are lonely, or need help. The ability to get support through healthy relationships is an important part of resilience.

Providing Strategies for Calming

Ms. Riley notices Yoon Sun and Indira hugging and rolling on the floor after coming inside, a sweet situation she knows is in danger of getting out of hand. Ms. Riley brings the girls a box of nesting cups and pop beads. "Here are some colorful beads and cups. You can work on the purple yoga mat." Ms. Riley rolls out the mat and places the box in the middle. The girls dig inside it. "Would you like to make a necklace or a bracelet?" Yoon Sun says, "Make necklace for Mommy." Ms. Riley smiles. "You can make a long one." The girls turn their attention to the colorful materials.

No matter how well prepared you are for a classroom of toddlers, you will experience challenges when they are together. Like Ms. Riley, you may need to step in when children are rolling on the floor and could hurt each other. When children are upset, you will need to turn the situation around quickly. In spite of your best efforts, children may cry.

The energy in a room full of toddlers can be high. In the morning, after being outdoors, and after naptime, prepare calming and soothing activities. The following will encourage closeness and help children adjust to the group setting:

- **Play soft, soothing music.** Meditative music with nature sounds or music with Celtic pipes, marimba, strings, or guitar can calm and relax the body.

- **Involve all the senses.** Children love to smell lemons, oranges, or cinnamon sticks. A smelling experience is both soothing and engaging.

- **Prepare water play.** Use individual dish tubs or a water table for washing dolls or cars, or for measuring and pretend cooking. The warm water is calming.

- **Encourage nurturing behaviors.** Children feel soothed when they rock dolls or cuddle stuffed animals.

- **Do toddler yoga.** With soft music on, model simple yoga positions that toddlers can do and enjoy. The books *Itsy Bitsy Yoga for Toddlers and Preschoolers* by Helen Garabedian, *Little Yoga: A Toddler's First Book of Yoga* by Rebecca Whitford, *Frog Yoga Alphabet* by Aruna Kathy Humphrys, and *Sleepy Little Yoga: A Toddler's Sleepy Book of Yoga* by Rebecca Whitford can get you started.

- **Give calming stickers.** When children are upset, you can often distract them with a piece of paper and a sheet of stickers. Peeling and sticking is repetitive and absorbing. It is perfectly fine if children press the stickers on their bodies.

- **Use calm-down bottles.** Fill child-safe plastic bottles with colored water and floating glitter or other fascinating objects.

- **Introduce turtle time.** Provide soft, round, green pillows. Show toddlers how to hug a turtle pillow and close their eyes to calm down or feel better. Keep these pillows in the soft, cozy area of your room. The purpose of turtle time is to withdraw and calm down (Kersey and Masterson 2013). Hug a turtle pillow with children until this becomes a natural way for children to find comfort or space from other children.

> **TEACHER TIP**
>
> ## Using Deep Breathing
>
> We taught the children to breathe deeply to calm down. I couldn't believe how quickly they tried it for themselves. The other day, Charlie was running around and was about to jump off a large dump truck. I put my arms around him and said, "I need you to be safe." He started deep breathing for himself. I said, "Charlie, you are awesome. You are breathing deeply to calm down." I was so excited to see that he was doing what we had practiced so many times before.

Unpacking Executive Function and Self-Regulation

"Whoa!" yells John. He runs across the room and slides toward the pillows. His body lands on the pillows, but his head just misses whacking the wall. Ms. Carla sits next to John. Placing her hands gently on his head, she says, "John, I love you. I love your head. Look with your eyes. Do you see the wall? When you land on the pillows, look for the wall. Slow down and keep your head away from the wall. I want you to be safe." She pats John's head and tousles his hair. "You okay?" "I'm okay!" says John.

Many times each day, you will see children beginning to regulate their bodies. John is learning to stop himself, but he still runs with wild enthusiasm. He aims for the pillows but nearly bumps the wall. He is learning to choose a path, aim for a target, and coordinate his body to reach his goal. He needs Ms. Carla to keep reminding him to be careful and to slow down. Over time, as his brain better coordinates his body, John's speed control, stopping, and watching for walls will become automatic.

Adults expect toddlers to come when called and to stop themselves when they want to touch everything in sight. They are supposed to walk instead of run. They need to steer themselves around other children. They are supposed to wait until adults are ready. All these expectations require effortful control.

Effortful control includes the ability to stop or refrain from a behavior on purpose when needed (Graziano, Keane, and Calkins 2010). For toddlers, this skill depends on adult support. Hands reach out to touch. Impulsively, a child grabs another child's food. With gentle consistency, you respond with verbal cues. "This bagel belongs to you." "Here is a truck you can play with." Toddlers cannot yet consistently resist a current desire to achieve another less relevant need, request, or goal (Liew 2012). They need continual, gentle guidance as they gain increasing competence.

FAST FACTS: WHY THIS WORKS

Exploring Effortful Control

Effortful control is part of executive function—a group of mental functions that direct and regulate thinking, remembering, and social behavior. The prefrontal lobe of the brain coordinates this management of behavior, focus, and planning. Experts call this the traffic control center of the brain (Center on the Developing Child 2011).

To regulate behavior, children must first direct their attention toward what needs to be done. They need to refrain from something else (inhibit behavior) in order to shift to a new behavior. Inhibitory control helps children handle conflict, delay gratification, and demonstrate compliance (Morasch and Bell 2011). They must shift attention from what they were doing, then start and follow through on the new task. Next children must activate energy to accomplish the task (Blair and Razza 2007).

This complex and essential system of control is not yet mature in toddlers. Effortful control is important for school readiness. It should be a focus for your learning and a priority as you evaluate and support children's emerging behaviors (Valiente et al. 2011).

How you respond to children's emotions and offer coping or regulation strategies influences children's ability to regulate (Spinrad et al. 2007). The ability to regulate both cognitive and emotional processes predicts better learning behavior and social competence in the classroom (Denham et al. 2012). Supporting the foundations of effortful control is an important priority for toddler teachers.

Lev Vygotsky, a leading child development theorist, explained that children's language and behavior control develop through interactions with adults (Vygotsky 1978). Adults talk through and assist the child with the steps needed. "Let's go wash hands. Let's climb up on the stool. Let's get a paper towel. Let's go to the table." But over time children internalize these words, steps, and behaviors. "We wash our hands before we eat." "We change our diaper before nap." "We put on a sweater to go outside." "We sit at the table to eat." "We are gentle with our hands." These habits become part of children's ability to self-regulate.

TEACHER TIP

Saying "I Can Stop Myself"

Our toddlers have so much energy. We were constantly saying, "Please jump on the mat." "Be careful with your hands." We had to physically separate children when they got wound up. One teacher finally said, "Please stop!" Sammie kept jumping. Then the teacher asked, "Can you stop your feet from jumping?" He looked up at her. The teacher prompted, "Sammie, say, 'I can stop myself.'" Much to our surprise, Sammie said, "I can stop myself."

And he stopped! We were amazed at the power of giving children words to tell their own bodies what to do. Now we teach all our children to say, "I can stop myself!"

STRATEGIES FOR SUCCESS

Building Self-Regulation

Building self-regulation depends on the setting, the child, and you. Here are the first steps to shift responsibility for children's actions to the children:

▶ **Survey the room.** Stay aware of children's ever-changing actions and needs. This will help you step in before problems occur.

▶ **Narrate steps, even after toddlers know them.** "We are going to read a story before naptime. Let's snuggle on the beanbags." Rehearsing steps helps children learn to tell themselves what to do.

▶ **Foster children's interactions with others as well as with you.** Guide children by supporting positive peer interactions through small-group activities. Toddlers' peer play requires adult assistance.

▶ **Invite children to take responsibility.** Toddlers have a natural desire to help. They imitate what you do and want to help. Ask them to arrange markers in a cup, feed the fish, or sweep the floor. Make these times enjoyable. "Our fish looks hungry. Can you feed it lunch?"

▶ **Stay connected.** Toddlers love to be with you. If you are washing your hands, they want to wash theirs, too. Make diapering and self-care routines fun, special, and personal. Children who feel emotionally connected also become more emotionally regulated.

▶ **Encourage.** Toddlers love cheers, fist bumps, and high fives. They want to see pride and excitement on your face when they accomplish a task. Everything is new for them, and verbal encouragement motivates them. Each time they practice a new skill, they build mental habits, including persistence and patience.

Teaching Early Social Skills

Ms. Everly has been sitting with Tommy on her lap during story time. She realizes he has fallen asleep. "Tommy fell asleep. Isn't he a sweet little pumpkin? Ms. Gia, can you help me get his cot ready?" Ms. Everly lifts Tommy gently and lays him down on his cot. She pats his back gently and tucks him in. Emma and Wiley come over to watch. "Can you help sprinkle sleepy dust on Tommy?" asks Ms. Everly.

Emma and Wiley both say, "Night-night, Tommy. Have a happy sleep." The three of them sprinkle sleepy dust over Tommy. Then they go with Ms. Everly to get ready for their own naps.

Toddlers learn about emotions through daily interactions. Other children hear Ms. Everly's affection in her voice. They perceive her gentleness by the way she touches Tommy soothingly. They internalize what kindness looks and feels like. As they sprinkle sleepy dust, they share Ms. Everly's emotion. Her words and actions have influenced their view of Tommy, too.

Watching others is how children learn about social skills. They see how you sit and eat. They notice that you take turns talking with your coteacher. They need to learn the simple manners and social rules that help them get along with others. These abilities will later enable children to share, take turns, and play successfully with others in the pre-K years.

Children need words to ask for what they need and want. Teach them to say, "I need help" or "I need you." Teach them to say, "Please," "Thank you," and, "May I have it?"

Children also need empowerment to stop what they don't want. Teach them to say, "No thank you." Teach words that protect their boundaries: "Please stop." Using puppet play, teach children that "stop" means "take your hands off." When one puppet touches the other, ask children, "What should the touching puppet do?" The children will tell you, "Stop touching."

When a child asks you to stop, respond, "I stopped. I am listening. What do you need?" When a child says, "I don't like that shirt" or "I don't want peas," it is important to say, "Thank you for telling me with words. We can choose something else to wear [or eat, play, or do]." When a child says, "Stop!" it is so important that you stop—and that you make sure other children stop.

Work with children to recognize their feelings and express emotions with words. When children express their feelings and needs and adults discount them, children revert to crying, hitting, pushing, or yelling. Respecting children's feelings will not spoil them. Rather, it encourages children to use words in the future—which is your goal. It also teaches them how to respect the feelings of others.

Helping Children Have Fun with Manners

Manners are simply habits that help people get along. They are socially expected ways of behaving. Toddlers learn that manners are a normal way to treat others. Don't expect perfection, but do teach and reinforce the following simple habits:

- **Saying please and thank you:** When you say these words consistently, they become part of children's vocabulary.

- **Taking turns:** Toddlers are just beginning to be able to take turns. Ample toys and materials should be available so that all children can participate. Large equipment, like swings and riding toys, must be shared. It is okay to say, "In five minutes, let's let David have a turn." Be sure to have an alternative ready. "Five minutes are up. Painting is waiting for you."

- **Table manners:** Show pride and enthusiasm over developing skills. "Wow. You are holding your spoon like a big boy." "I am so happy you drank all by yourself." When eating gets creative, you can say, "Food stays on the plate." "Let's eat with the fork."

- **Waiting:** Use the word *patient* when you are modeling patience. "I am patient. I will wait for you." Teach toddlers to "wear a patient hat." They can point their hands together over their heads. Say, "You can swing for a few minutes, and then we'll let Chris have a turn." Set a timer if necessary, and get the child involved with another toy or activity.

Exploring Differences in Temperament

Mr. Rosty is reading *Mindy and Her Blue Socks* by M. Ruth Smith to Leyton. Leyton is leaning on Mr. Rosty and looking at the pictures. "Which socks do you want to wear?" Mr. Rosty asks. Leyton puts his hand under his chin and sighs. "Um . . . I think I would like to have . . ." He considers his options. "I think I would like to have . . . these ones." Mr. Rosty says, "Those socks are a good choice. Where will you go when you put on your blue socks?" Leyton says, "I'm goin' for a walk with Jimmy."

The other children don't seem interested in this book, but Mr. Rosty knows Leyton has a great deal of focus and interest in details. Leyton's quiet demeanor really changes when Mr. Rosty interacts with him over the book. He lights up and has so much to say. Mr. Rosty spends time each day getting to know each child well.

You may hear that some children are difficult or easy, sensitive or flexible. It is true that children come into the world with unique ways of being. But the key aspect of how you perceive a toddler's temperament is how it fits with yours. If you are energetic and have a sense of humor, you may enjoy a child with this personality. If you are soft-spoken and thoughtful, you may be drawn to quiet, creative children. If you are sensitive to your environment, you can relate to children with this temperament. It is the responsiveness of adults to the temperamental needs of children—the goodness of fit—that matters (Brock and Curby 2016).

Some children are more cautious or fearful. Some may be more anxious or sensitive to environmental stimulation. Some may react strongly to changes or have particular ideas about how things should be done. They may be less flexible and dislike unpredictable circumstances. Some children can't wait for a new challenge. These individual traits affect children's social development because of how children respond to the environment and how others respond to them (Laible, Panfile, and Makariev 2008). The key is to know each child well and support children's growing skills. Your ability to understand and support children's unique strengths is what matters most.

As you interact with children, consider each situation from their perspective. When you show affection and caring, you actually create a lifetime of believing "I am worthy of love." Children internalize the words they hear and learn about their strengths and value by how you respond to them (Tanyel 2009). A child-centered view can help you know best how to give support.

STRATEGIES FOR SUCCESS

Building Children's Strengths

▶ **Invest in personal time.** Spend a few minutes with children when things are going well. "I love watching you play with the trains. Will you show me how they go up the tracks?"

▶ **Nurture children's self-esteem.** Tell children what you see and enjoy. "You have a great sense of humor! I like to laugh with you." "You are so creative. I like to paint with you."

▶ **Speak positively about children while they are listening.** When you are with your coteacher or other adults, including family members, highlight children's positive accomplishments and words. Your words are powerful. Cultivate the habit of affirming others' strengths.

SEEING FROM THE CHILD'S POINT OF VIEW

Honoring My Fears

I don't know how the world works. I sometimes feel afraid. See my concern and reassure me. Here are some fears and what to say:

▶ **Fear of loved one not coming back:** "I know you are sad that Daddy is leaving. After you play and take a nap, Daddy will come back to get you."

▶ **Fear of getting head stuck in shirt:** "We are going to pull off your shirt. I will be gentle. You won't get stuck. Let's do it together."

▶ **Fear of toilet flushing:** "Let's cover our ears. The toilet is noisy." Over time sensitive toddlers will take their hands off of their ears to see if they can tolerate the sound for a few seconds.

▶ **Fear of bad weather:** Often toddlers see their families show anxiety when a thunderstorm, tornado, or other bad weather is in the area. Children need reassurance. "The storm is outside, and the wind is going to blow it away. I will keep you safe."

▶ **Fear of being left behind:** "You can come with me. I will stay with you while we get your coat on. You can hold my hand while we go outside."

▶ **Fear of animal sounds:** Before activating a toy that makes animal sounds, say, "The rooster is going to crow very softly." Make sure this sound and other noisemakers are muted.

▶ **Fear of choking:** Some children don't like certain textures in their mouths, such as dry, slippery, fuzzy, or grainy foods. Honor children's refusal to eat certain foods. These sensory issues are often related to the fear of choking. When children shake their heads or say no, honor that choice.

▶ **Fear of adult reactions:** When toddlers feel strong emotions, they may also feel fear. They may fear there won't be a solution. They may fear that adults will get upset. Remain calm.

Young children depend on safe and supportive care, especially during self-care routines, such as eating, toileting, dressing, napping, and handling transitions. Your respect for their concerns helps them feel secure away from home. Reassure children that they are safe and that you understand how they feel.

Fostering Positive Interactions with Peers

Ms. Peggy is sitting with the children and looking at the family tree, which is at the children's eye level. Its trunk is made from brown paper. Leaves are sprinkled at the end of each branch. The leaves carry laminated photos of the children and their families. "Where are *you*, Lidia? Where are *you*, Sheena?" "Where are *you*, Ma'Kai?" "Is this your mom? Is this your puppy? What is your puppy's name? What do you like to play with your mom?"

Ms. Peggy is teaching the children about one another. They spend just a few minutes at a time highlighting three families, but over time they talk about all the families. Ms. Peggy knows the children are beginning to understand that families are the same and different. As the children answer questions, they learn to think about one another as individuals.

Toddlers are very expressive about their love and concern for others. They have strong feelings and preferences. Theory of mind refers to the ability to understand the self and others as having independent thoughts, beliefs, and desires (Allen and Kinsey 2013). While this skill is emerging, you can build children's awareness of and enjoyment of others.

STRATEGIES FOR SUCCESS

Encouraging Positive Peer Interactions

Toddlers can't sustain prolonged play in groups without teacher support. When you actively facilitate peer interaction in the following ways, you nurture children's growing awareness of others:

▶ **Make positive links to what others are doing.** "You are eating toast for breakfast. George has a bagel." "Jasper is enjoying the playdough. You are working on your drawing." Toddlers need help to notice what others are doing. Noticing others encourages awareness and empathy.

▶ **Talk about the need for space.** "Livy needs space to play with her toys." "David needs space for his milk." "Let's give Joshua space to sit with us." Awareness of space is a skill reinforced over time.

▶ **Keep hands busy.** Children enjoy helping. Ask them to pass out cups, crayons, or small beanbags. Ask them to "wash" cookie sheets, tables, or doors with a spray bottle of water.

▶ **Keep bodies busy.** Play follow-the-leader. Crawl like puppies, slither like snakes, tiptoe like turtles, hop like bunnies, sway like elephants, jump like kangaroos, or skip to music.

▶ **Monitor the need for privacy.** Toddlers become overstimulated when they are constantly around other children. They need to feel limits around them. In group settings, children need time to play alone. For toddlers, parallel play is part of development. Encourage use of places and spaces for children to be alone, including a soft, cozy area that is not used for play.

RESOURCES FOR GROWTH

Great Books about Toddler Emotions

Toddlers prefer recognizable photos or drawings that depict their own experiences. Focus on the pictures and describe what you see. Ask children what the child in each picture is doing and feeling. Children may point to the pictures and repeat what you say. The following are popular toddler stories about emotions:

- ▶ *Calm-Down Time* by Elizabeth Verdick
- ▶ *Feelings* by Aliki
- ▶ *Hands Are Not for Hitting* by Martine Agassi
- ▶ *Let's Talk about Feeling Angry* by Joy Berry
- ▶ *Lots of Feelings* by Shelly Rotner
- ▶ *Love Waves* by Rosemary Wells
- ▶ *Sometimes I'm Bombaloo* by Rachel Vail
- ▶ *Talk and Work It Out* by Cheri J. Meiners
- ▶ *The Temper Tantrum Book* by Edna Mitchell Preston
- ▶ *Tessa Tiger's Tantrum Book* by Barbara deRubertis
- ▶ *The Way I Feel* by Janan Cain
- ▶ *When I Feel Angry* by Cornelia Maud Spelman

———

Quick question: If I don't get angry at children for hitting or pushing, how will they know that it is wrong to hit and push?

Simple solution: Like yelling at a child to be quiet, getting angry to make a child stop being angry is counterproductive. A child learns to become calm by seeing your calm response. Using anger, fear, or shame makes it less likely that children will focus on the needed skill—and more likely that they will fear you or your reaction. Adult verbal aggression increases child physical aggression (Wilson et al. 2008). Staying calm and creating a positive outcome through talking and problem solving helps children remember the calm, positive option next time.

———

Quick question: Can you recommend a book to help boys develop healthy social and emotional skills?

Simple solution: *Raising Cain: Protecting the Emotional Life of Boys* by Dan Kindlon and Michael Thompson is a wonderful book that shows how emotions can develop into positive resources for children. See www.penguinrandomhouse.com/books /92664/raising-cain.

Guiding Toddler Behavior

Toddlers are highly sensitive to adults' body language, facial expressions, actions, and words. They respond in the best way they are able to the many new experiences they face each day. This chapter addresses toddlers' need for consistency, preparation, and support as they navigate the behavior expectations of a group setting. It presents positive relational guidance strategies that keep your connection strong and secure while you help children get what they need. It provides practical skills for calming upsets, handling behavior challenges, and helping you better understand toddler behavior dynamics.

Guiding with Respect

Laura pulls on Ms. Evelyn's arm. "Just a minute, Laura. I am helping Alex." Ms. Evelyn wipes Alex's tears and brushes the hair from his forehead. She says, "It's okay, Alex. I will help you." Laura leans over to pat Alex's hair, too. She says, "Don't cry, Alex." Ms. Evelyn responds to her as well. "Laura, you are sweet to care about Alex. Let's pat his back and rub his arm. We can talk with him until he feels better."

The close connection between a teacher and each child is an important part of behavior guidance. Ms. Evelyn shows empathy for Alex's sadness. Her gentle, quiet soothing teaches an important lesson to the children watching. When Ms. Evelyn includes Laura in showing empathy to Alex, both children learn what kindness feels like.

The greatest influence in guiding behavior is your modeling. When you are warm and sensitive, toddlers are, too. They imitate your tone of voice, mannerisms, and even your sense of humor. Over time children learn from you how to be respectful and caring.

To guide toddlers effectively, you need to respect their limits and build on their potential. Knowing the unique characteristics of this age group can help you see how sensitive they are to your modeling:

- **Toddlers respond to others' emotions.** They absorb and react to the energy level they feel. They are calmed when adults respond calmly to them. They use these external cues to regulate their own emotions.

- **Toddlers are rarely flexible.** When they don't know what to expect or their schedules are inconsistent, toddlers are not likely to adapt quickly. They respond best when procedures and routines are predictable.

- **Toddlers are absorbed in the moment.** Toddlers are egocentric, and therefore hyperfocused on their current interest or need. They may not notice the cues or activities of others around them.

- **Toddlers are inconsistent.** They may not be able to sustain tomorrow behaviors they demonstrated independently yesterday. Developing skills can be as frustrating to the child as to the adult.

- **Toddlers are curious.** Their desire to explore drives their behavior. Their instinct to investigate is how they learn. They want to touch anything within reach and figure out how it works.

- **Toddlers desire competence.** The words "I want to do it myself" express the need for mastery. Toddlers want and need to gain control over themselves and tackle new challenges.

- **Toddlers want a close connection with you.** They seek to be with you and want to participate in what you are doing. They need your time and full attention.

- **Toddlers learn from you.** They watch how you respond to challenges. They gather information about what to say and what to do from your words and emotions.

When you consider toddlers from a strength-based view, you can see that when they are upset or discouraged, they simply need love, support, comfort, and reassurance. When they dash around a small area and bump into others, they need enough space and time to run. When they melt down, they are exhausted or not feeling well. Toddlers' behaviors signal their needs.

Until toddlers gain more language, they use their bodies to communicate their needs. When they can identify and ask for what they need, or figure out a better plan of action, they will. But while these skills are developing, you need to assist them as they navigate the challenges and excitement of a group setting.

Respecting Children's Strengths

What does deeper respect for children's strengths look like? We talk a lot about seeing children as competent. Maybe we see they are interested in puppies. So we put a puppy in the housekeeping area. But is this enough? Have we looked deeper? Are the children seeking comfort? Do they want to nurture the puppy? Of course children will get something from having a puppy to play with. But we have learned to take the time to listen more intently to each child. Every conversation gives us an opportunity to find meaning behind the children's words. The more we know, the more we understand children's real needs.

Successful behavior guidance is anchored in the belief that every child should be honored, respected, and cherished. As an early childhood professional, you must look for and nurture each child's gifts and abilities. You must provide the highest-quality experiences to ensure the best possible future.

STRATEGIES FOR SUCCESS

Respecting Personal Boundaries

Toddlers learn respect by being respected. When you need to touch children's personal belongings, ask first. "I need to put your sweater in your cubby. Is that okay? Do you want to help me?" When children need a diaper, ask first. "Would you like to choose your diaper?" Respect is a fundamental part of all self-care routines.

A teacher shared, "At first I thought, 'Are you kidding me? I am supposed to ask a child before I check his diaper or go into his cubby?' Then the lightbulb went on. I realized that when I ask children first, they learn to ask me first before touching my things. When I show respect for children's things, they accept that respecting other people's belongings is part of what we do."

Setting Up for Success

Aria runs to pick up a foam soccer ball from the sandbox, where it landed. She kicks it across the playground. In the same instant, she grabs a plastic pail and throws it after the ball. Sand sprays everywhere and just misses Emily, who is playing in the sandbox.

Ms. Hannah quickly joins Aria and gets down next to her. She holds Aria's hands gently and speaks quietly. "Where does the bucket go?" Aria looks at the sandbox.

Ms. Hannah nods. "Yes. Sand toys in the sandbox. Can you say, 'Sand toys in the sandbox?'" Aria repeats, "Sand toys in the sandbox." Ms. Hannah helps her return the pail to the sand. Ms. Hannah says, "Thank you, Aria. You may throw the ball. But the pail stays in the sand. Keep your friends safe." Ms. Hannah fist-bumps Aria. She runs off to find the ball.

Ms. Hannah knows Aria is excited. In an energetic moment, she throws a pail. Ms. Hannah joins Aria on her eye level and states a simple rule. "Sand toys in the sandbox." She encourages Aria to repeat the words to help her remember. She fist-bumps to end the interaction in a positive way.

Ms. Hannah makes a note to watch Aria when she is near the sandbox. Next time she wants to support her *before* she throws a pail. Over time Aria will be better able to control her impulses. Until then she may need additional gentle reminders and quiet talks. Ms. Hannah knows that behavior guidance means to teach, coach, and support children's success.

The first rule of behavior guidance is that consistency leads to success. You want to respond to children the same way each time. Your patient eye-level connection, asking the same question, repeating the simple rule, and parting on a positive note helps children practice needed skills. Your matter-of-fact, positive demeanor helps children focus on the issue at hand and remember the lesson better than if they feel upset.

Expectations and routines also need consistency. Because toddlers depend on doing tasks the same way every time, a set sequence for snacks, self-care, naptime, and transitions will minimize behavior issues. Whatever routines and procedures you and your coteachers choose, stick to them. The repetition gives children many opportunities to practice needed skills.

The second rule of behavior guidance is to identify and build skills needed for success. Set up each interaction so it results in a successful moment for the child. Show and review needed steps and skills. Then help the child achieve those steps.

Self-efficacy means seeing oneself as capable of reaching a desired result. Children take pride in knowing what to do to achieve a goal (Bandura 1982). Each experience of mastery—when children handle a situation well—increases their ability to succeed again.

To ensure success, expectations must be achievable for children's specific abilities and understanding. At sixteen months, children need a lot of ongoing assistance. At two years, they need more opportunities to try for themselves with you nearby to support their growing independence. By age three, children can follow simple verbal steps with your encouragement more consistently.

Planning Ahead

Looking and planning ahead is essential to successful toddler behavior guidance. The following steps will help you use anticipatory guidance:

▶ **Be proactive.** Supervise closely, anticipate children's needs, and be ready to step in. Distract and intervene in behavior that may lead to more serious issues.

▶ **Meet sensory needs.** When children are understimulated, they seek something to explore, learn, do, or manipulate. Provide materials that are new and interesting, that engage curiosity and build children's skills. Ensure plenty of outdoor time with adequate physical exercise and play.

▶ **Plan, communicate, and coordinate daily activities with your coteacher(s).** Take time daily to review what is ahead and reflect on completed routines, activities, and events. Talk about what went well and what you can adjust. Reflecting together can help you better collaborate to support each child's needs.

Staying Connected

Jackson shouts, "Look, Ms. Jana! My car is sliding down the slide!" At the same time, Lilly throws her arms around Ms. Jana's neck and says, "I love you!" Jackson runs over and falls on top of Lilly and Ms. Jana. "Love you!" he shouts. Ms. Jana helps Jackson turn around and sit next to Lilly. "I love you both!" she says. She squeezes them tight. "Now, Jackson, do you want to show me your car? Lilly, do you want to slide cars down the slide with us?" The three go off together to play.

Toddlers are emotionally expressive. Without prompting, Jackson and Lilly throw their arms around Ms. Jana's neck to demonstrate their love. They say, "Love you!" and associate these words with the happiness they feel when they are with her. They snuggle next to her and want to see happiness on her face.

Your relationship means everything to a child. Children's desire to feel safe, happy, secure, and connected is your greatest source of influence. The stronger your connection, the easier it is to guide behavior. When children feel close, they seek your comfort and want to do what you are doing.

TEACHER TIP

Staying Calm

My colleague is so effective. When children are upset, she gets down and holds their hand gently. Even if they are on the verge of losing control, her calm demeanor works magic. She tells them, "I am going to help you. I am going to stay here and talk with you." I have learned so much from watching her. The children trust her, and you can see how much impact she has.

When you gently help children get dressed, they return the gentleness toward you when you help them manage frustration during play. Frustrated children who feel safe coming to you will seek your help to feel better rather than hurt another child.

Many caregivers know touch and gentle massage are important for infants, but this practice often diminishes in the toddler classroom. However, during this time of development, toddlers frequently need to feel physically connected, reassured, and soothed.

Physical touch is a healthy part of a nurturing relationship. An interaction may last for a few seconds or a few minutes as a child sits next to you, leans on your arm, or enjoys a gentle tickle on the back. Appropriate and safe touch shows respect at all times. Pay attention to and honor each child's comfort level. The following techniques for safe touch can be soothing for toddlers throughout the day:

- **Hand gestures:** Give high fives, fist bumps, pinky kisses (touch pinky fingers and make a kissing sound), or caterpillar kisses (wiggle fingertips on the back of a child's hand).

- **Figure eight:** Draw a small figure eight with your index finger on the back of the child's wrist and lower arm. This gentle touch (firm or light) can help children relax, especially during circle time, reading time, or at rest time or naptime.

- **Puppy tug:** Gently grasp each fingertip with your own thumb and forefinger. Gently press and rotate back and forth. Begin with the thumb and end with the pinky.

- **Palm dance:** Walk your fingertips around the inside of the child's palm. Press gently, like walking on a soft mattress or pillow.

- **Squeeze walk:** This gentle traveling squeeze and release is done on the forearm between the wrist and elbow.

- **Hand pat:** Gently stroke the top of a child's hand, lifting your hand and fingertips at the end of each stroke.

- **Back rubs:** During small-group or circle times, a coteacher can sit next to a child and gently scratch or rub between the shoulder blades. Use an up-and-down or circular motion.

Safe and soothing touch depends on an existing respectful, caring, and warm relationship. You must always observe and stay tuned into children's physical and verbal cues. Honor any pulling away—even slight—as a "no." A child's comfort with physical affection is rooted in the family. Some children do not want to be touched in a certain way, or may only want to be touched as part of a rest or nap routine. When it comes to touch, the child is in charge.

FAST FACTS: WHY THIS WORKS

Exploring the Link between Relationships and Behavior

Toddlers are relationship dependent. Your close connection, warmth, and caring support directly influence their behavior. Your commitment to using positive guidance and protecting their emotional lives profoundly affects their development in the following ways:

▶ A high-quality relationship between you and a child is mediatory, protective, and predictive of higher developmental outcomes and greater self-regulation (Blair 2013; Phillips 2010; Phillips and Meloy 2012).

▶ For children at risk, your close relationship directly influences the neurobiological, social-emotional, and cognitive strengths that predict school and life success (Adams, Tout, and Zaslow 2007; Camilli et al. 2010; Fuller, Gasko, and Anguiano 2010; Mashburn 2008).

▶ Research shows consistently that punitive behavior guidance increases aggression, lowers compliance, decreases internalization of values, and exacerbates misbehavior (Gershoff 2010; Gershoff and Bitensky 2007; Straus 2010).

▶ NAEYC prohibits corporal punishment and gives the following guidance: "Above all, we shall not harm children. We shall not participate in practices that are emotionally damaging, physically harmful, disrespectful, degrading, dangerous, exploitative, or intimidating to children. This principle has precedence over all others in this Code" (NAEYC 2011).

▶ Punishment has both short- and long-term detrimental impacts on children, especially those who are already at risk due to deficits in health, education, language, or socioeconomic and community resources (Duncan et al. 2013).

▶ Shame-based approaches undermine children's sense of self-worth and dignity and are emotionally damaging (Sterns and Sterns 2017). Research consistently shows that punitive approaches create more problems than they correct (Osher et al. 2010).

Using Effective Behavior Strategies

Ms. Mandy says, "Time to wash hands, Patrick." Patrick does not move. He sits and stares at a book. Ms. Mandy sees that he does not realize it is time for lunch. She sits next to Patrick and points at the page where he is staring. "Do you want to be a worker?" Patrick replies, "I wish I could be a painter, Ms. Mandy. I wish I could be a painter, because I am going to help the bears." Ms. Mandy asks, "What are the bears doing?" Patrick points. "The bears are working. I want to jump into the book and help the bears."

After talking about the bears, Ms. Mandy asks, "Will you help the bears wash their hands? It's time for lunch, and all the bears need to wash their hands." Patrick puts down the book and walks with Ms. Mandy to the sink.

Ms. Mandy knows that she needs to help Patrick shift his focus away from his book. She recognizes that his early obsession with books is positive. She shifts his attention in a way that teaches what is needed and supports his strengths. She wants to work with his skills rather than against them.

Toddlers may not have the ability to shift their focus independently. They do not have the capacity to step back, be emotionally objective, evaluate a situation, or think ahead to make a plan of action. These are adult abilities. You are the one who has a great deal of influence over the way interactions turn out.

To encourage toddlers' cooperation, you can first minimize power struggles. Power struggles happen when adults try to force children's compliance rather than building self-control and cooperation. Power struggles include the following:

- **Asking a question when something needs to done:** "Do you want to take a nap?" This is a power struggle, because the child can say "no." The child's "no" often results in a demand by the adult.

- **Issuing a demand:** "Stop touching her." "Give that back." Trying to stop a behavior may work for a minute, but it doesn't teach or show a child what to do instead.

- **Making a threat:** "Come here now, or I am leaving you." "If you don't stop doing that, we will have to go inside." A threat, like a demand, may cause a child to do something in the moment, but it does not teach skills for what to do next time. Demands and threats do not transfer responsibility for the behavior to the child. The goal is to build skills and teach the satisfaction of self-chosen cooperation.

Positive guidance keeps children and you focused on creating good solutions. It fosters cooperation and avoids typical power struggles that can be frustrating to the child and to you. Positive guidance helps you focus on how toddlers learn best.

Positive Behavior Guidance for Toddlers

Guidance means to teach and train positive habits of behavior and to strengthen self-regulation. There are five basic positive guidance strategies that are effective with toddlers. You can use these strategies individually or combine them as needed. The desired outcome is to help children succeed.

Prepare children for what is coming next. "First we will wash hands. Then we will eat lunch."

Give positive feedback. Draw attention to effective strategies. "How kind. You shared your wagon with Skye." "You stepped over Bryon's puzzle. Good for you to notice he was working."

Use effective redirection. Rather than mentioning what a child should not do or telling a child to stop, describe a safe, positive choice or solution. Redirection is an incompatible alternative, because the new positive behavior replaces the behavior you do not want to continue.

▶ To a child steering a riding toy toward another child, say, "Drive around Tommy," rather than, "Don't hit Tommy."

▶ To a child who bumps into another child while walking, say, "Look for your feet," rather than, "Look out. Don't bump Charlie."

▶ To a child throwing a beanbag at another child, say, "Throw the beanbag into the basket," rather than, "Don't throw the beanbag at Remy."

Offer choices. Make a simple statement that describes a needed behavior, then add two choices to shift responsibility to the child, as in the following examples:

▶ "Naptime. Do you want to snuggle with your blanket or teddy bear?"

▶ "Time to wash hands. Do you want help with the soap, or can you squirt it by yourself?"

▶ "Time to pick up toys. Do you want to help pick up the cars or the bears?" If needed, repeat. "Time to pick up toys. Cars or bears?" If the child does not choose, offer the container, help put the bears in, and talk about the upcoming activity.

Keep it simple. Toddlers have a short attention span. Give brief, one-step instructions:

▶ For a child climbing, say, "Feet on the floor," rather than, "Look out, Shalynn. You will fall off that chair and hurt yourself."

▶ For a child wanting to play at naptime, say, "Naptime. I will pat your back," rather than, "Honey, if you don't sleep now, you will be tired when Momma comes, and I promised her I would help you take a good nap."

▶ For a child waving a book around, say, "Book on your lap. Let's read together," rather than, "If you wave that book around, you will bop yourself on the head and get hurt."

Always invite cooperation. Early childhood standards and best practices recommend positive redirection as a substitute for telling children "no." When a toddler is climbing the stairs to reach the sink when it is not time to wash hands, what are your options? If you say "no," children are more likely to reply "no" in return. They may return to the forbidden activity to see what will happen. The following strategies are alternatives to "no" that shift children's attention forward to a positive activity:

- Move the child (or the item) without discussing the activity or item of interest.

- Redirect or distract. "I have a box of squishy balls. You can roll them down the slide." Hand the box to the child and demonstrate.

- Offer a choice. "Would you like to paint at the easel or make handprints with Ms. Kelly?" Help the child get started.

- Engage the child in a new activity with other children. "Let's blow bubbles with Jasmine and Sam." Guide the child to the children with bubbles.

When you simply stop a behavior by saying "no," children stop because you have made them. When you replace a behavior, children learn and practice the skills they need for successful behavior choices. They learn positive strategies to get what they need.

Children live up to the positive words and labels they hear you say. "Three cheers for my kind children! You were helping each other." "Awesome! We had fun cleaning up together." "I am so happy to read with you. You are a good book reader." This positive spirit will infuse everything you do—and make your own day satisfying and meaningful. Children will feel confident and happy.

Positive guidance fosters social skills and strengthens children's ability to get along with others. It instills caring ways of thinking, needed habits, and strategies for success. Over time children learn how to ask for what they need and how to look out for others' well-being.

SEEING FROM THE CHILD'S POINT OF VIEW

Wanting Your Approval

I watch for your face. When you are mad, I worry you are mad at me.
When you are worried, I think there is something to be afraid of.
When you are quiet, I wonder if I have done something wrong.
When you are happy, I think that I caused your smile.
When I wake up and you are watching for me, I feel my own smile.
When I am laughing and you laugh with me, it is the funniest fun I know.

Understanding What Toddlers Need

On the playground, Ms. Sara says, "Jody, Mitchell likes your ball. Can you kick the ball to Mitchell?" Jody hugs the blue ball to her chest. She stares at Mitchell as if he is an intruder.

"Can you share the ball, Jody?" Ms. Sara urges her. Jody answers. "I *can* share. I don't *want* to." Ms. Sara and Ms. Megan smile. Ms. Megan finds a red ball for Mitchell and says, "Let's both kick the red ball. When you kick it to me, I will kick it back to you. Jody will kick the blue ball to Ms. Sara. We can all kick the balls back and forth."

These teachers wisely decide to model sharing skills rather than try to make the children share one ball. Getting another ball is a simple solution to the challenge. The teachers use this opportunity to show the children how sharing works. "We can all kick the balls back and forth." Stepping in with additional equipment and then modeling skills is an important strategy for age-appropriate behavior guidance.

Jody does not yet fully understand the concept of sharing. But she does understand what it means to have something taken away. She worries that if she gives up the ball, it will not come back to her. Telling her to share will not be successful. However, showing how to kick a ball with someone else—and have fun doing it—leaves a lasting impression.

Adults may think of toddlers as little preschoolers and use ways of redirecting behavior that are ineffective, such as giving detailed reasons or launching into long explanations. "Now, boys, we have to share. Here are two monkeys. Can you each take one? George, you have the blue one. Seth, you have the orange one. Let's be nice and share." In order to digest that long sentence, toddlers need to stop what they are doing, interrupt their emotional reaction, calm down long enough to listen, focus on a long explanation, and understand the difference between *blue* and *orange* and the link between *nice* and *share*. That response involves a lot of steps and more cognitive comparison than a toddler can muster. Those are complex skills that toddlers do not yet have.

Toddlers are bound by the limits of their developmental stage. When you understand and honor children's needs, you gain insight into how your words and approaches can affect their responses. Their limited vocabulary, emotional sensitivity, and dependence on you guide their responses.

From sixteen to thirty-six months, toddlers' emotions are immediate, switching from delight to frustration within seconds. As they pass the two-year milestone, they begin to use words. However, just like adults, they cannot easily retrieve words when they are upset. Toddlers are naturally egocentric, absorbed in their own physical sensations and emotions. They often don't notice they are hungry until they are ravenous. They don't recognize their thirst until their throat is scratchy and they feel irritable. They rely on you to notice and assist them in meeting these needs.

Toddlers feel safe within firm, consistent boundaries. Toddlers know and believe to be true what you show them is true. If the rule is to go down the slide feet first, but you laugh or ignore when children turn upside down, then they learn that expectations are not firm. If you want children to keep their feet on the floor, but you ignore a child who kneels on the chair, they learn that sometimes rules are to be followed, and sometimes they are not. When expectations are clear, children are quick to adopt them.

When you are sensitive and responsive to toddlers' limitations and needs, you will see how much influence you have on how situations turn out. When you understand the limits of toddlers' capability, are consistent in age-appropriate expectations, and seek to meet their underlying needs in positive ways, you will find that they trust you and look to you for guidance.

STRATEGIES FOR SUCCESS

Meeting Children's Needs

▶ **Teach simple words or cues that children can use when they need help.** Teach them to say, "Stop!" or "Help!" or to tap you on the arm. When children follow through, thank them for coming to get you.

▶ **Give a child time.** Be patient. Toddlers need time and assistance to leave what they are doing and come to a calmer place or a new activity.

▶ **Keep rules few and positive.** State what needs to be done, rather than what should not be done. "We are gentle with our hands." "We help our friends." "We use a quiet voice."

▶ **Minimize issues and make behavior a nonissue.** Address children's frustrations quietly and quickly. Draw children's attention forward by quickly shifting the conversation. Your goal is to build skills and create successful solutions.

▶ **Explain what is happening.** When a child is struggling, reassure other children. "Maureen is sad, but I am comforting her. She will come and play in a few minutes." "Marcus is crying. He feels upset that his dad left. We are going to sit together and read a book."

▶ **Hug a lot.** Often a frustrated child does not need anything fixed. A gentle hug and invitation to come with you to a quiet place for a few minutes is enough to soothe. Being with other children all day long can be stressful for toddlers, just as it is for adults. Listening to gentle music or curling up with a blanket on a soft floor pillow with picture books may be just what a toddler needs to regroup. A few minutes later, the child may be off playing again as though nothing happened.

Addressing Common Behavior Issues

Jose puts the cows and pigs into the barn. He tries for several minutes to fit them all and latch the door. Once he does so, he can't get the door back open. He groans in frustration. Ms. Melissa slips over quickly and says, "I am sorry the latch stuck. To open it, pick up the square part of the latch and pull it up." She shows Jose how and then says, "You try." Jose picks at the latch with his fingers. As it opens, Ms. Melissa says, "Good for you. Now the farm animals can come out."

Ms. Melissa has been watching Jose play and noticing his physical cues. She is careful to show him and then ask him to try, rather than simply open the latch for him. She stays near to assist him. Stepping in early allows her to talk with Jose before his frustration escalates.

Toddlers sometimes need you to do something for them, like turn on a water fountain or reach for a toy that is stuck. However, when a skill is within children's developmental ability, it is important to show them how and then give them an opportunity to practice the skill. Ms. Melissa assists Jose when he cannot open a latch. She demonstrates the skill with a clear, simple explanation. Then she asks him to try. This is a highly effective two-step strategy.

You will notice the signs when a child is about to flip out or give up. A trembling upper lip, eyebrows knit together, or a growl of frustration tells you it is time to intervene. If you wait too long, the frustration can escalate into tears.

It helps to understand that toddlers are goal oriented. Two children's simultaneous need for one toy is not about selfishness. Children simply see and decide to play with the same toy at the same moment. They are absorbed in play and need the equipment to carry out their actions.

The following strategies will help you build skills and respond to behavior as an opportunity to teach and train. Because toddlers are learning everything for the first time, your patience and encouragement are essential. The scenarios below represent the most common challenges toddlers face.

Assisting When One Child Wants What Another Has

After washing his hands, Noah sees Ms. Rose put a muffin on Charlie's plate. He walks with hand outstretched toward Charlie's muffin. Ms. Rose steps in front of Charlie. "This is Charlie's muffin. *Your* muffin is on *your* plate."

Interception is the best intervention for attempted snatching. Ms. Rose gets in front of and on the eye level of the moving child. She states the facts simply. "This is Charlie's muffin." No other explanation is needed. Noah doesn't have issues with Charlie. He simply wants a muffin and needs redirection toward his own.

Use the same intervention when children take toys from other children. Provide an alternative item and state the facts simply. "Samantha is playing with her truck. Here is your truck." Quickly lead the children forward into productive play. "Let's drive our trucks to the orchard to load the apples." Show the children how to load large beads into the backs of the trucks. Evaluate the situation to be sure adequate space, supervision, and materials are in place.

Turning Around Frustration and Biting

Toddlers sometimes bite when they are over- or understimulated. They bite when they are excited or frustrated. They may bite an arm, leg, or back just because it is nearby. NAEYC suggests that toddlers bite to relieve teething pain, to explore cause and effect, to experience the biting sensation, and to satisfy their oral-motor simulation needs (NAEYC 2016). Research shows that toddlers are more likely to bite if they have not interacted individually with adults in more than five minutes (Claffey, Kucharski, and Gratz 1994). You can address biting with consistency and calm intervention in the following ways:

- **Anticipate problems.** Notice when excitement or activity is getting frenetic. Step in and guide children to a quieter activity. Redirect *before* biting occurs. Stay nearby and anticipate potential problems.

- **Ensure adequate space and materials.** Biting happens more often when children are in close physical proximity.

- **Meet sensory needs.** Fingers and objects in children's mouths are signs of oral needs. Offer safe biting necklaces and teething rings. Chewy bars and other textured foods may help. Teething may increase desire for oral stimulation.

- **Stay calm.** Biting usually brings immediate, intense adult attention, which can be both frightening and reinforcing. Children may repeat the behavior to see what happens.

- **Give verbal alternatives.** "Biting hurts. You can bite a teething ring." "You can bite food." "We use our mouths to blow kisses."

- **Move the child gently to a safe place.** The child who bit may feel upset or surprised. This is a time to be calm.

- **Attend to the bitten child.** Give hugs and kisses. If skin is not broken, wash with soap and water. If staff need to administer first aid, follow the licensing procedures and requirements of your state for notifying families.

- **Use the opportunity to teach.** Never yell, shame, or punish. Toddlers need assistance to regulate emotions and behaviors. Stay consistent. When adults work together, children move past this behavior. Teachers find that when they use the advice above and give adequate supervision, biting subsides. As children mature, their need to bite disappears.

Calming Hitting or Aggression

By nature, children explore. When toddlers are not engaged, they are more likely to struggle with behavior regulation (Aguiar and McWilliam 2013). Hitting may happen due to fatigue, frustration, hunger, or overexcitement. It happens when space, materials, and supervision are inadequate. Children use their hands when they do not have words. Prepare ahead, and respond consistently:

- Keep transitions short and routines consistent.

- Set out all materials for easy access by multiple children.

- Stay nearby and provide adequate support during play.

- Adjust furniture to give children ample space.

- Increase physical activity for all children. Outdoor active play and vigorous music and motion help release energy.

- Keep naptimes consistent. Rested children have more patience and self-control.

- Keep activities age appropriate—stimulating but not too challenging.

- Stay calm. Intervene by gently holding the child's hands. Say, "Hands are for hugging." "We are gentle with our hands."

- Teach words to get help. "When you need help, say, 'Help me!'" "Tell your friend, 'No thank you.'" "Tell your friend, 'Walk away.'"

Soothing Tantrums

Tantrums are not misbehavior. They are ways for children to tell adults that they cannot or do not want to handle a stressful situation. When tantrums have worked at home to get what children want, they may become a way to get attention from teachers. When children have tantrums, they often receive attention, pleading, threats, promises, and inconsistency from adults. These responses can complicate, reinforce, and prolong tantrums. The following steps can help you intervene successfully:

- Note what happened before, during, and after the tantrum. Set up the situation differently next time so a similar response is less likely. Intervene before a tantrum occurs.

- Step in and move the crying child to a quiet place. Remain near the child and say, "I am going to wait for you." Ask a coteacher to reassure and engage the other children in an activity.

- Tantrums can be scary for the children who are upset. When they stop crying, hug and reassure them of your care. Lead them forward to a new activity. Reassure other children as well.

- Teach alternatives. Read books about anger and frustration that show positive strategies to handle emotions. Teach children to say, "Hugs and help!" You can model this with a coteacher or a puppet. When a child uses this strategy, say, "Thank you for coming for hugs and help!"

Toddlers cannot control intense emotion. They depend on you to set up situations differently or reorganize events so you can give comfort before they are overwhelmed. Your consistent response to tantrums and positive teaching can quickly change this behavior.

Respecting Children's Natural Limits

Michael keeps rubbing his eyes. Instead of running after Jose and Maria, he lingers near Ms. Jen. When Maria grabs Michael's shirt to make him come play, Michael bursts into tears. Ms. Jen says, "It's okay, Michael. You can stay with me and play with playdough. See the roller? We can make tracks." Ms. Jen hugs Michael and reassures him.

When children are tired, frustrated, hungry, or upset, there are many ways to meet their needs. Ms. Jen sees that Michael is tired. She knows the playdough will soothe and engage him. Time with her will match his need for personal connection and rest. In a few minutes, Michael will be ready to join the others.

Life with toddlers can go from fun to frustrating quickly. Their strengths bring both benefits and challenges. The most important element of toddler behavior support is recognizing that social skills, language, and behavior habits are just taking root. Toddlers need your ongoing assistance to strengthen each area of development:

- **Toddlers are masters of imitation.** The benefit is that they love to help. They enjoy taking part in goal-oriented tasks like stacking books and putting things away. The challenge is that toddlers copy aggression and other unsafe behaviors. They may imitate what other children do to get attention. What to do? Redirect quickly when needed, and separate children who are reinforcing each other. Give positive feedback for helpful behaviors.

- **Toddlers are developing prosocial skills.** The benefit is that they love to cooperate and be part of activities. The challenge is that toddlers can suddenly shift from friendly to ferocious. What to do? Stay nearby and be ready to step in immediately when needed. Narrate the successful strategies you see.

- **Toddlers are strengthening the link between language and behavior.** The benefit is that they add vocabulary quickly, often learning new words after only a few exposures. The challenge is that toddlers can experience frustration when feelings come faster than words. What to do? Use and teach emotion words. Help children learn words to set boundaries and get help. Teach them to say, "Please stop," and "No thank you."

- **Toddlers are increasing their ability to regulate their emotions and bodies.** The benefit is that they use emotion words, demonstrate sensitivity to others, and develop preferences in friends. The challenge is that toddlers are still immature and need adults to help them manage emotions and behaviors (Bruno 2011). What to do? Keep expectations realistic and continue to provide support.

Toddlers need consistent repetition for good habits to form. Experiencing success wires the toddler brain for ongoing growth in coordination, regulation, and language competence. As language grows, emotions mature. Your patience and consistency will pay off when you celebrate many new accomplishments.

STRATEGIES FOR SUCCESS

What to Do with Persistent Behavior Issues

If behavior issues persist, you may be tempted to focus on the child and the behavior, rather than on evaluating the circumstances and shifting the adults' preparation, supervision, and response. Review this chapter with your colleagues. Evaluate each part of the behavior sequence. The following questions will help you decide what a child needs:

▶ **What leads up to the behavior?** Observe carefully and record what happens first. Are children crowded into a corner? Are they playing without close adult supervision? Are there enough materials and space? Have the children gotten enough exercise? Rest? Are the expectations age appropriate? Have children had too much stimulation? Not enough stimulation?

> ▶ **How are you currently responding to the behavior?** Is the child receiving a lot of attention? Is the adult response increasing anxiety? Is the response teaching needed skills and redirecting in positive ways?
>
> ▶ **Does the child need soothing?** Stress, fatigue, or a busy morning can increase frustration and anxiety for toddlers. Look first through the lens of soothing and support. Spend time with children on your lap, in one-on-one reading time, or in physical contact before naptime. When problem behaviors occur, often a hug and reassurance is the best plan of action for toddlers.
>
> Look for changes you can make to set toddlers up for success and apply positive behavior guidance and soothing strategies. You will quickly see a change in yourself and in the way children respond.

Using Reflective Practice

George watches Ms. Ellie put the book back onto the shelf. He reaches to pull out the book. Ms. Ellie responds, "Are you trying to help me, George? Can you slide this one into the space?" She helps him press another book into a space on the bookshelf. Then she hands George a few board books. "Will you help me load these into the book bin?" She sits with George and hands him book after book, and he drops them into the plastic bin. "Will you please help me carry the bin over to the shelf?" George holds one end, and Ms. Ellie holds the other. They slide the bin onto the shelf. "High five! You are a great helper. Thank you."

Ms. Ellie understands that George is not trying to undo her work. She knows he is curious about how the books fit together on the shelf. She invites him to help her, then shifts his attention to a task better suited to his development. She knows George cannot manage the large books and thin slots on the bookshelf. So she invites him to help her put the smaller books into the plastic bin. She wants George to know that helping others is satisfying and fun.

Over time George will learn how to shelve books independently. But today he is learning that putting away books is fun. He knows that his teacher enjoys his company. He is learning that the big books go next to the big books, and the small books go in the bin. This experimentation will continue as George gains greater physical dexterity. He will also develop increasing language skills. Both boost his ability to learn even more. Cognitive, language, and social learning go hand in hand.

Reflective practice helps you become thoughtful about your choices and active in evaluating your effectiveness. When you try a new strategy, you may find that it doesn't work perfectly. You might need to tweak your approach, change your words, or use the strategy at a different time. You make a new plan of action. "I waited until Megan was crying before I helped her. Tomorrow I am going to notice what happens before she starts playing with the dolls. Maybe I can figure out what she needs before she gets upset." Evaluating what happens before, during, and after an incident can give you information to help you adjust your approach.

When challenges continue, ask others for feedback. Maybe someone else is experiencing the same problem. "What should I do when the children are restless but we can't go outside?" "How do we help children release their energy without getting them too wound up?" "How can I encourage interest in reading when toddlers have such a short attention span?" You can save time, get help, and learn quickly when you reflect on your challenges with others.

Over time you may decide to meet regularly with your colleagues to improve your teaching. This is called a community of practice (Saint-Onge and Wallace, 2003). You may meet informally at first and then set regular times to explore issues. You may want to explore both what is working well and what needs attention. You can share challenges and brainstorm ideas and solutions. At the same time, you will gain a cheering team to encourage you.

TEACHER TIP

Observing Others

Observing in another classroom is an amazing opportunity. You are outside the action. You can see missed opportunities. You can see what works and how it works in a way that you might miss in your own teaching. When others observe your teaching, they can see what you missed. Their feedback helps you see things in a more meaningful and intentional way.

RESOURCES FOR GROWTH

Learning More about Positive Guidance

The following resources provide additional tips and strategies that you can use in your classroom and also share with families:

▶ For a comprehensive approach to positive behavior guidance, including strategies for toddlers, see *101 Principles for Positive Guidance with Young Children: Creating Responsive Teachers* by Katharine Kersey and Marie Masterson.

> ▶ To communicate with and encourage families to use strength-based approaches, appropriate boundaries, and effective positive guidance, see *Enjoying the Parenting Roller Coaster: Nurturing and Empowering Your Children through the Ups and Downs* by Marie Masterson and Katharine Kersey.
>
> ▶ The CDC's "Essentials for Childhood" framework promotes relationships and environments to help children grow up to be healthy and productive: www.cdc.gov /violenceprevention/childmaltreatment/essentials.html.

———

Quick question: What do you think of telling toddlers to share? If they prefer to play on their own, does telling them to share help? When I tell them to share, it doesn't seem to make a difference.

Simple solution: With toddlers, the best way to teach sharing is to model it. For example, choose two teddy bears you like. Brush each bear. Tie a bow on each. Then say to a child, "I would like to share my bears with you—one for me, one for you. Let's put our bears in the wagon. You can pull them. I like sharing with you."

When you see children sharing, make a big deal about it. "Josiah, I saw you share your blocks. That made Maddie so happy." Drawing attention to kindness you see is the best way to encourage it.

———

Quick question: Two children seem to bother each other no matter what we do. Should we separate them, or should we try to make them get along?

Simple solution: Children with complementary personalities often get along well. A child who is easily stimulated or affected by noise may be drawn to play with a child who is quiet or focused. When you find that two toddlers reinforce each other's behavior, such as getting overly silly or frenetic, the best plan is to guide them gently to separate activities and spaces.

Over time you can reintroduce happy play by setting up activities that involve both children. For example, you can help each of them use a dough press while they sit near each other at a low table. Eventually, parallel play with your close supervision can influence their dynamic. With new and successful experiences, the two may begin to play well near each other.

7

Nurturing Language and Early Literacy

anguage skills help toddlers express their needs and connect with teachers and peers in positive ways. Language itself boosts social skills and self-regulation, which in turn act as early anchors for learning. This chapter explores the remarkable explosion of language that takes place during toddler development and shows how to strengthen children's growing skills. You will find practical strategies for choosing books, with tips for reading and storytelling that engage children in delightful interaction and foster a lifelong love of reading.

Activating the Power of Language

Camila and Tandy run across the bridge, listening to their feet thumping the wood. Ms. Piper laughs. "I can hear your feet going *pitter-pat* over the bridge. I have to run fast to keep up with you." "Wait up!" yells Sam. Ms. Piper says, "You mean, 'Wait for me.'" "Wait for me!" Sam yells. Ms. Piper waits for Sam and says, "Let's run together across the bridge." They hold hands and follow Camila and Tandy.

Ms. Piper narrates the children's actions. She helps Sam use a sentence to express his needs. Ms. Piper knows these toddlers are adding new words and learning how to express themselves while they run and play.

A child's communication development happens rapidly. Adults respond to infants' vocalizations, use gestures, and match babies' facial expressions. Infants soon know that *dog* means a furry bundle of action that wags its tail and barks. They watch and listen as liquid is poured into a cup and hear the word *water* or *milk*. They taste and see that water is not the same thing as milk. They soon will attach labels to objects and use this vocabulary to communicate.

Infants are not merely learning words for objects. By ten months, they have picked up voice inflections, local accents, and unique family pronunciations. As children reach their second year, they adopt the everyday language that is unique to the region where they live. When milk spills, they may repeat, "Oh boy, oh boy," or "Ooooh, that's a bad one!" or "Uh-oh!" just as they hear their families say. In this way, language reflects each family's way of communicating.

Learning and language go hand in hand. Children discover that a big dog is different from a little cat. A white poodle is different from a black Lab. Children recognize that *running, jumping,* and *talking* are words that describe actions. They realize that *desk, chair,* and *car* are names for objects. In this way, language is more than communication. It is the foundation for learning and understanding.

Toddlers also use emotional and social cues to make sense of what they hear. They watch your facial expressions to interpret what is happening. They notice your voice tone and inflection. They use this information to decide how they should feel and to find out what is expected. Toddlers use social referencing by tuning in to your reactions to decipher the meaning of words and emotions.

Children learn how to listen and how to take turns in a conversation. These social rules vary from situation to situation and culture to culture. At home a child might push on his brother's arm and say, "Hey yah. You sittin' on my leg." But at school, he would be expected to use more formal language. "Excuse me. I want to get up."

In some situations, it is acceptable for people to talk over each other in excitement or agreement. In other settings, children are expected to listen, be quiet, or take turns. These social rules are an important part of language learning.

For these reasons, language development is much more than learning to talk. It both reflects and expresses a child's unique experience and identity. It also influences toddlers' social skills, learning, and behavior adjustment. Your day-to-day conversations and interactions have a direct impact on children. What toddlers experience with you can prepare them for successful future experiences in school and in life.

FAST FACTS: WHY THIS WORKS

Examining the Priority of Language

Your decision to create rich language experiences is an investment that keeps paying off. When children have strong language ability, they draw others into conversation easily. Children's ease in connecting with teachers and peers in turn leads to stronger social skills. Frequent positive social experiences lead to greater learning opportunities. In this way, language and social skills are self-reinforcing as they continue to strengthen and increase development (Cuhna and Heckman 2010).

The interdependent benefit of language and social skills is called a skill multiplier. With strong language and social skills, children will be prepared for kindergarten. Language and social skills are the foundations of competence that give children early and lasting advantages in learning and life (Denham and Brown 2010; King and Dockrell 2016). An early strong start during the toddler years creates a foundation for future social interactions, learning, and ongoing school success.

Why does a rich language experience matter so much to each child? Here are several reasons:

- A child's vocabulary at age three is a key predictor of the child's ability to read at third grade, which is a powerful indicator of subsequent academic success (Head Zauche et al. 2016).

- Language nutrition, early language exposure that is rich in quantity and quality, is created through talking, interacting, and reading with children. There must be enough language enrichment and interaction to impact a child's brain positively (Weldon 2014).

- There must be high-quality interaction that stimulates and challenges children each day to positively influence language expression and vocabulary (Weisleder and Fernald 2013; Rowe 2012).

- Child-centered conversation increases cognitive processing skills and vocabulary (Suskind et al. 2013).

- Language-enriched environments with responsive interactions positively influence outcomes for children at risk (Kuhl 2011).

- Language-rich interactions, along with sensitive, responsive caregiving, can positively influence brain development (Fox, Levitt, and Nelson 2010; Shonkoff 2010).

- By two years of age, disparities in language are equivalent to a six-month gap between children from rich and poor families in both language processing skills and vocabulary knowledge (Fernald, Marchman, and Weisleder 2013).

- Toddler teachers tend to use interactions to give directions, rather than respond to individual children and provide rich personal conversation (Hallam et al. 2009).

- Most interactions focus on telling children what to do. "Renie, put your book on the shelf." Teachers don't realize how important it is to respond to the needs and interests of a single child (Gloeckler, Cassell, and Malkus 2013). "Emi, your basket is full. What did you put inside?"

- Toddler teachers need to understand how to use emotionally rich language and provide a sufficient amount of language and cognitive stimulation (Landry et al. 2014).

Words do more than communicate. Through language, children think about, talk about, and build understanding about the world (Vygotsky 1978). Language allows children to make friends, regulate their behavior, and express their ideas and feelings. Strengthening language skills is a critical priority during the toddler years.

Helping Language Grow

Daniel opens the toy barn doors and peeks inside to see the farm animals. Mr. Tom says, "There is Goose. Goose is big and fat and says, 'Honk, honk.'" "Honk, honk," says Daniel as he puts the goose on top of a block wall. Daniel reaches for a pig and puts it next to the goose. Mr. Tom narrates Daniel's actions. "Oink, oink. Pig wants to sit next to Goose." Daniel repeats, "Oink, oink." He wiggles the pig up onto the block wall. Mr. Tom continues, "Are Goose and Pig sitting on the wall?" The animals fall. "Uh-oh," Daniel says. "My animals all fall down." "Yes," Mr. Tom responds. "Your animals fell off the wall. Can you help them climb back up? What will your animals say when you help them?" Daniel smiles. "They will say, 'Thank you!'"

Each day as Mr. Tom plays with the children, he helps their language grow. He zeros in on Daniel's actions and describes them. He encourages Daniel to talk about his play. He is pleased to see that Daniel gives the animals polite manners.

Children don't absorb language; they learn it through direct and purposeful interaction with you. There are many ways to make conversation engaging. Children love the close feeling of conversation. They think that conversation is part of play. You can be confident that this warm and interesting interaction builds children's skills. Here are specific ways to make your interactions rich in words:

- **Use self-talk.** Self-talk is "thinking out loud" to narrate what you are doing or feeling. "Let's see where the green frog is. We can dig down in the basket to look for him." "Where should I put this doll? Let's put him in the cradle and cover him up with a blanket."

- **Use parallel talk.** Parallel talk is describing what you see children doing. "I see you are hiding under the blue blanket."

- **Ask questions.** You can draw children into conversation by asking a question after parallel talk. "You are pushing the shopping cart. What will you buy at the store?"

- **Use descriptive words.** "Here is the big black horse. It is running through the thick green grass." "The little black caterpillar tickles when it crawls on your arm." Rich words make details come to life and add vocabulary to toddlers' communication toolbox.

- **Repeat and extend.** When children give one-word answers, repeat and extend what they say. A child says, "Fire truck." You can respond, "You have a big red truck with a siren. You saw a fire truck at the parade. Is your fire truck in a parade?" This process encourages conversation and draws children into deeper thinking and expression about their play.

- **Recast.** Toddlers often use grammar rules incorrectly. For example, children may say, "I putted the plate on the table." You can respond, "You put the plate on the table." Children may say, "I goed to the park." You can respond, "Yes, you went to the park to play." Recasting models the correct forms of words.

- **Use expansion.** Expansion extends an idea by adding onto what a child says. It introduces related concepts to encourage a child's thinking. "Yes, that is a big elephant. It uses its trunk to drink water."

- **Talk with children during play.** Play gives you the opportunity to use rich action and position words. Action verbs include *building, stacking, touching, balancing,* and *climbing.* Position words describe where objects are in space and include *up, down, on, above, around, under, beside,* and *between.*

Boosting Daily Conversations

Miya and Petra stuff the mailbox with letters and take them out. They stuff letters again, then take them out. Some letters land in the tray, and others slide onto the floor. Ms. Sara says, "I am the mail carrier. Do you want to put your letters into my bag?" She holds up a leather purse, and the girls stuff in the letters and a stuffed dog, a hammer, and three plastic pancakes. Ms. Sara says, "Thank you for the packages. I will put them in my mail truck and drive them to the post office."

Ms. Sara extends toddler play in an age-appropriate way. While the girls are content putting letters in and pulling them out of the mailbox, Ms. Sara knows how to build on their words and actions. She doesn't mind that some letters fall. She doesn't try to change or fix the items the children stuff into her letter bag. She follows their lead.

How can you get started saying more and engaging children? The following strategies will help you expand children's skills:

- **Make language loops.** Language loops are the turn-taking pattern of listening and talking. They are like a tossing a ball back and forth—first you, then me. For example, say, "Oh, you have a sandwich. How does Mommy make your sandwich?" Then listen and respond to the child's reply.

- **Play with words.** Ms. Sandy says, "Oh boy. What happened to those pumpkins?" She spits out the *p* and slides up and down dramatically on the word *pumpkins.* The children giggle. She says again, "Oh boy, oh boy, oh boy. What happened to those . . ." She lets the children finish her sentence. They yell, "Macaroni!" "Muffins!" "Vegetables!" Playing with spoken words helps children enjoy and learn about sounds long before they are aware of printed letters and words.

- **Introduce sign language.** Using signs for the words *drink*, *more*, *please*, and *all done* helps younger toddlers express their needs and reduces their frustration. Model the signs to the children as you say the words. Signs for daily needs can enhance language development.

- **Honor individual development.** Children add vocabulary at different rates, just as they learn to roll over, sit up, and walk at different times. While one child is saying the word *doggie*, another may be able to say the sentence "I see a Dalmatian." You can encourage and celebrate each child's progress.

- **Enjoy each moment.** Children say the dearest things. One teacher said, while pointing to pictures in a book, "We can run around in our bare feet on the beach, but we wouldn't run around on crunchy leaves in our bare feet." "Oh no. We wouldn't do that," responded a two-year-old. "Our feet would get crunchy." Toddlers are fun, funny, and unique. As Dana Suskind suggests: tune in, take turns, and talk more (Suskind 2016). Everyone benefits.

Making Reading Meaningful

Ms. Katelyn sits with three children who have woken up from their naps. She is wearing a straw farmer's hat and an oversize flannel shirt while she reads *Big Red Barn* by Margaret Wise Brown. In front of her is an assortment of stuffed animals. As the pig squeals, the rooster crows, the cows moo, and the cat meows, the children make the sounds, too. Ms. Katelyn holds up the animal and shakes it as it makes the noise. The she hands the animals to the children, who hug them and hold them on their laps. When she gets to the part where the animals are asleep, she tips her head, closes her eyes, and gives a big snore.

Even when a book has all the characters toddlers enjoy, it isn't the book itself that toddlers love. It is the way you bring it to life. Personal interaction and shared emotions make reading delightful.

A simple scarf draped over your head can bring a story to life. A booming firefighter's voice or a sweet, melodic kitten's voice can captivate toddlers' attention. Your movements, props, and tone of voice can transform the words and pictures into a magical experience.

Toddlers do not distinguish between make-believe and real life, so they can "fall into" reading time with you with complete absorption. Book reading is an active conversation with children. Your responses are contingent on children's expressions, body language, and words.

When you draw attention to the details of picture book illustrations, you are actually showing children how to entertain themselves with the pictures. Children who experience book reading that includes pointing and talking about pictures will soon do this for themselves. They will pick up a book independently and move their eyes across the page to look for the interesting details.

As you ask questions, children really do want to know the answers. What is that sheep doing? Is she eating? Is she watching Farmer John hoe the tomatoes? Is the farmer saying, "Be careful. Don't step on my tomatoes!" to the sheep? Reading satisfies children's endless curiosity about how the world works.

As children gain language, they will talk directly to a book. They will repeat your tone of voice, point, and say funny things to the animals. They will begin to use books to self-teach, repeating the same questions they have heard you ask. "What is this?" "What is he doing?" "What is she saying?" They will use the same funny voices you use. They will hold the book and turn the pages as you do. They will even go to sit with the book on the same beanbag or chair where you read with them. Soon books will be a favorite choice in children's play.

When children bring you a book, you can respond, "You found the best book to read. I love that book. That is the one about the farmer and her tractor." Be sure to tell families, "Jason loves reading. He just loves to find out what the people in the book are doing." Your enthusiasm will encourage families to read with their children.

All this excitement over books can happen in the toddler years, even though toddlers themselves are not reading a single word. These preliteracy activities instill a love of the experience of books. Children associate book reading with close physical connection and positive feelings.

Over time adults can draw attention to words they see in the environment. They can point to a big red sign and say, "Here we are at Target!" Conversations in the grocery store also bring meaning to signs and symbols. When crossing the street, adults can point to a stop sign and say, "Stop!" Children naturally begin to associate signs, symbols, and pictures with places and things. All this talking and pointing helps children become more aware of words in their environment.

As you point at pictures in books, children hear you say, "What is that? It's a turkey. Gobble, gobble!" Soon children will answer the question with you. "Gobble, gobble!" This conversation will happen outdoors as well. "What is that noise? It's a helicopter." "Look at the bird. It's a robin." You are teaching children to notice and care about the details around them.

It will be some time before children will know that individual letters combine to make sounds and that sounds make up parts of words. But toddlers do get the idea that there are words and sounds, and that these are fun. With many enriching experiences, written words will one day become labels for what children already know and understand.

Book reading isn't just a moment in the day or a planned activity. With you, children learn that reading is a pleasure. They will love to read because they will associate books with the joy of shared moments and the thrill of figuring things out. This is a gift you can give that will bring pleasure to children's personal lives and success to their learning for years to come.

STRATEGIES FOR SUCCESS

Preparing for Reading with Toddlers

Make it comfortable. At home, children associate reading with snuggling. Re-creating this feeling in a group setting is important. As much as possible, read with smaller groups or with individual children. Once a pattern of warm, responsive reading is set, larger reading sessions can include individual pillows, blankets, or stuffed animals. Soft beanbag chairs, a child-size sofa, and upholstered chairs make an inviting and cozy space for individual reading.

Vary book placement. Place several books with beautiful and inviting covers on top of a blanket, on low tables, in well-spaced baskets, or on toddler-friendly bookstands, where the covers will capture children's attention. Engaging children visually will encourage them to choose books independently.

During group reading, make sure all children can see. If possible, sit on the children's level. Be sure to hold the book outward and sweep the book around so that each child has a few moments to look closely at the pictures when the book comes near them.

Fostering Creative Group Book Reading

Ms. Mallory is reading Elivia Savadier's *Time to Get Dressed!* She is sitting on the floor with a pile of clothing next to her. As Ms. Mallory points to the book, she says, "Solomon and his daddy need to go to the store today. They have to buy some milk for Momma. They have to go to the gas station. They have to go to the library."

"Before they go outside, Solomon needs to get dressed. What should he wear?" She puts down the book, holds up a bright red shirt, and says, "Here is Solomon's shirt. Does it go here?" She puts it over her foot. The children laugh. "No!" Ms. Mallory puts the shirt on her head. "Does it go here?" "No!" "Does it go here?" She slips her hand in the sleeve. The children laugh and say, "Yes!"

As Ms. Mallory reads the book, she points to the illustrations. Solomon tries on his shirt, pants, socks, and shoes in the wrong places. Finally, she asks, "Do *you* know how to get dressed by yourself? In the dress-up box, there are lots of hats and shirts to put on. You can put them on."

Ms. Mallory has fully engaged these children. As she tries to put on the clothing in the wrong way, she makes dramatic faces and sighs loudly. The children are captivated by her antics. At the same time, this is a situation they know personally—how hard it is to get dressed.

By connecting book reading to the children's experiences and extending the topic into play, Ms. Mallory has given the children something meaningful to think about. She will read this book many times over the next few weeks. She will repeat the dressing antics and encourage the children to practice dressing during play. These connections capture the children's attention and interest.

The following strategies will help you prepare for toddler-appropriate book reading. Choose one or two ideas to use at first. Gradually, you will find many ways to integrate book activities. Both you and the children will find that these are some of your favorite times together.

Make Reading Connections

In addition to your reading area, place books with related items to engage children. Add books about trains to cardboard boxes linked like a train. Keep books about cooking or food in a basket with play kitchen utensils. Store picture books about babies next to a doll bed and rocker to invite children to read to their dolls. Place books about families in a basket with child-safe mirrors and laminated photos of the children's own families to encourage self-exploration. These integrated experiences communicate that books are a natural part of daily life.

Make Engagement Physical

During book reading, provide a handheld prop for each toddler. When the butterfly flies away home, children can wave and flap a butterfly in the wind. When the kitten crawls into bed and meows, children can tuck their kittens underneath their armpits and say, "Meow." Props engage active participation. Children will tell their families that they "read a book to the kitten" and "played with a butterfly." To the children, these make-believe activities are the same as real-life experiences. Below are some suggestions for physical objects to enhance reading:

- **Hand props:** Props can include beanie-size stuffed animals, laminated pictures, or objects cut from colored foam craft paper. You can reuse hand-made props the next time you read a book. Store the items for each book in a large, clear ziplock bag. Write the name of the book in permanent marker on the bag. File bags in alphabetical order in a tub labeled "Book Reading Props for Toddlers."

- **Finger and hand puppets:** You can make simple finger and hand puppets from infant- or toddler-size socks. Use permanent marker to draw a face, and sew on felt ears to make an animal. Tuck the puppets into a clear, labeled ziplock bag and store for future use.

- **Lap friends:** During reading time, when a child holds a small stuffed animal or doll, this focuses the child's attention on "helping kitty read" or "helping dolly see the book." By assisting the doll, toddlers also direct their own attention.

- **Loveys:** Pass out small "lovey" blankets for cuddling during reading. You can cut these with pinking shears to make twelve-inch squares of flannel. Toddlers love to reach into a basket and choose a color or pattern to snuggle with. These washable loveys can become a favorite part of reading times, especially for younger toddlers.

- **Laminated book characters:** Many toddler teachers find that color-copied, cut-out, and laminated book characters bring the stories to life. Each child may hold a character. At first, give all the children identical characters. Over time children will get used to holding different characters.

- **Flannel boards:** Old-fashioned flannel boards are a toddler favorite. Children are captivated as they see the characters jump out of the book onto the board. Flannel pieces should be large enough for children to manipulate easily and for everyone to see. The pieces may be manipulated by the teacher alone or by children who show a desire to participate.

- **Costumes for children:** Passing out firefighter hats, caps, scarves, or aprons before reading a book about a firefighter, playing outside, or cooking makes the story come to life. Toddlers like to run in place to chase the fire truck, stir a pot of stew, or pull down their caps to stay warm. Collect these props over time and use them for multiple purposes.

Using Handheld Props for Reading

I create hand-size characters to match our stories. We use pigs cut from pink-colored foam sheets when we read *The Big Red Barn*. We use blue caterpillars with red faces for *The Very Hungry Caterpillar*. While the caterpillar in the book gobbles the leaves and fruit, the children wiggle their caterpillars and make gobbling sounds.

When we read *Butterfly Butterfly: A Book of Colors*, the children make their handheld butterflies fly around the room. When we are finished reading, I carry around a ziplock bag, and the children place their items in the bag. I store these bags with the matching books. The stories are short and keep their attention. The children's hands are busy following along with the story.

Choosing Books for Toddlers

Ms. Karen is reading *Good Morning, City* by Pat Kiernan. She points to the bakery and says, "Does your daddy get a bagel at the bakery?" She listens to the children's answers. "Mommy got a bagel." "Daddy got coffee." She points to the garbage truck and says, "*VROOM!* Does your garbage truck make a big noise, too? What does it sound like?" In this urban setting, children relate to the sounds, pictures, and words of the book's morning in the city.

Ms. Karen received a stack of books from her friend, a preschool teacher. She traded some because they were for older children. She kept the books with colorful, clear illustrations. This book about going to the city was one of the books she knew her toddlers would enjoy. The morning sights and sounds reflect their daily experiences. They have a lot to say as she points to the pictures.

Toddlers are becoming aware of experiences in their daily lives. They don't yet realize there are children on the other side of the world. But they know children and grown-ups live in their community. They are curious about the people and events they know.

Toddlers also understand experiences they have had with their families. They participate in cooking, shopping, bathing, and using transportation. Books that depict these experiences help children recall and talk about events. You can use books to reinforce toddlers' feelings and experiences.

Perhaps, like Ms. Karen, you have received books from another teacher, and you are not sure which ones are best for the children in your care. The following tips can help you sort your books or choose new books:

- **Choose books with bright, familiar images.** Picture books that capture toddlers' experiences with objects from their own world can bring endless excitement. "I see the car!" "I like ice cream!" "I help my daddy!"

- **Introduce culturally diverse books.** Reflect the ethnicity and culture of your own families. Also include other cultures and perspectives. You know your children best. You can personalize book reading to match their setting (city, suburb, farm), cultural understanding, and experiences.

- **Create homemade books.** Make books with photos of the children engaging in classroom activities. Children love to see themselves playing. You can slip photos into clear sheet protectors and keep them in a half-inch binder, which is small enough for toddler hands to hold.

- **Choose books written specifically for toddlers.** The end of this chapter offers a list of tried-and-true books that toddlers will enjoy over and over. These are just some of the books appropriate for children sixteen to thirty-six months.

Supporting Dual-Language Learning

"Moo!" Ms. Ceci moans. Then she squeaks, "There is the cow, *peeeeeking* around the barn!" The toddlers laugh. "How will that farmer catch the cow? What if the cow runs away? What will the farmer do?" She looks at the children with her eyebrows raised and opens her arms in a shrug. The children shout, "The farmer will catch her." Ms. Ceci says, "Yes, the farmer will run fast to catch the cow." Mr. Lin repeats the words in Chinese. All the children are laughing.

Mr. Lin and Ms. Ceci work together to invite lively engagement at reading time. They make sure all the children are actively involved. They know that bilingual book reading benefits all the children in the classroom and provides specific support for the children who speak Chinese (Semingson, Pole, and Tommerdahl 2015).

Mr. Lin reads individually with the bilingual children in both English and Chinese. He and Ms. Ceci also make photo books that reflect the families' experiences. They know that all the toddlers will benefit.

Children are born with the capacity to learn multiple languages. Dual-language learners follow a similar pattern of learning as do children who speak only one language. All toddlers learn how words work and how they sound, and love to be read to. They enjoy playing with the sounds of words. They string words together and use gestures to show what they need and mean. All toddlers map new words and information onto existing words and understanding.

Studies show advantages for dual-language learners. Over time they have increased ability to solve problems. They develop the ability to focus attention and to ignore distractions, which are skills beneficial to school success. Dual-language learners can have improved reading and academic performance over time (Espinoza and Calderon 2015). In addition skills from one language, such as phonological awareness, can boost skills in the second language.

While very young bilingual children may take longer to add vocabulary to both languages, over time—when they are in a rich language environment—they excel. But like all toddlers, they depend on you to provide sensitive, responsive caregiving and a variety of language-rich experiences matched to their capabilities and needs (Magnuson and Duncan 2014).

A language-rich environment is especially important for toddlers who are dual-language learners. Since they are just becoming verbal, getting support in both languages is a priority. In addition supporting the home language connects children to the rich heritage, stories, and daily communication with all members of their families.

STRATEGIES FOR SUCCESS

Engaging Dual-Language Learners

The following book-reading practices will benefit all the toddlers in your setting:

▶ Read books that contain pictures representing a variety of cultural practices. Books should contain stories and illustrations that children identify as their own and that depict their daily lives.

▶ Invite dual-language learners' family members to read picture books in their home language to all the children.

▶ Ask families if they are willing to record stories and songs in home languages.

▶ Make many happy emotional connections with shared reading. Point to illustrations and photographs and enjoy talking, laughing, and smiling together.

For classroom communication, use the following strategies:

▶ Learn favorite songs the children hear at home. Teach these songs to all the children.

▶ Learn phrases in the home language to greet the children and their family members.

▶ Learn and use phrases for daily communication. "Time to wash hands." "Let's change your diaper." "Time to go outside."

▶ Learn lullabies and comfort words that families use. For example: "Love you." "You are okay." "I am sorry you are sad."

▶ Learn words for foods you frequently serve and use.

▶ Adopt the familiar words children use for their family members.

▶ Ask families to contribute photos of their children with family members.

▶ Ask families to bring in games, art materials (fabrics, artifacts, papers, crafts), and familiar household utensils. These items woven into daily classroom activities and play make the classroom itself feel like home.

Screen hearing and speech as purposefully with dual-language learners as with English-only speakers. Be sure children are assessed in their home language. For children who need speech services, locate a specialist who can provide care in their home language. If you use an interpreter to communicate about the need for services, make sure this person shares the family and neighborhood culture. Find resources in the family's community so others involved understand the family's beliefs and culture.

Making Stories Come Alive

Ms. Julia is reading *Say Aah! My First Trip to the Doctor* by Jen Green. Merci says, "The doctor peeked into my mouth." Ms. Julia asks, "Did the doctor see your teeth and throat?" Merci responds, "He looked in my mouth." Ms. Julia says, "The doctor looked into your mouth and saw your teeth and throat. Did he poke your tummy, too?"

Ms. Julia thinks of book reading as a conversation. She uses a three-part strategy to engage children. She focuses their attention, asks what will happen, and responds to the children. She knows toddlers don't need someone to read *at* them. She includes them in conversation and reads *with* them. Below are effective strategies for engaging with toddlers during book reading.

- **Think of book reading as a conversation.** Your responsiveness is the most important ingredient. Match your pace, energy, and questions to your children:

  - *Draw attention.* "The doctor says, 'Open your mouth and say, "Ahhhh!"'" Let's all open our mouths and say, 'Ahhhh!'"

  - *Make it personal.* Connect the story to children's experiences. "Did you go to the doctor with your mommy? Did the doctor peek into your mouth, too? Did he poke your tummy?"

  - *Respond to children.* Take time to listen. When children want to tell you something, it is okay if what they say doesn't match what you are reading or telling. Follow children's lead and respond to the questions they ask. Affirm and extend their interest or ideas.

- **Connect reading to daily sights and sounds.** When you hear a siren through the window, say, "Let's get a book and look at the fire trucks." Toddlers make active connections between the outside world and reading.

- **Connect to children's own experiences.** For stories about families, point to the pictures and ask questions. "There is a stroller. Do you go for a walk with your momma in a stroller?"

- **Encourage participation.** When reading *The Happy Man and His Dump Truck* by Miryam, all the children can say, "Wheeeeee!" as the animals slide down into a heap. In the city, children can roar like a truck or chirp like a bird.

- **Use books to remember together.** Choose books that follow up on shared experiences. After a petting zoo visit, a book can remind children of what they did or saw. "Look, there is a little goat! Did we see a little goat, too? Did it say, '*Maaaa, maaaa*'? Do you say, '*Maaaa, maaaa*,' too?"

- **Match books to daily routines.** During snack or lunch, choose a book about food and point out the shapes, colors, and textures. "Oh, those carrots are so crunchy! They are so tasty!" Toddlers will surprise their families by repeating at home, "Carrots are so crunchy! They are tasty!"

- **Modify when needed.** To draw children into a book, modify the text when children need a shorter version story or simpler words, or when you want to talk about the illustrations. However, many predictable or rhyming books are perfect for toddlers. And many storybooks match toddlers' direct experiences.

Extending Stories through Dramatic Play

"Today we are going to take care of our puppy. What do we need to do?" The puppy puppet says, "*Woof! Woof! Woof!*" The children laugh. With a higher pitch, it comes near Ms. Anna's face. "*Woof! Woof! Woof!*" The children laugh. Ms. Anna says, "Oh dear. Puppy is barking. What do you think Puppy wants?" The puppy puppet licks Ms. Anna's face. It licks Ms. Anna's hand. It jumps up and down. The children are smiling.

Ms. Anna asks, "What do you think Puppy wants me to do? Does Puppy need a hug?" She hugs Puppy. "Should we brush Puppy's fur?" Ms. Anna sprays the fur with a tiny water bottle and brushes it. She dries Puppy with a little towel. "Shall we take Puppy on a walk?" She clips on a red leash, and the puppy puppet dances around Ms. Anna. "My puppy keeps barking! What do you think we should do? Do you think Puppy is hungry?"

The children say, "Hungry. Puppy hungry. Breakfast. Make breakfast." "Yes!" says Ms. Anna. "Our puppy needs breakfast. Here is our dog food, in the container. I can use a scoop." She scoops food into a dish. The puppy puppet gobbles the food, and the children laugh.

Ms. Anna knows that many of the children have dogs at home. She has been reading the Carl books by Alexandra Day. Today she reads *Carl's Afternoon in the Park*. "The puppy goes for a walk. The puppy takes baby to the park. The puppy jumps in the flowers . . ." When she is finished reading, Ms. Anna says, "I hear barking. Can you help the puppies? Can you feed and brush your puppies? You can scoop out dog food and feed them. Ms. Martha will help you spray and brush them. You can take your puppies for a walk."

Ms. Anna uses new words along with familiar ones. "We take care of our puppies. We help our families. You can take care of your pet." When Ms. Anna points to pictures and tells stories, she uses position words. "Baby gets on top of Carl." "Carl runs down the stairs." When she says "up," her voice slides up, and when she uses "down," her voice slides down. She tells the children Carl has curled up "next to" the baby. When Ms. Anna reads, children forget their teacher is reading and think a puppy is talking.

At one table, Ms. Anna has prepared small blocks in dish tubs with scoops of different sizes. Next to the tubs are dog bowls. In the middle of the table is a basket of plush puppies. Here the children will feed their puppies. At another table, she has set out doll brushes and small spray bottles of water, with flour-sack towels the children can handle easily. Here the children can wash and brush their puppies before "going on a walk."

In the housekeeping area, Ms. Anna has set a laundry basket of hats, mittens, and scarves so the children can "get dressed" before they take their animals on a walk. Her coteacher is pushing a baby buggy with some animals in it—also wearing a hat and mittens. She helps some of the children put on hats and mittens. They put their puppies in a wagon to pull.

During play, the teachers have conversations with children as though the events are actually happening. "Your dog got all muddy. Are you washing off the mud?" "Is your dog all clean now?" "Do you need help putting your puppy in your backpack?"

When a few children seem aimless, Ms. Martha turns on music. The children dance with their stuffed animals and sing, "Puppy dog, puppy dog, turn around. Puppy dog, puppy dog, touch the ground."

Even at snacktime, the teachers enjoy talking with the children about their pets. They ask the children how they help their families take care of their animals. When it is time to go outside, the teachers encourage the children to run like puppies. By naptime, these children are ready to sleep.

The teachers and children have shared a meaningful day of fun. Their interactions have brought laughter and excitement. There will be many happy stories to share with families later in the day.

When you read with toddlers, make the most of their ability to shift from reality to fantasy. Use the strategies below to purposefully teach words and draw children into the enjoyment of book reading:

- **Animate words with exaggerated expression.** In the same way that you use a singsong voice with infants, continue to exaggerate vocal range when you read with toddlers. Your higher-pitched voice illustrates natural communication and draws interest. "'*Squeak, squeak!*' Little Mouse is calling his daddy. '*Squeak, squeak!* I want some food.'"

- **Act out words.** When you are saying words like *rock*, *jump*, *rat-a-tat-tat*, *pat-pat*, and so on, use hand gestures that show what the words mean.

- **Use repetition.** "Here is a puppy. '*Woof, woof!*' The puppy is happy. Do you hear the puppy barking?" Repeating the word in multiple sentence forms reinforces vocabulary.

- **Point and ask.** "Where is Momma? Do you see Momma? Here is Momma!" Another version: "Who is this?" Wait for child to answer. "This is Momma!" Repeat.

- **Point and make sounds.** This helps children pair what they see to the sounds. "Fire truck." Point and make a siren sound.

RESOURCES FOR GROWTH

Choosing Books for Toddlers

Animals

- ▶ *A Ball for Daisy* by Chris Raschka
- ▶ *Baby Animals* by Dorothea DePrisco
- ▶ *Baby Animals on the Farm* by R. F. Lewis
- ▶ *Bears* by Elizabeth Carney
- ▶ *Brown Bear, Brown Bear, What Do You See?* by Bill Martin Jr. and Eric Carle

- *Dear Zoo* by Rod Campbell
- *Farm Animals* by Laaren Brown
- *Farm Animals* by Nancy Dickmann
- *Giraffes* by Laura Marsh
- *Let's Learn about . . . Birds!* by Cheryl Shireman
- *Let's Learn about . . . Cats!* by Cheryl Shireman
- *Let's Learn about . . . Horses!* by Cheryl Shireman
- *Llama Llama Red Pajama* by Anna Dewdney
- *My Big Animal Book* by Roger Priddy
- *My Pet* by Debbie Bailey
- *National Geographic Little Kids First Big Book of Animals* by Catherine D. Hughes
- *National Geographic Little Kids First Big Book of Bugs* by Catherine D. Hughes
- *National Geographic Little Kids First Big Book of the Ocean* by Catherine D. Hughes
- *Owl Babies* by Martin Waddell
- *The Runaway Bunny* by Margaret Wise Brown
- *The Very Hungry Caterpillar* by Eric Carle
- *We're Going on a Bear Hunt* by Michael Rosen

First Experiences

- *The Berenstain Bears Go to the Doctor* by Stan and Jan Berenstain
- *Corduroy Goes to the Doctor* by Don Freeman
- *Curious George Visits the Dentist* by Margret and H. A. Rey
- *Going to the Doctor* by Anne Civardi
- *The New Baby* by Mercer Mayer

Weather and Seasons

These books should match the climate where you live. Northerners have the advantage of four seasons. For those of you in warm climates, share books about animals such as lizards, plants such as cacti, and other reflections of the nature around you.

- *I See Summer* by Charles Ghigna
- *Sneezy the Snowman* by Maureen Wright
- *Snow* by P. D. Eastman
- *Summer Days and Nights* by Wong Herbert Yee
- *Who Likes Rain?* by Wong Herbert Yee

Food and Eating

▶ *Eating the Alphabet* by Lois Ehlert

▶ *Eating the Rainbow* by Star Bright Books

▶ *Farmers' Market Day* by Shanda Trent

▶ *Food from Farms* by Nancy Dickmann

▶ *Hands Can* by Cheryl Willis Hudson

▶ *I Eat Fruit* by Hannah Tofts

▶ *Llama Llama Yum Yum Yum!* by Anna Dewdney

▶ *Pancakes for Breakfast* by Tomie dePaola

▶ *We're Going to the Farmers' Market* by Stefan Page

Emotions

▶ *Bye-Bye Time* by Elizabeth Verdick

▶ *Calm-Down Time* by Elizabeth Verdick

▶ *Full, Full, Full of Love* by Trish Cooke

▶ *Hands Are Not for Hitting* by Martine Agassi

▶ *Hugs and Kisses* by Roberta Grobel Intrater

▶ *I Love You All Day Long* by Francesca Rusackas

▶ *I Love You Through and Through* by Bernadette Rosetti-Shustak

▶ *I Was So Mad* by Mercer Mayer

▶ *Listening Time* by Elizabeth Verdick

▶ *Llama Llama Misses Mama* by Anna Dewdney

▶ *Peek-a-Boo!* by Roberta Grobel Intrater

▶ *Sharing Time* by Elizabeth Verdick

▶ *Splash!* by Roberta Grobel Intrater

▶ *Teeth Are Not for Biting* by Elizabeth Verdick

About Myself

▶ *The Babies and Doggies Book* by John Schindel and Molly Woodward

▶ *Baby Dance* by Ann Taylor

▶ *Baby Faces* by DK Publishing

▶ *Global Babies* by the Global Fund for Children

▶ *Let's Pretend* by Debbie Bailey

▶ *Marvelous Me* by Lisa Bullard

- *My Face Book* by Star Bright Books
- *Peekaboo Morning* by Rachel Isadora
- *Please, Baby, Please* by Spike Lee and Tonya Lewis Lee
- *Shades of Black* by Sandra L. Pinkney
- *Smile!* by Roberta Grobel Intrater
- *Whose Knees Are These?* by Jabari Asim
- *Whose Toes Are Those?* by Jabari Asim

Family

- *Are You My Mother?* by P. D. Eastman
- *Carry Me* by Rena D. Grossman
- *Global Baby Bedtimes* by Maya Ajmera
- *Global Baby Boys* by Maya Ajmera
- *Global Baby Girls* by The Global Fund for Children
- *Good Night, Little Bear* by Patsy Scarry
- *Goodnight Moon* by Margaret Wise Brown
- *Grandma* by Debbie Bailey
- *Grandpa* by Debbie Bailey
- *Join Hands! The Ways We Celebrate Life* by Pat Mora
- *My Dad* by Debbie Bailey
- *My Family* by Debbie Bailey
- *My Mom* by Debbie Bailey
- *We Can Go Anywhere: My Adventures on Daddy's Chair* by Glen Dick

Around the House

- *Doing the Washing* by Sarah Garland
- *We Help Daddy* by Mini Stein

Authors: Ezra Jack Keats

- *Hi, Cat!* by Ezra Jack Keats
- *Jennie's Hat* by Ezra Jack Keats
- *Peter's Chair* by Ezra Jack Keats
- *The Snowy Day* by Ezra Jack Keats
- *Whistle for Willie* by Ezra Jack Keats

Authors: Mem Fox

▶ *Baby Bedtime* by Mem Fox

▶ *Hello Baby!* by Mem Fox

▶ *Ten Little Fingers and Ten Little Toes* by Mem Fox

▶ *Time for Bed* by Mem Fox

▶ *Whoever You Are* by Mem Fox

Authors: Jan Brett

▶ *Daisy Comes Home* by Jan Brett

▶ *On Noah's Ark* by Jan Brett

Authors: Margret and H. A. Rey

▶ *Curious George* by Margret and H. A. Rey

▶ *Curious George and the Birthday Surprise* by Margret and H. A. Rey

▶ *Curious George and the Firefighters* by Margret and H. A. Rey

▶ *Curious George Goes Camping* by Margret and H. A. Rey

▶ *Curious George Visits a Toy Store* by Margret and H. A. Rey

▶ *Sweet Dreams, Curious George* by Margret and H. A. Rey

Classic Golden Books

▶ *Baby Listens* by Esther Wilkin

▶ *Daddies* by Janet Frank

▶ *A Day at the Seashore* by Kathryn Jackson

▶ *The Fire Engine* by Tibor Gergely

▶ *The Fuzzy Duckling* by Jane Werner Watson

▶ *Mommy Stories* by Jean Cushman and Margo Lundell

▶ *The Poky Little Puppy* Janette Sebring Lowrey

▶ *The Shy Little Kitten* by Cathleen Schurr

Things in My World

▶ *Best Word Book Ever* by Richard Scarry

▶ *Farm Machines* by Nancy Dickmann

▶ *First 100 Animals* by Roger Priddy

▶ *First 100 Machines* by Roger Priddy

▶ *First 100 Words* by Heather Amery

> ▶ *Jobs on a Farm* by Nancy Dickmann
> ▶ *The Little Blue Truck* by Alice Schertle
> ▶ *Look Inside Things That Go* by Rob Lloyd Jones
> ▶ *Pull-Back Busy Train* by Fiona Watt

———

Quick question: I heard that it is okay to start teaching toddlers to read. Is this true?

Simple solution: Armed with rich language exposure and many stimulating life experiences, toddlers will be ready to notice print in the environment, such as on stop signs and in store logos, when they are a bit older. Here are strategies to use now to ensure a strong foundation:

- *Talk about life events.* Describe what is going to happen and talk through the steps in activities.

- *Read picture books many times a day.* Happy book talk will engage children in greater independent book exploration.

- *Display colorful pictures, photos, posters, and artwork to inspire conversation.*

- *Enjoy fingerplays, songs, and rhymes.* The rhythms and word patterns encourage language learning.

- *Have more fun.* Keep enjoying daily life with toddlers, sharing and talking about their activities and the world around them. These conversations nurture the love of words and learning.

———

Quick question: What should I do when I am reading to one or two toddlers and they get up and walk around while I read to them?

Simple solution: Toddlers are active. Stay tuned in to their level of engagement. If they are standing up and wiggling but are still actively listening to the book and answering your questions, you know they still want to read. If they walk away and get busy with another activity, then you know their time for reading is over for now.

––––––

Quick question: It seems like no matter how much fun I make book reading, toddlers aren't interested in a whole book. What should I do?

Simple solution: Toddlers have short attention spans. Choose shorter books that match the children's interests, and keep reading time short. Modify length by focusing conversation about illustrations. As children's language ability increases, they will gradually increase their focus time.

––––––

Quick question: What is the best way to conduct a whole-group book reading?

Simple solution: When you find an engaging book, use props and invite active participation. Make sure all adults in the room are sitting with the children. They should participate with and support the children. Start with shorter stories and provide children with items to hold. Quickly shift to a whole-body activity after the book reading or encourage free-choice play.

8

Fostering Partnerships with Families

Family partnerships knit together all the pieces of success for young children. Communication and collaboration with family members provide the information, coordinated caregiving approaches, and cultural knowledge you need to effectively support the development of toddlers in your care. This chapter will show how family, school, and community collaboration can ensure the best possible outcomes for children.

Building a Relationship of Trust

Ms. Chloe says to Kieran, "Do you want to show your mom your treasure box?" Together Kieran and his mom sit in the window seat. They open the box and take out the leaves, pebbles, and pieces of bark that Kieran collected on his morning walk.

Ms. Peggy holds a blue bead steady while Tory pushes the end of a thick cord through the opening. "I make Mommy a necklace." Ms. Peggy smiles. "You are making a beautiful pattern for Mommy. Do you want to add a red bead?" Next to them, Wyatt takes beads from a tray and drops them one by one into a cup. "I can hear your beads dropping—*kuplink, kuplank, kuplunk*—just like Sal's blueberries in *Blueberries for Sal*." Ms. Peggy notices that Tory's mom has arrived. "Hello, Ms. Linton. Tory made you a necklace." Tory runs across the room to hug her mom.

During afternoon pickup, Ms. Peggy stays busy with children at the table while Ms. Chloe coordinates greeting families near the door. These teachers know how important family members feel when they are invited into the room to see what children are doing and making. They understand that some people can't spend extra time in the morning but can do so at the end of the day.

An open classroom shows families the kinds of work and learning that happen during the day. It allows family members to participate in special moments with their children. Children feel the setting is theirs to share with their families, rather than a place of separation. The children sense that this is a place to belong. Spending a few minutes together at drop-off or pickup helps families feel like full partners. Securing their trust is a necessary foundation for collaboration.

At drop-off and pickup time, you may greet different family members, nannies, or babysitters. Of course you will have signed agreements that give these caregivers permission to retrieve children. Building trust with all the adults in children's lives is important. Practice the same warm and caring communication with everyone involved in children's lives. Here are a few strategies to help you:

- **Make it personal for all who drop off and pick up children.** Learn the names of children's family members and caregivers so you can address or ask about them. "Is Johanna feeling better today?" You will also be able to have personal conversations with children. "Do you and your sister Sofie play in the yard?" These connections help everyone feel important and invested in the child's experience.

- **Make building trust a priority.** Building trust is the first step in fostering partnerships with families. Trust is a firm belief in the reliability, truth, ability, or strength of another person. For building trust, consistency with families is as important as consistency with children. Your reliability and professionalism can validate families' confidence in the care of their child.

- **Follow through with parental requests.** Be sure to follow through when you tell a family member you will check on something or get something for them. Keep a stack of index cards, a clipboard, or a notebook to record your responsibilities. For example, if you say you will check on a policy or find out the date of an event, be sure to do so. Your follow-through shows your interest in the family's needs.

- **Keep communication positive.** Sometimes family members will ask about a child's behavior at pickup time. Always tell them something positive the child did. It won't help anyone to hear in the afternoon about something that happened in the morning, such as bumping into another child or spilling food. The conversation may cause embarrassment to the family and to the child, and others will hear. If a family member wants to talk about a personal issue, set a time when you can talk privately.

Focusing on Children's Strengths

I love to share a child's strengths. This gives Mom or Dad something fun and happy to talk about as they go out the door with their child. I tell about something special a child did. It makes a parent's day and reinforces the happy event with the child.

Consider your positive communication with families to be an investment in trust. Strengthening trust when things are going well can help things go more smoothly when you need to discuss concerns. Children will sense that you are working together in their best interest. This coordination of care between you and families will have a positive influence on children.

Overcoming Communication Barriers

Raelyn arrives at lunchtime to pick up her daughter, Laura, for an early afternoon doctor checkup. She watches Tanya, a lunchtime assistant, who is sitting with Laura at the table. Tanya tells Laura, "It's okay, honey, you don't need to finish. Your mom is here." Raelyn interrupts, "Laura, finish your potatoes." To Tanya she says, "I don't want my daughter to be a fussy eater. I want her to eat what you give her." Tanya responds, "Okay, Laura. Your mom is going to wait for you while you finish eating lunch."

It takes time and effort to establish cooperative relationships with families. They may hold differing ideas about self-care routines, child rearing, behavior, or what children should be doing or playing. Raelyn has strong feelings about how Laura should eat. She wants Laura to finish what she is given and believes that children who are catered to may become fussy eaters. However, as part of her early childhood training, Tanya was taught to let children choose how and what they eat.

You may have established routines and ways of caring with which you feel most comfortable. At the same time, families may worry that you won't take care of their child in the same way they do. Your approach may conflict with what families prefer for their child. You may assume that others share your beliefs and values, but often there are subtle differences.

In addition family members may have hidden feelings that require sensitivity. They may feel threatened by your close relationship with their child. Maybe a child cries because she doesn't want to leave you. A parent may hear the child calling you "Momma." Perhaps you tell a parent, "Gianni ate all his lunch and then slept like a lamb for two hours," but Gianni's mother has been struggling to get him to nap at home. You may be thrilled to say, "Finn pulled himself up today for the first time!" But mom may feel badly that she missed the milestone—and worry that you are getting too close to her child emotionally.

Sharing positive moments can make family members' day. They will enjoy hearing about sweet moments and funny experiences. You can frame these experiences to help families feel part of the special moments. "We love hearing Sharon laugh with the other children. You must enjoy her wonderful sense of humor at home." "I love the way Sharon plays with the dolls so gently. You must have shown her how to do that." This approach lets family members know you see children's strengths as emerging from their positive nurturing.

Learn as much as you can about each child's family. Get to know their approaches and preferences. Invite them to share with you. "What activities does John enjoy at home that we can introduce here?" "What new words has John been using?" "How has John been eating and sleeping?" Your questions communicate that you value family input.

When you involve parents and families, you learn so much about nurturing and child rearing that can help you make each child feel more comfortable. Families want to share their hopes and desires for their child. They want you to understand the strengths and values they want to have nurtured. By communicating about home routines and ways of comforting, eating, singing, and soothing, families show how you can be more effective.

Without trusting communication, you have only a partial view of what children need. Talking with families can help you develop shared goals. You may coordinate strategies for soothing, reading books, or encouraging self-feeding. Cooperative goals ensure consistency. Toddlers thrive with shared support.

STRATEGIES FOR SUCCESS

Boosting Interpersonal Competence

The following tips can help you be sensitive to a parent's point of view and build bridges that overcome concerns:

▶ **Guard professional boundaries.** Parents are your professional investment partners. You are together for a limited time for a specific purpose: to build the strengths of a child. Resist the urge to spill details or feelings about your personal life to parents. When you keep a healthy boundary between personal and professional issues, you will have trust when you need to hold the line on a rule, regulation, or health issue.

▶ **Hold conversations privately**. Don't converse about children in front of children or other parents. There will always be pressure to do so. Repeat your rule often: "I am happy to discuss your concerns in private. Would you like to set a time to call me?"

▶ **Guard confidentiality**. Guard privacy as though it is your most essential responsibility. Beware of saying, "Kathy mentioned that issue as well." Or "The Perez family is struggling with that issue, also." Even when you are aware of an issue, say, "I appreciate your feelings. Thank you for sharing this with me." A trusting relationship depends on privacy.

▶ **Be a peace broker.** If one parent comes to you about a parent or child, say, "I am glad you trust me to share this with me; however, it would be best for you to talk individually with that parent." If you hear something negative, say, "I am sorry. I don't know that to be true of that person. If you have a concern, I encourage you to talk directly with her." Often people want to release their feelings but don't really want to talk directly with the other person. Your unwillingness to discuss the issue can put a stop to negativity. Quickly change the subject with positive information. Say, "I want to tell you something funny Tiffani said today. She was delightful." The conversation will shift forward to a positive subject.

Inviting Meaningful Conversation

Evan's mom says, "I know how active Evan can be. I have been worried that he takes so much of your attention in the classroom. I feel relieved to know you feel he is doing fine and getting along well with the other children." Ms. Sylvia responds with a smile, "We love having Evan with us and enjoy his happy smile and caring ways."

Ms. Sylvia reassures Evan's mom that her son is doing well. The time they share together is warm and friendly. Evan's mom leaves feeling reassured. Ms. Sylvia feels proud of her work with Evan and knows she has made his mom feel good about his progress in her classroom.

Talking with families may be a concern for them and for you. What is the best way to ask questions? What should you say to bring up an issue? Which kind of meeting works best for parents of toddlers? Planning ahead can make your time together go well.

Honoring family strengths means viewing the parent or primary caregiver as the expert and nurturer and welcoming open and ongoing communication. At times it may be difficult for someone to identify and explain what they do at home or to share their point of view. An authentic partnership involves inviting parents or primary caregivers to share and demonstrate their ways of nurturing. It means focusing on children's strengths and ways to encourage their development.

The following strategies can help you jump-start conversations with families. Each strategy requires scheduled time, but the trust you build and the information you learn will help you so much in your teaching. You will get to know each family well and better understand each child's needs.

Conducting an Interview with Each Family

Meeting privately with parents or primary caregivers can give you a great deal of insight about their experiences. To schedule a meeting, ask them to suggest two dates that work for them. Avoid a public sign-in sheet to protect privacy.

If there is a language difference, invite a friend of the family or someone who shares the same cultural background to translate. If you can, conduct the interview at the family's home. If a parent wants to come to school or meet you at a local library or coffee shop, that is okay. The key is to be sure families are comfortable. The following questions can guide your interview:

- Tell me about your family. Who are the members?

- Where is your home of origin? What languages are spoken in your family?

- How long have you lived in this community? What do you value most about your community experiences?

- Do other members of your family take care of your child? What does your child call them?

- What are some activities you enjoy with your child and your family?

- What strengths do you see in your child? How would you like me to support these?

- What are your earliest memories of school? What do you wish for when your child goes to school?

- What experiences, phrases, or sayings does your family use to teach your child? How do you comfort your child?

- What dreams and goals do you have for your child's future? What values do you want to instill?

- What would you most like me to do to build your child's strengths and talents?

End a family interview by saying, "Is there anything else you want to ask me or want me to know?" Sometimes parents will ask a question or tell you there is still something they are worried about. They may tell you that they are concerned about how a family event or situation is affecting a child. You can respond, "Thank you for telling me."

If a parent raises a question that requires a brief response, you can answer right away. If the issue is more complex, you can say, "That is important, too. Let's set a time to meet and talk about that. I want to be sure we have time to address your question completely."

Be sure to thank families for their time and for sharing their experiences with you. You can say, "I appreciate your confidence in me. I will be sure to support your child." Let them know that you look forward to talking with them again in an upcoming meeting.

Inviting Parents to Touch-Base Meetings

The phrase *parent conference* can sound formal and intimidating. Instead, invite parents or primary caregivers to a touch-base meeting. Rather than schedule all families on the same day, set up these meetings over several months. You will be better able to accommodate families' schedules and bring focus and energy to each meeting. Here is a checklist for touch-base meetings:

- **Share strengths you observe at school.** Write down several specific examples that you want to share with families. "Samuel shows creativity through his questions and terrific sense of humor. He loves to point to the farm pictures in his favorite book. I encourage you to ask Samuel to point to pictures as you name objects when you read at home."

- **Ask families to describe strengths they observe at home**. "What strengths do you see in Samuel at home?" Take notes on what is shared. Say, "Thank you for sharing Samuel's strengths. I will encourage them when Samuel is at school."

- **Ask families to describe a skill or strength they would like you to support.** Families may mention washing hands, practicing manners, using the potty, or saying please and thank you. You can say, "Yes. Let's work on this together. I will remind Samuel to say please and thank you at school, and you can do this with him at home."

- **Conclude with positive words.** "Thank you. I am so glad we spent this time together. I am happy to work with you to support Samuel's strengths."

Touch-base meetings are a way for you to celebrate children's progress. Rather than describe an area to work on together as a "weakness" or a "problem," you can explain that all toddlers need support as they develop and grow. Present a need for support as a way to build a child's strengths.

When questions involve medical, psychological, or developmental issues, ask families to discuss their concerns with their children's pediatricians. Perhaps a parent says, "I am not sure Samuel's speech is coming along fast enough." Or, "I am concerned about Samuel's readiness for potty training." These conversations should happen between families and their health care providers. Say, "Your pediatrician is the best source for guidance about that issue."

Family interviews and touch-base meetings will help you accomplish your goal of knowing children well. When you communicate with families, always consider how your words will affect them. A collaborative partnership will mean so much to families, and you will continue to learn so much about them, their child, and yourself.

TEACHER TIP

Building Trust through Positive Phone Calls

When we made plans to reach out to parents, I thought, "I don't have time for that." But then I realized that I could invest my time before problems occurred instead of after. It takes only a few minutes to call a parent and leave a positive message. I do it right when the children go down for a nap. I call one family per day. Most of the time I leave a message, but the parents tell me this means so much to them. They know I am thinking of them. That makes all the difference.

Establishing Greater Collaboration

Ms. Tamara notices that Emmy's mom has been quiet the last few days during pickup. She is usually talkative and cheerful. This change has motivated Ms. Tamara to check on her. On Friday, Emmy's mom is the last one to come in. She asks Ms. Tamara, "Do you have a few minutes to talk?" Ms. Tamara replies, "Yes. All the other children have gone, and Emmy is busy playing with puzzles. Let's sit together for a few minutes. I want to be sure everything is okay for you."

When you get to know your families well, you will notice subtle changes from day to day and week to week. You will hear when a happy event is ahead and notice when struggles are happening. This deep knowledge of families will help you show sensitivity to their needs.

For toddlers, open communication and collaboration with families is essential. You can build on parents' strengths and insights and empower them to participate in making choices about their child's care (Eichner and Johnson 2012). Your communication can have a lifetime impact on parents' expectations for children. Your partnership with parents is necessary to ensure healthy mental and physical development for each child (APA 2017).

STRATEGIES FOR SUCCESS

Ensuring Open Communication

The following strategies will help you keep communication channels open and positive:

▶ **Gather information.** A clipboard with a sentence starter should be available where families enter daily. Parents and primary caregivers can respond to the prompt "Something I want you to know today about my child is . . ." or "Today my child is feeling . . . and needs . . ." Provide a two-part check box at the bottom that says, "I need to schedule a call," or "I just wanted you to know." Provide a large envelope on the back of the clipboard for families to submit their requests to you privately.

▶ **Make phone calls.** Set aside a specific time each week when you are available to receive calls from parents and primary caregivers. In addition call one family each day just to check in. "Just checking in. I was so excited to watch Marley build a tower today. She seems so happy. I wanted you to know."

▶ **Take notes.** When families tell you something or ask a question, make a note of it. Write down the question and revisit it a week or more later. "I have been watching Marley. I remember that you asked me about her balance. She's been scooting along the table and is getting so strong! I wanted to give you a progress update."

▶ **Use a daily activity sheet or app.** All families will appreciate photos of their children at play. You may use a digital app for this purpose. Apps like Baby Connect, Daycare Tracker Pro, Tadpoles, Kaymbu, and HiMama allow sharing of real-time updates.

▶ **Email during naptime.** Send along a quick note. "Just checking in to tell you Joshua is having a wonderful day."

▶ **Send a weekly email.** A short group email can say, "Guess what I learned this week?" Include tips on sleep, healthy snacking, exercise, or positive guidance.

▶ **Create a simple newsletter.** Highlight activities and share plans. Add a section of quick tips to focus on child development and milestones and share positive guidance advice. Ask families to share cute or funny things their children said in a Child Moments corner. Share books you are reading to the children so these can be read to children at home. You can attach a single-page newsletter to an email.

▶ **Always communicate positively in writing.** What is written remains forever. If parents want to discuss complicated issues or want an answer that you cannot give in a few brief sentences, invite them to talk with you in person at another time. Follow the steps that keep you focused on building children's strengths.

▶ **Set healthy time boundaries.** Answer emails before children arrive in the morning and in the minutes after they leave. Assure parents and primary caregivers that you want to talk, but that you have set phone hours. Enforce talking privately when children are not present. When families know your availability, they will honor those times.

Using Family-Friendly Technology

We use a technology program that is a very helpful tool for teachers, parents, and administrators. We use it to check children in and out, input lesson themes, and communicate about meals, diapers, feedings, naps, and special moments. Parents receive a report at the end of each day. We can also take photos, save videos, write notes, track our learning goals, and keep track of development. We rely on it to connect us with parents, and they appreciate having this connection with their child.

Understanding Family Resilience

At eleven o'clock, Rachel and her mom arrive. "I just got Rachel to sleep when Kellan woke up. The whole night went like that. The morning wasn't much better. I totally forgot to bring a change of clothes for Rachel. I'm sorry. I hope she won't need them until tomorrow." "We'll be fine," assures Ms. Kay. "I have some extra things if Rachel needs them."

For a toddler's parents, life can be a roller coaster. They don't always get enough sleep. Often exhausted, they have to figure out meals, deal with constant messes, and try to keep the family centered while meeting the needs of a growing child. If a toddler is in all-day care, it is likely that parents are working, commuting, and trying to juggle the demands of work and home. Being a parent is not easy.

A typical family is balancing life events with the daily stress of getting up early, preparing children to leave the home, and handling unexpected challenges. Mom or Dad may be caring for an aging parent in addition to young children. Family life is complex, and the dynamics affect children.

A National Scientific Council on the Developing Child report suggests that young children can tolerate the kinds of stress that happen during typical life situations because they learn that life reorients quickly (NSCDC 2005/2014). They can handle more serious but temporary stress when it is buffered by supportive relationships. Perhaps a child lives with a teenage mom or a grandmother. There may be only one parent at home, or perhaps a new stepparent is involved in the family. Maybe a family is struggling to cover financial needs or a parent has lost a job. When major transitions affect a child directly, teachers and families can work together to provide needed support.

Stressors may be more serious when they persist over time. Early physical health issues, poverty, inadequate prenatal care, substance abuse, mental health issues, and other family factors can greatly challenge family resources. Death and loss, neighborhood violence, poverty, and divorce can tax families' ability to cope. These more serious and prolonged stressors can take a lifetime toll on children's physical and mental health (Shonkoff and Garner 2012).

According to national research, the more stressors that exist, the more severe is the impact on the child (NCCP 2017). However, close, warm, secure relationships can serve as a protective factor for children, even from serious stressors. Sensitive, responsive caregiving can act as a powerful buffer against a child's stress (NSCDC 2005/2014). You can be sure that your emotional and physical resources provide protection to young children (Masten 2007).

The American Academy of Pediatrics defines resilience as the ability to use one's protective factors to navigate a stressful situation successfully (AAP 2017). Resilience is the ability to bounce back or recover from a stressful event. Protective factors include the surrounding resilience of parents and caregivers, social connections, tangible help and resources in times of need, parent and caregiver knowledge of child development, and the developing social competence of the child.

Infants and toddlers are entirely dependent on their caregivers to offer reassurance, consistency, and ongoing comfort in challenging situations. They are vulnerable to their caregivers' choices, emotions, and actions. Adults must provide the secure experiences young children need for stability, nurturing, and care (Masterson and Kersey 2016).

It helps to understand the personal experiences, stresses, and challenges families face so you can be sensitive and supportive to each child. By better understanding the context of the child's social, emotional, and physical experiences, you can promote resilience and buffer the negative effects of stress.

Toddlers are too young to understand when things around them are topsy-turvy. They become anxious when family routines change. They may have a physical response when they experience sadness, depression, or anxiety, such as a change in eating, sleep, and emotional patterns. They may not have the words to tell you what they feel, so it is important to stay in touch with changes. When there is a death, a move, a financial change, or a new sibling, it is important to know.

When you learn about stress that children are experiencing, provide practical support. Children may need extra comfort during meals and naptimes. They may need extra lap time or rocking time. You can revisit the soothing sensory experiences in chapter 3 and read books that help children talk about their feelings. When you know extra support is needed, you can be proactive and provide responsive care.

FAST FACTS: WHY THIS WORKS

The Impact of Family Engagement

Positive communication and coordination between families and other caregivers is paramount. This "environment of relationships" supports or detracts from development (Center on the Developing Child 2014). The day-to-day success of your work depends on your specific knowledge of each family and your responsiveness to each child's needs.

The term *family engagement* (as opposed to *parent engagement*) represents the multigenerational nature of families and includes extended family members and nonrelatives who are involved in a child's life (Halgunseth, Jia, and Barbarin 2013). When children have this collaborative support from family and teachers, they gain the strengths and skills they need to be ready for school and learning (Schwarz and Easterbrooks 2014; Forry et al. 2011). When families partner with teachers to communicate and support children's development and learning, children achieve more, do better in math and reading, and have better social skills.

Open, two-way communication boosts family well-being as well. It increases satisfaction in parenting (NCPFCE 2014). A full coparenting approach, with open communication and coordinated care, benefits children (Ruprecht, Elicker, and Choi 2016). This level of open sharing and conversation between you and parents, primary caregivers, and families is essential for toddlers.

Exploring Family Culture

Cari and her mother arrive breathless, with a dripping umbrella and a sack of clothes. "I am sorry I can't stay this morning, but I need to drop off the boys at school. Nonna will come for Cari today at four o'clock." Ms. Hana responds, "*Buenos días*, Imira. Let me help you with those." She takes the clothing and smiles at Cari. "You brought raindrops on your cheeks today. We will watch for Nonna to come after naptime." Ms. Hana touches her own cheeks and then points to Cari's cheeks. "*Mojado las mejillas.* Your cheeks are wet from the rain."

Ms. Hana has children from many backgrounds in her classroom. She is from Japan. Ms. Ibarra is from Brazil. In the metropolitan area where they live, up to 35 percent of children speak a language other than English at home. In this toddler room, one of the families speaks Chinese and another Korean. Three of the families speak Spanish. Ms. Hana has learned welcome words for each family. She greets each one warmly when they arrive. At thirty months, Cari is just beginning to speak both Spanish and English.

Learning different languages didn't come easily for Ms. Hana. She spent time with her coteacher to learn words and phrases. Even more importantly, she works hard to convey welcome and acceptance to families. Coming from another country herself, Ms. Hana understands how a smiling face, a hug, and sincere care translates to families and children. This is a warm, inviting place where every child is special.

Communication about care, especially between people from different cultures, can present challenges. Sometimes parents may not be able to explain the differences they see in what you are doing. Both they and you may feel something is not quite the same, yet neither of you may be sure how to put your perceptions into words, especially if there is a language barrier.

It helps to understand that subtle ways of communicating are different for each family. The ways people walk, speak, and use their hands to express meaning are unique. The same is true of the ways people care for children. What seems completely natural to you may feel foreign to someone whose ways of nurturing and caregiving are different.

FAST FACTS: WHY THIS WORKS

Honoring Funds of Knowledge

Cultural and social norms influence the ways parents interact with their children. Subtle differences exist in parents' level of control, the ways they comfort, and their approaches to behavior guidance (Hill and Tyson 2008; Mah and Johnston 2012). If a child cries, is upset, or expresses a need, the way a parent responds emotionally and physically varies by culture (Vinall, Riddell, and Greenberg 2011). How much choice and whether a parent is gentle or assertive, or explains what needs to be done, can vary (Köster et al. 2016). Culture also determines how parents, family members, and extended family contribute to a child's upbringing.

These unique strengths and ways of parenting are called funds of knowledge. This is how we describe the life values, resources, knowledge, and social networks of a people group (Wolf 1966; Vélez-Ibañez 1988). A strength-based mind-set helps us look for and support contributions to a child's sense of identity and well-being. This fully informed partnership is called a cocaring framework of care (Lang et al. 2016). Cocaring includes mutual support, comfort, communication, encouragement, and trust. Families and teachers share a philosophy of respect and commitment to foster each child's full resiliency and development.

Assuming that other people share your views about children is easy to do. However, you may value independence, while a parent may value dependence. You may think toddlers should walk, but their parents carry them. Maybe a child uses a pacifier, bottle, or blanket longer than you think is appropriate. While you value independence, a parent may feel that the toddler years are an extended time of dependence that affords extra time to transmit values and teach a child important ways of living.

Parents may "do everything" for their children, just when you are trying to teach children to dress themselves independently. You may feel frustrated when children are "babied." These contradictions between home and group expectations can feel stressful to both you and to a parent.

Another conflict may occur when children are allowed to sleep in and are brought to school late—or inconsistently. You may have worked hard to put together an activity and feel slighted by families who don't seem to notice their children are missing important events. You may feel that unpredictable attendance is lazy or uncaring. However, families may simply be enjoying a close and caring time at home or the option of a flexible work time.

Getting to know specific cultural dynamics and beliefs is essential to forming a trusting partnership. Valuing parents as children's first and most important teachers can help you work with compassion and empathy to bridge misunderstandings and create the best possible support for each child. You will need sensitivity to cultural differences and knowledge of different caregiving approaches in order to open caring communication.

STRATEGIES FOR SUCCESS

Increasing Cultural Responsiveness

Authentic partnerships involve more than simply accommodating family requests. A partnership means that you acknowledge family ways of child rearing as foundational to the optimal health and well-being of children. By communicating about home routines and ways of comforting, eating, singing, and soothing, parents can teach you to be more effective in your guidance and interactions. Here are approaches that work:

▶ **Build trust.** Tell parents frequently that you see them as full partners in their children's care. Say often that you honor and appreciate their love for their children. Make it plain that you value all they are doing to nurture and care for their children.

▶ **Make the classroom feel like home.** Represent children's identities by displaying photos of families. Rotate music that represents children's home cultures, and have music playing when children arrive. Display inspirational messages in families' home languages near the door.

▶ **Find a cultural broker.** Find someone who can serve as a cultural broker—someone connected to the community and family who can not only translate effectively but also explain to you the needs of the family.

▶ **Become an expert.** Learn all you can about the families, their countries of origin, neighborhood resources, and extended families. Learn frequently used greetings and phrases.

▶ **Challenge your own assumptions.** Reflect often on your words and actions. Don't assume that parents understand what you are saying. Be aware that you are participating in a mutual learning experience. Be flexible, patient, and ready to see the needs and perspectives of other people.

Inviting Family Participation

Raul's father comes on Friday morning. He sits on the floor and reads to two of the children. He makes funny voices and uses puppets to entertain the children. Ms. Perez can see Raul's happiness with his father present. Ms. Perez says to her director, "I am amazed how the children respond when a parent volunteers. They love the individual attention. They ask someone to read to them much more after parents visit. And they show more interest in the puppets."

In Ms. Perez's room, family members enjoy time with the children. Children take pride in having their families participate. They get excited about reading, block play, and other games modeled by family members. They have so much to offer through their time, ideas, insights, and energy.

The more you can connect families to the classroom and to one another, the better. The sense of community and collaboration will boost energy and morale. Your classroom will become a hub of creative ideas and events.

Family involvement takes many forms, through active participation in the classroom and through families supporting their children's development and learning at home. In addition many community resources can help your families as they seek to enrich their children's learning. The following are strategies you can use to increase family involvement:

- **Keep an open-door policy.** Invite families to share activities, be guest readers, demonstrate circle games, and share songs with the children.

- **Create a class or group website.** Your website should be fully password protected so that your location, photos, and other identifying information are not available to the public. WordPress, Weebly, Wix, and other free web hosting sites allow you to create resource-filled communications as well as activity and learning calendars for your families. If you enjoy writing, you can share your insights and creativity on a classroom blog. Be sure your blog summarizes activities or insights rather than highlighting a particular child or situation. Of course, all communication will be positive and encouraging. Remember that everything on the web is permanent. Protect privacy and edit carefully.

- **Share adventure challenges**. Challenge families to involve toddlers in "I spy" experiences. An "I spy" trip to the grocery store might introduce a child to a new fruit or vegetable. Children might spy a baker or a grocer. An "I spy" trip to the park might include looking for a tree or a squirrel or collecting pinecones and seedpods.

- **Schedule mini parent-child events.** Hold music, reading, dance, or language activities focused on parents and children. Local libraries, music schools, dance studios, parks, and other organizations are often available to lead such events. A thirty- or forty-five-minute event can bring joy to everyone.

- **Share the creative power.** Invite families to make decisions about classroom events and activities. Are you deciding on a learning theme or art project? Ask families to weigh in and share their ideas and talents. Perhaps you have a photographer, painter, cook, or designer in your midst who can teach, create, or enrich the children's activities.

- **Warm up the welcome with food.** Invite families for donuts and coffee one morning a month. A cheerful table set with coffee and muffins or donuts (or fruit as a healthy alternative) can warm up the welcome at the start of each week or month.

- **Encourage parent mentoring.** Partner a new parent with a parent who has been part of your school, center, or home care longer to ease the transition and build friendships. Offer a corner of the classroom for parent meetings and connect parents with similar interests and needs.

- **Connect families.** A simple family meeting or coffee and cookies can encourage a sense of community. At the meeting, ask parents and primary caregivers to introduce their children and share exciting milestones or special traits. Create special topic events and ask a child development expert, behavior coach, or pediatrician to field questions. Common interests and personalities will inspire friendships among families.

Building Your Strengths

In this book, you have explored many ways that you can instill an early love of learning. Importantly, you have seen how rich language interactions influence learning and behavior. You have learned more about the need for culturally and linguistically responsive teaching that honors each child's background and family experience. You have seen how a warm and responsive relationship with you is the foundation for children's healthy development. These critical elements of teaching directly influence children's success.

As a toddler teacher, you will leave a legacy of positive impact on each child you teach. Over the months, you will provide encouragement and support for parents and families. You will develop deeply connected relationships with children. Some of the most important growth you experience will take place in the setting of your classroom and in your day-to-day experiences with children.

Your influence may help a family through a difficult week or encourage a child through a difficult moment. As these moments add up, a blueprint for self-esteem and positive relationships is formed. Your positive words help families understand their children's potential. The way you make children feel will nourish empathy and compassion for themselves and for others. The love you instill in them for learning will set them on the right path for school ahead.

As you grow in your teaching journey, the following steps can remind you of your personal and professional goals. As you keep these in mind, you can be confident knowing that you are making a difference today—and that your influence will live on in the children you teach for the rest of their lives.

- **Believe the best about others.** Your positive spirit and energy will be contagious and will continue to influence others around you. The positive regard and respect you give to others will be returned to you.

- **Embrace challenges as opportunities to grow.** When change feels uncomfortable, remind yourself that change is part of life. Patience and steady steps in the moment will lead to greater understanding and wisdom.

- **Celebrate small steps of growth.** Stay tuned in to the special and extraordinary moments that happen every day: a child's new understandings, milestones reached, a child's laughter, or a spontaneous hug.

- **Be active in gratitude.** Let others know how thankful you are for the things they do. Express appreciation for encouragement from colleagues and friends.

- **Be an expert listener.** When you notice what is really present, you can connect with and encourage others more effectively. You will find authentic ways to support the needs of others. You will also benefit from others' wisdom and perspective.

- **Aim for integrity.** Be an inspiration by being trustworthy. Be a safe place for a child, a parent, and a friend. You will gain the respect and trust of your colleagues and families. You will teach children that they are worthy of respect and trust.

- **Share your passions.** As you share your love of learning, others will experience your energy and commitment. Your love of children and joy in teaching will energize your daily work. Connect with others who share your passions, and together you will inspire positive change in your school and community.

- **Take risks.** Try something new. Offer to teach a seminar. Share a book you have read or webinar you have taken. Embrace positive change and use your talents to encourage others.

- **Think big.** Early childhood professionals are motivated by a shared purpose: we want to change the world. What could be more inspiring than that? Keep your eye on the bigger purpose of positively influencing children. Keep aiming for growth, and make good things happen for yourself and others. What you aim for, you can achieve.

- **Pursue professional growth.** Take a class toward a child development or education degree. Pursue a new credential. Willingness to grow can open professional doors. Conferences, webinars, and training modules are available to address many topics of interest to you as a toddler teacher. The Quality Rating and Improvement System (QRIS) National Learning Network has compiled a comprehensive list of QRIS contacts and websites for each state: https://qrisnetwork.org/qris-state-contacts-map. These resources will connect you with others like yourself who are dedicated to making a difference in the lives of children and families.

———

Quick question: What should I do when parents stay and talk a long time during pickup and monopolize my time so I can't talk with other parents?

Simple solution: When you find that a parent is going into a lot of detail or moving beyond a daily exchange, say, "This is an important subject. I would like to talk with you further. Let's schedule a phone time, since we cannot talk now." Or say, "I would like to talk about this issue more with you when we can speak privately. Let's schedule a touch-base meeting. Will you please email and let me know two times that work for you?" If the parent says, "Oh, this will only take a minute," respond, "I know this is important, but since I need to greet the other parents, let's talk in detail when we can speak privately." Keeping healthy boundaries is important.

———

Quick question: There is so much I want to learn. How do I get started?

Simple solution: Big goals begin with small steps. Keep a notebook or journal. Be faithful in writing down questions and concerns. Try writing these on the left side of a column. On the right side, as you gain insight, use a new strategy, or try something new, write down what you did, how it worked, and what you learned. Keeping track of a lesson learned each day can revolutionize your teaching.

Appendix

Crosswalk by Topic and Page Number

Supporting Quality Improvement

Let's Talk Toddlers provides practical information, background research, and effective strategies to help you use high-quality interactions in your toddler setting. It encourages family partnerships that foster resilience and success for children, including those with special needs and dual language learners. In addition to the guidance provided, you should follow all health and safety practices required by state and national licensing agencies. The scenarios and book features can help you in your journey of professional growth and encourage continuous quality improvement as you participate in your early childhood quality improvement system.

Alignment with Toddler CLASS

For the Classroom Assessment Scoring System Toddler (La Paro, Hamre, and Pianta 2012) the following chart identifies the location of chapter content that supports continuous quality improvement in the following content areas:

Content Area	Chapter	Topic
Postitive climate	1: Making a Difference in the Lives of Toddlers	Creating a Foundation of Nurture — 9 Creating a Positive Emotional Climate — 13 Strategies for Success: Making Common Routines Special — 14 Strategies for Success: Encouraging Children — 21
	4: Setting Positive Routines and Expectations	Ensuring Positive Morning Routines — 71 Meeting Individual Needs — 76 Making Mealtimes Happy — 84 Nurturing Effective Self-Care Routines — 78 Connecting During Dressing and Diapering — 79 Making Self-Care Fun — 80
	5: Strengthening Social Skills	Exploring Differences in Temperament — 115 Fostering Positive Interactions with Peers — 117

Content Area	Chapter	Topic
Postitive climate (*continued*)	6: Guiding Toddler Behavior	Guiding with Respect — 121 Staying Connected — 125 Exploring the Link between Relationships and Behavior — 127
	8: Fostering Partnerships with Families	Building a Relationship of Trust — 167
Teacher sensitivity	1: Making a Difference in the Lives of Toddlers	Caregivers as an Important Source of Attachment — 10 Examining Attachment Theory — 11 Using Developmentally Appropriate Practice — 14 Strategies for Success: Planning Ahead — 19
	2: Preparing the Environment for Play	Strategies for Success: Honoring What Children Need — 45
	3: Boosting Learning through Guided Play	Honoring the Child's Way of Being — 49
	4: Setting Positive Routines and Expectations	Meeting Individual Needs — 76 Nurturing Effective Self-Care Routines — 78 Connecting During Dressing and Diapering — 79
	5: Strengthening Social Skills	Exploring Emotional Competence — 97 Capturing the Immediacy of Toddlers' Feelings — 99 Providing Strategies for Calming — 109 Exploring Differences in Temperament — 115
	6: Guiding Toddler Behavior	Fostering Emotion Recognition and Expression — 101 Strategies for Success: Meeting Children's Needs — 132 Respecting Children's Natural Limits — 136
	8: Fostering Partnerships with Families	Understanding Family Resilience — 176

Content Area	Chapter	Topic
Regard for child perspectives	1: Making a Difference in the Lives of Toddlers	Using Developmentally Appropriate Practice — 14 Strength-Based Practice — 20
	2: Preparing the Environment for Play	Understanding the Impact of Space and Materials — 27 Inspiring Engagement and Imagination — 33 Strategies for Success: Making Playtime Work — 34 Strategies for Success: Planning Space for Toddlers — 28
	3: Boosting Learning through Guided Play	Strategies for Success: Following Children's Lead — 67
	4: Setting Positive Routines and Expectations	Planning a Predictable Schedule — 74 Meeting Individual Needs — 76 Nurturing Effective Self-Care Routines — 78 Supporting Sensitive Toilet Training — 81 Taking Care of Nose Blowing — 83
	5: Strengthening Social Skills	Unpacking Executive Function and Self-Regulation — 111 Strategies for Success: Building Self-Regulation — 113 Fostering Positive Interactions with Peers — 117
	6: Guiding Toddler Behavior	Respecting Children's Natural Limits — 136
Behavior guidance	1: Making a Difference in the Lives of Toddlers	Understanding Daily Needs — 18 Strategies for Success: Planning Ahead — 19 Strength-Based Practice — 20 Strategies for Success: Encouraging Children — 21
	2: Preparing the Environment for Play	Strategies for Success: Honoring What Children Need — 45
	4: Setting Positive Routines and Expectations	Minimizing Transitions — 90 Planning a Predictable Schedule — 74

Content Area	Chapter	Topic
Behavior guidance (*continued*)	5: Strengthening Social Skills	Capturing the Immediacy of Toddlers' Feelings — 99
		Fostering Emotion Recognition and Expression — 101
		Holding Realistic Expectations — 104
		Using Stories and Puppets to Teach Emotions — 106
		Providing Strategies for Calming — 109
		Unpacking Executive Function and Self-Regulation — 111
		Teaching Early Social Skills — 113
	6: Guiding Toddler Behavior	Guiding with Respect — 121
		Setting Up for Success — 123
		Strategies for Success: Planning Ahead — 125
		Using Effective Behavior Strategies — 128
		Strategies for Success: Positive Behavior Guidance for Toddlers — 129
		Understanding What Toddlers Need — 131
		Addressing Common Behavior Issues — 133
		Respecting Children's Natural Limits — 136
		Strategies for Success: What to Do with Persistent Behavior Issues — 137
		Using Reflective Practice — 138
Facilitation of learning and development	1: Making a Difference in the Lives of Toddlers	Ensuring Each Child's Success — 15
	2: Preparing the Environment for Play	Inspiring Engagement and Imagination — 33
		Strategies for Success: Making Playtime Work — 34
		Promoting High-Quality Learning through Play — 44
		Resources for Growth: Evaluating the Purpose of Play — 46

Content Area	Chapter	Topic
Facilitation of learning and development (*continued*)	3: Boosting Learning through Guided Play	Boosting Learning with Purposeful Conversation — 51
		Strategies for Success: Following Children's Lead — 67
		Expanding Concepts with Themed Boxes — 58
		Understanding the Need for Guided Play — 61
		Promoting Art Appreciation — 64
		Activating Nature and Outdoor Experiences — 66
		Engaging Children in Music and Movement — 62
	4: Setting Positive Routines and Expectations	Ensuring Positive Morning Routines — 71
		Meeting Individual Needs — 76
		Making the Most of Songs and Games — 91
	5: Strengthening Social Skills	Fostering Emotion Recognition and Expression — 101
		Unpacking Executive Function and Self-Regulation — 111
	7: Nurturing Language and Early Literacy	Making Reading Meaningful — 148
		Fostering Creative Group Book Reading — 150
		Making Stories Come Alive — 156
		Extending Stories through Dramatic Play — 157
Quality of feedback	3: Boosting Learning through Guided Play	Boosting Learning with Purposeful Conversation — 51
		Understanding the Need for Guided Play — 61
	4: Setting Positive Routines and Expectations	Nurturing Effective Self-Care Routines — 78
		Supporting Sensitive Toilet Training — 81
	5: Strengthening Social Skills	Exploring Emotional Competence — 97
		Fostering Emotion Recognition and Expression — 101
		Holding Realistic Expectations — 104
		Strategies for Success: Building Children's Strengths — 116

Content Area	Chapter	Topic
Quality of feedback (*continued*)	6: Guiding Toddler Behavior	Strategies for Success: Positive Behavior Guidance for Toddlers — 129 Respecting Children's Natural Limits — 136
	7: Nurturing Language and Early Literacy	Helping Language Grow — 146
Language modeling	2: Preparing the Environment for Play	Supporting Socio-Dramatic Play — 40 Resources for Growth: Evaluating the Purpose of Play — 46
	3: Boosting Learning through Guided Play	Boosting Learning with Purposeful Conversation — 51 Understanding the Need for Guided Play — 61
	4: Setting Positive Routines and Expectations	Ensuring Positive Morning Routines — 71 Nurturing Effective Self-Care Routines — 78
	5: Strengthening Social Skills	Fostering Emotion Recognition and Expression — 101 Using Stories and Puppets to Teach Emotions — 106
	6: Guiding Toddler Behavior	Respecting Children's Natural Limits — 136
	7: Nurturing Language and Early Literacy	Activating the Power of Language — 143 Helping Language Grow — 146 Boosting Daily Conversations — 147 Supporting Dual Language Learning — 154 Making Stories Come Alive — 156

Alignment with ITERS-3

For the *Infant/Toddler Environmental Rating Scale*, Third Edition (Harmes, Cryer, Clifford, & Yazejian 2017), the following chart identifies the location of chapter content that supports continuous quality improvement in the following content areas:

Content Area	Chapter	Topic
Indoor space	2: Preparing the Environment for Play	Understanding the Impact of Space and Materials — 27 Strategies for Success: Planning Space for Toddlers — 28 Making Small Changes for Big Results — 30
Furnishings for care, play, and learning	2: Preparing the Environment for Play	Strategies for Success: Planning Space for Toddlers — 28 Creating Indoor Space for Big-Body Play — 31 Strategies for Success: Reflecting on Play Support — 39
	5: Strengthening Social Skills	Providing Strategies for Calming — 109
	6: Guiding Toddler Behavior	Strategies for Success: Respecting Personal Boundaries — 123 Strategies for Success: Meeting Children's Needs — 132
Room arrangement	1: Making a Difference in the Lives of Toddlers	Strategies for Success: Planning Ahead — 19
	2: Preparing the Environment for Play	Understanding the Impact of Space and Materials — 27 Making Small Changes for Big Results — 30 Strategies for Success: Reflecting on Play Support — 39
	4: Setting Positive Routines and Expectations	Planning a Predictable Schedule — 74 Meeting Individual Needs — 76
	5: Strengthening Social Skills	Strategies for Success: Encouraging Positive Peer Interactions — 118
	6: Guiding Toddler Behavior	Strategies for Success: What to Do with Persistent Behavior Issues — 137

Content Area	Chapter	Topic
Display for children	1: Making a Difference in the Lives of Toddlers	Strategies for Success: Making Common Routines Special — 14
	3: Boosting Learning through Guided Play	Promoting Art Appreciation — 64
	7: Nurturing Language and Early Literacy	Quick Question: Teaching Toddlers to Read — 164
Meals/snacks	4: Setting Positive Routines and Expectations	Meeting Individual Needs — 76 Making Mealtimes Happy — 84
Diapering/ toileting	4: Setting Positive Routines and Expectations	Nurturing Effective Self-Care Routines — 78 Connecting During Dressing and Diapering — 79 Quick Questions: Books for Self Care — 94
Health practices	1: Making a Difference in the Lives of Toddlers	Strategies for Success: Planning Ahead — 19
	4: Setting Positive Routines and Expectations	Understanding the Science of Hand Washing — 81 Taking Care of Nose Blowing — 83 Providing Support for Napping — 85 Minimizing Transitions — 90
	6: Guiding Toddler Behavior	Strategies for Success: Positive Behavior Guidance for Toddlers — 129 Strategies for Success: Meeting Children's Needs — 132
Safety practices	1: Making a Difference in the Lives of Toddlers	Understanding Daily Needs — 18 Strategies for Success: Encouraging Children — 21
	2: Preparing the Environment for Play	Strategies for Success: Planning Space for Toddlers — 28 Loose Parts — 35 Strategies for Success: Reflecting on Play Support — 39
	3: Boosting Learning through Guided Play	Activating Nature and Outdoor Experiences — 66 Strategies for Success: Following Children's Lead — 68

Content Area	Chapter	Topic
Safety practices (*continued*)	6: Guiding Toddler Behavior	Exploring the Link between Relationships and Behavior — 127
		Addressing Common Behavior Issues — 133
		Turning Around Frustration and Biting — 134
		Calming Hitting or Aggression — 135
		Soothing Tantrums — 135
		Strategies for Success: What to Do with Persistent Behavior Issues — 137
Talking with children	1: Making a Difference in the Lives of Toddlers	Creating a Foundation of Nurture — 9
		Caregivers as an Important Source of Attachment — 10
		Strategies for Success: Encouraging Children — 21
		Quick Question: Talking with Children — 24
	3: Boosting Learning through Guided Play	Exploring the Impact of Language-Rich Interactions — 54
		Following Children's Lead — 68
	4: Setting Positive Routines and Expectations	Meeting Individual Needs — 76
		Nurturing Effective Self-Care Routines — 78
		Connecting During Dressing and Diapering — 79
		Making Self-Care Fun — 80
	5: Strengthening Social Skills	Fostering Emotion Recognition and Expression — 101
Encouraging vocabulary development	2: Preparing the Environment for Play	Supporting Socio-Dramatic Play — 40
		Resources for Growth: Evaluating the Purpose of Play — 46
	3: Boosting Learning through Guided Play	Boosting Learning with Purposeful Conversation — 51
		Expanding Concepts with Themed Boxes — 58
	4: Setting Positive Routines and Expectations	Ensuring Positive Morning Routines — 71
		Nurturing Effective Self-Care Routines — 78
	6: Guiding Toddler Behavior	Fostering Emotion Recognition and Expression — 101
		Using Stories and Puppets to Teach Emotions — 106

Content Area	Chapter	Topic
Encouraging vocabulary development (*continued*)	7: Nurturing Language and Early Literacy	Activating the Power of Language — 143 Helping Language Grow — 146 Boosting Daily Conversations — 147 Supporting Dual Language Learning — 154 Making Stories Come Alive — 156 Extending Stories through Dramatic Play — 157
Responding to children's communication	1: Making a Difference in the Lives of Toddlers	Caregivers as an Important Source of Attachment — 10 Examining Attachment Theory — 11 Ensuring Each Child's Success — 15 Strategies for Success: Planning Ahead — 19
	3: Boosting Learning through Guided Play	Honoring the Child's Way of Being — 49
	4: Setting Positive Routines and Expectations	Strategies for Success: Nurturing Successful Self-Care Routines — 78 Supporting Sensitive Toilet Training — 81 Making Mealtimes Happy — 84
	5: Strengthening Social Skills	Fostering Emotion Recognition and Expression — 101 Understanding the Role of Stress — 106
	6: Guiding Toddler Behavior	Strategies for Success: Planning Ahead — 125 Strategies for Success: Positive Behavior Guidance for Toddlers — 129 Respecting Children's Natural Limits — 136
	7: Nurturing Language and Early Literacy	Helping Language Grow — 146 Boosting Daily Conversations — 147 Supporting Dual Language Learning — 154
Encouraging children to communicate	1: Making a Difference in the Lives of Toddlers	Caregivers as an Important Source of Attachment — 10 Examining Attachment Theory — 11
	3: Boosting Learning through Guided Play	Boosting Learning with Purposeful Conversation — 51 Understanding the Need for Guided Play — 61

Content Area	Chapter	Topic
Encouraging children to communicate (*continued*)	4: Setting Positive Routines and Expectations	Ensuring Positive Morning Routines — 71 Nurturing Effective Self-Care Routines — 78
	5: Strengthening Social Skills	Fostering Emotion Recognition and Expression — 101 Using Stories and Puppets to Teach Emotions — 106 Strategies for Success: Building Self-Regulation — 113 Strategies for Success: Building Children's Strengths — 116
	6: Guiding Toddler Behavior	Respecting Children's Natural Limits — 136
	7: Nurturing Language and Early Literacy	Activating the Power of Language — 143 Helping Language Grow — 146 Boosting Daily Conversations — 147 Supporting Dual Language Learning — 154 Making Stories Come Alive — 156
	8: Fostering Partnerships with Families	Building a Relationship of Trust — 167
Staff use of books with children	3: Boosting Learning through Guided Play	Expanding Concepts with Themed Boxes — 58
	5: Strengthening Social Skills	Fostering Emotion Recognition and Expression — 101 Using Stories and Puppets to Teach Emotion — 106 Resources for Growth: Great Books about Toddler Emotions — 118
	7: Nurturing Language and Early Literacy	Making Reading Meaningful — 148 Strategies for Success: Preparing for Reading with Toddlers — 150 Fostering Creative Group Book Reading — 150 Choosing Books for Toddlers — 153 Strategies for Success: Engaging Dual-Language Learners — 155 Making Stories Come Alive — 156 Quick Questions: Reading to Toddlers — 164

Content Area	Chapter	Topic
Encouraging children's use of books	4: Setting Positive Routines and Expectations	Choosing Books to Share for Napping — 89
	7: Nurturing Language and Early Literacy	Making Reading Meaningful — 148 Strategies for Success: Preparing for Reading with Toddlers — 150 Choosing Books for Toddlers — 153 Resources for Growth: Choosing Books for Toddlers — 159
Fine motor	2: Preparing the Environment for Play	Loose Parts — 35 Fine-Motor and Logic Play — 37
Art	3: Boosting Learning through Guided Play	Promoting Art Appreciation — 64
Music and movement	3: Boosting Learning through Guided Play	Engaging Children in Music and Movement — 62
	4: Setting Positive Routines and Expectations	Making the Most of Songs and Games — 91 Fast Facts: Why This Works, Using Music to Boost Self-Regulation — 93
Blocks	2: Preparing the Environment for Play	Construction Activities — 36
	3: Boosting Learning through Guided Play	Boosting Learning with Purposeful Conversation — 51
Dramatic play	2: Preparing the Environment for Play	Supporting Socio-Dramatic Play — 40 Community and Career Play — 40 Cooking and Homemaking — 41 Dolls and Nurturing Play — 41 Dress-Up Clothing — 42 Themed Buildings and Accessories — 42 Cars and Trucks and Things that Go — 42
	7: Nurturing Language and Early Literacy	Extending Stories through Dramatic Play — 157
	8: Fostering Partnerships with Families	Strategies for Success: Increasing Cultural Responsiveness — 180

Content Area	Chapter	Topic
Nature/science	2: Preparing the Environment for Play	Indoor Science and Nature Play — 43 Sensory Play — 43
	3: Boosting Learning through Guided Play	Activating Nature and Outdoor Experiences — 66
Math/number	2: Preparing the Environment for Play	Loose Parts — 35 Construction Activities — 36 Ramps and Tubes — 37
	3: Boosting Learning through Guided Play	Engaging Children in Music and Movement — 62 Quick Question–Simple Solution: Teaching STEM — 69
Appropriate use of technology	3: Boosting Learning through Guided Play	Examining the Impact of Media and Technology — 57
Promoting acceptance of diversity	1: Making a Difference in the Lives of Toddlers	Understanding Your Influence — 21
	2: Preparing the Environment for Play	Supporting Socio-Dramatic Play — 40 Cooking and Homemaking — 41 Dolls and Nurturing Play — 41 Cultural and Local Tradition Play — 42
	3: Boosting Learning through Guided Play	Traveling — 60
	4: Setting Positive Routines and Expectations	Making the Most of Songs and Games — 91 Exploring Differences in Temperament — 115 Honoring Fears — 116
	7: Nurturing Language and Early Literacy	Activating the Power of Language — 143 Boosting Daily Conversations — 147 Choosing Books for Toddlers — 153 Engaging Dual-Language Learners — 155
	8: Fostering Partnerships with Families	Exploring Family Culture — 178 Honoring Funds of Knowledge — 179 Strategies for Success: Increasing Cultural Responsiveness — 180

Content Area	Chapter	Topic
Gross motor	2: Preparing the Environment for Play	Creating Indoor Space for Big-Body Play — 31 Fast Facts: Why This works—Understanding Sensory Integration and Movement — 31
	3: Boosting Learning through Guided Play	Activating Nature and Outdoor Experiences — 66 Quick Question: Constructive Outdoor Play — 69
Supervision of gross motor play	2: Preparing the Environment for Play	Strategies for Success: Planning Space for Toddlers — 28 Creating Indoor Space for Big-Body Play — 31 Strategies for Success: Reflecting on Play Support — 39
	3: Boosting Learning through Guided Play	Engaging Children in Music and Movement — 62 Activating Nature and Outdoor Experiences — 66 Quick Question: Constructive Outdoor Play — 69
	6: Guiding Behavior	Fostering Emotion Recognition and Expression — 101 Strategies for Success: Planning Ahead — 125 Strategies for Success: Meeting Children's Needs — 132 Respecting Children's Natural Limits — 136
Supervision of play and learning (non-gross motor)	1: Making a Difference in the Lives of Toddlers	Ensuring Each Child's Success — 15 Understanding Daily Needs — 18
	2: Preparing the Environment for Play	Inspiring Engagement and Imagination — 33 Strategies for Success: Making Playtime Work 34 Strategies for Success: Reflecting on Play Support — 39 Promoting High-Quality Learning through Play — 44 Resources for Growth: Evaluating the Purpose of Play — 46 Understanding the Need for Guided Play — 61

Content Area	Chapter	Topic
Supervision of play and learning (non-gross motor) (*continued*)	3: Boosting Learning through Guided Play	Boosting Learning with Purposeful Conversation — 51
		Expanding Concepts with Themed Boxes — 58
		Understanding the Need for Guided Play — 61
		Engaging Children in Music and Movement — 62
		Promoting Art Appreciation — 64
		Activating Nature and Outdoor Experiences — 66
		Strategies for Success: Following Children's Lead — 67
	4: Setting Positive Routines and Expectations	Ensuring Positive Morning Routines — 71
		Meeting Individual Needs — 76
		Making the Most of Songs and Games — 91
	5: Strengthening Social Skills	Fostering Emotion Recognition and Expression — 101
		Unpacking Executive Function and Self-Regulation — 111
	7: Nurturing Language and Early Literacy	Making Reading Meaningful — 148
		Fostering Creative Group Book Reading — 150
		Making Stories Come Alive — 156
		Extending Stories through Dramatic Play — 157
Peer interaction	2: Preparing the Environment for Play	Promoting High-Quality Learning through Play — 44
		Strategies for Success: Honoring What Children Need — 45
	4: Setting Positive Routines and Expectations	Ensuring Positive Morning Routines — 71
	5: Guiding Toddler Behavior	Fostering Positive Interactions with Peers — 117
Staff-child interaction	1: Making a Difference in the Lives of Toddlers	Caregivers as an Important Source of Attachment — 10
		Examining Attachment Theory — 11
		Providing Security and Consistency — 12
		Using Developmentally Appropriate Practice — 14
		Strategies for Success: Encouraging Children — 21

Content Area	Chapter	Topic
Staff-child interaction (*continued*)	2: Preparing the Environment for Play	Strategies for Success: Honoring What Children Need — 45
	3: Boosting Learning through Guided Play	Honoring the Child's Way of Being — 49 Using Observation to Understand, Document, and Support Learning — 54
	4: Setting Positive Routines and Expectations	Meeting Individual Needs — 76 Nurturing Effective Self-Care Routines — 78 Connecting During Dressing and Diapering — 79
	5: Strengthening Social Skills	Exploring Emotional Competence — 97 Capturing the Immediacy of Toddlers' Feelings — 99 Holding Realistic Expectations — 104 Understanding the Role of Stress — 106 Providing Strategies for Calming — 109 Exploring Differences in Temperament — 115
	6: Guiding Toddler Behavior	Fostering Emotion Recognition and Expression — 101 Strategies for Success: Meeting Children's Needs — 132 Respecting Children's Natural Limits — 136
	8: Fostering Partnerships with Families	Understanding Family Resilience — 176
Providing physical warmth/touch	1: Making a Difference in the Lives of Toddlers	Creating a Positive Emotional Climate — 13 Strategies for Success: Making Common Routines Special — 14 Ensuring Each Child's Success — 15
	4: Setting Positive Routines and Expectations	Providing Support for Napping — 85 Strategies for Success: Patting Backs at Naptime — 87 Using Snuggle Routines for Waking — 89
	5: Strengthening Social Skills	Understanding the Role of Stress — 106
	6: Guiding Toddler Behavior	Staying Connected — 125 Strategies for Success: Meeting Children's Needs — 132

Content Area	Chapter	Topic
Guiding children's behavior	1: Making a Difference in the Lives of Toddlers	Understanding Daily Needs — 18 Strategies for Success: Planning Ahead — 19 Strength-Based Practice — 20 Strategies for Success: Encouraging Children — 21
	2: Preparing the Environment for Play	Strategies for Success: Honoring What Children Need — 45
	4: Setting Positive Routines and Expectations	Planning a Predictable Schedule — 74 Minimizing Transitions — 90
	5: Strengthening Social Skills	Exploring Emotional Competence — 97 Capturing the Immediacy of Toddlers' Feelings — 99 Fostering Emotion Recognition and Expression — 101 Holding Realistic Expectations — 104 Using Stories and Puppets to Teach Emotions — 106 Providing Strategies for Calming — 109 Unpacking Executive Function and Self-Regulation — 111 Teaching Early Social Skills — 113
	6: Guiding Toddler Behavior	Guiding with Respect — 121 Setting Up for Success — 123 Strategies for Success: Planning Ahead — 125 Using Effective Behavior Strategies — 128 Strategies for Success: Positive Behavior Guidance for Toddlers — 129 Understanding What Toddlers Need — 131 Addressing Common Behavior Issues — 133 Respecting Children's Natural Limits — 136 Strategies for Success: What to Do with Persistent Behavior Issues — 137 Using Reflective Practice — 138
Scheduling and transitions	4: Setting Positive Routines and Expectations	Planning a Predictable Schedule — 74 Meeting Individual Needs — 76 Minimizing Transitions — 90

Content Area	Chapter	Topic
Free play	1: Making a Difference in the Lives of Toddlers	Encouraging Children — 21
	2: Preparing the Environment for Play	Understanding the Impact of Space and Materials — 27
		Strategies for Success: Planning Space for Toddlers — 28
		Inspiring Engagement and Imagination — 33
		Strategies for Success: Making Playtime work — 34
		Strategies for Success: Reflecting on Play Support — 39
		Supporting Socio-Dramatic Play — 40
	3: Boosting Learning through Guided Play	Activating Nature and Outdoor Experiences — 66
	4: Setting Positive Routines and Expectations	Ensuring Positive Morning Routines — 71
		Planning a Predictable Schedule — 74
		Meeting Individual Needs — 76
	5: Strengthening Social Skills	Strategies for Success: Encouraging Positive Peer Interactions — 118
	7: Nurturing Language and Early Literacy	Helping Language Grow — 146
Group activities	1: Making a Difference in the Lives of Toddlers	Creating a Positive Emotional Climate — 13
		Using Developmentally Appropriate Practice — 14
		Understanding Daily Needs — 18
	2: Preparing the Environment for Play	Strategies for Success: Planning Space for Toddlers — 28
		Creating Indoor Space for Big-Body Play — 31
		Inspiring Engagement and Imagination — 33
		Strategies for Success: Making Playtime Work — 34
	3: Boosting Learning through Guided Play	Boosting Learning with Purposeful Conversation — 51
		Strategies for Success: Following Children's Lead — 67

Content Area	Chapter	Topic
Group activities (*continued*)	4: Setting Positive Routines and Expectations	Planning a Predictable Schedule — 74 Meeting Individual Needs — 76 Nurturing Effective Self-Care Routines — 78 Minimizing Transitions — 90
	7: Nurturing Language and Early Literacy	Quick Questions: Engaging During Reading — 164

References

Chapter 1

Ahnert, Lieselotte, and Michael E. Lamb. 2011. "Child Care and Its Impact on Young Children (2–5)." *Encyclopedia on Early Childhood Development*, May. www.child-encyclopedia.com/sites/default/files/textes-experts/en/857/child-care-and-its-impact-on-young-children-2-5.pdf.

Barnett, W. Steven, and Jason T. Hustedt. 2011. "Improving Public Financing for Early Learning Programs." *Preschool Policy Brief*, April. National Institute for Early Education Research (NIEER). nieer.org/resources/policybriefs/24.pdf.

Bergin, Christi, and David Bergin. 2009. "Attachment in the Classroom." *Education Psychology Review* 21:141–70.

Bowlby, John. 1969. *Attachment and Loss: Volume 1: Attachment*. New York: Basic Books.

———. 1988. *A Secure Base: Parent-Child Attachment and Healthy Human Development*. New York: Basic Books.

Bowlby, Richard. 2007. "Babies and Toddlers in Non-Parental Daycare Can Avoid Stress and Anxiety if They Develop a Lasting Secondary Attachment Bond with One Carer Who Is Consistently Accessible to Them." *Attachment and Human Development* 9 (4): 307–19.

Braveman, Paula A., Tabashir Sadegh-Nobari, and Susan Egerter. 2008. "Early Childhood Experiences: Laying the Foundation for Health across a Lifetime." *Issue Brief 1: Early Childhood Experiences and Health*, June. Robert Wood Johnson Foundation: Commission to Build a Healthier America. www.commissiononhealth.org/PDF/095bea47-ae8e-4744-b054-258c9309b3d4/Issue%20Brief%201%20Jun%2008%20-%20Early%20Childhood%20Experiences%20and%20Health.pdf.

CDC (Centers for Disease Control and Prevention). 2017. "Developmental Monitoring and Screening." www.cdc.gov/ncbddd/childdevelopment/screening.html.

Center for High Impact Philanthropy. 2014. "Investing in High Quality Preschool: Q & A with Dr. Robert C. Pianta." University of Pennsylvania: Center for High Impact Philanthropy. February 20. www.impact.upenn.edu/investing_in_high_quality_preschool_qa_with_dr-_robert_c-_pianta/.

Child Care Aware. 2016. "Parents and the High Cost of Child Care." http://usa.childcareaware.org/wp-content/uploads/2016/12/CCA_High_Cost_Report.pdf.

Cozolino, Louis. 2014. *The Neuroscience of Human Relationships: Attachment and the Developing Social Brain*, 2nd ed. New York: W. W. Norton.

Dearing, Eric, Kathleen McCartney, and Bret A. Taylor. 2009. "Does Higher Quality Early Child Care Promote Low-Income Children's Math and Reading Achievement in Middle Childhood?" *Child Development* 80 (5): 1329–49.

Duncan, Greg, Katherine Magnuson, Tom Boyce, and Jack Shonkoff. 2013. "The Long Reach of Early Childhood Poverty: Pathways and Impacts." National Forum on Early Childhood Policy and Programs: National Science Council on the Developing Child. www.orionchildreninternational.org/uploads/2/2/4/7/22473078/the_long_reach_of_early_childhood_poverty_pathways_and_impacts.pdf.

Ebbeck, Marjory, and Hoi Yin Bonnie Yim. 2009. "Rethinking Attachment: Fostering Positive Relationships between Infants, Toddlers, and Their Primary Caregivers." *Early Child Development and Care* 179 (7): 899–909.

Ebbeck, Marjory, Dora Mei Youg Phoon, Elizabeth Chai Kim Tan-Chong, Marilyn Ai Bee Tan, and Mandy Lian Mui Goh. 2015. "A Research Study on Secure Attachment Using the Primary Caregiving Approach." *Early Childhood Education* 43:233–40.

Ferguson, Ronald F. 2016. "Aiming Higher Together: Strategizing Better Education Outcomes for Boys and Young Men of Color." Urban Institute, May. www.urban.org/sites/default /files/publication/80481/2000784-Aiming-Higher-Together-Strategizing-Better -Educational-Outcomes-for-Boys-and-Young-Men-of-Color.pdf.

Fraga, Lynette, Dionne Dobbins, and Michelle McCready. 2015. "Parents and the High Cost of Child Care: 2015 Report." Child Care Aware. usa.childcareaware.org/wp-content /uploads/2016/03/Parents-and-the-High-Cost-of-Child-Care-2015-FINAL.pdf.

Fuller, Bruce, John W. Gasko, and Rebecca Anguiano. 2010. "Lifting Pre-K Quality: Caring and Effective Teachers." *Institute of Human Development, UC Berkeley*. www.elcmdm.org /Knowledge%20Center/reports/Fullerhighquality.pdf.

Gloeckler, Lissy, and Karen M. La Paro. 2015. "Toddlers and Child Care: A Time for Discussion, Dialogue, and Change." *Zero to Three* 36 (2): 45–52.

Goldhaber, Dan, John Krieg, and Roddy Theobald. 2014. "Knocking on the Door to the Teaching Profession? Modeling the Entry of Prospective Teachers into the Workforce." *Economics of Education Review* 43:106–24.

Granot, David, and Ofra Mayseless. 2012. "Representation of Mother-Child Attachment Relationships and Social-Information Processing of Peer Relationships in Early Adolescents." *Journal of Early Adolescence* 32 (4): 537–64.

Halle, Tamara, Elizabeth Hair, Mirjam Nuenning, Debra Weinstein, Jessica Vick, Nicole Forry, and Akemi Kinukawa. 2009. "Primary Child Care Arrangements of US Infants: Patterns of Utilization by Poverty Status, Family Structure, Maternal Work Status, Maternal Work Schedule, and Child Care Assistance." *ChildTrends*, June. Office of Planning, Research, and Evaluation. www.acf.hhs.gov/sites/default/files/opre/child_trends_9a.pdf.

Hamm, Katie. 2015. "How Child Care Is Becoming a Crisis in America." *ThinkProgress*, September 11. https://thinkprogress.org/economy/2015/09/11/3700668/childcare-cap -report-guest-post/.

Howard, Eboni C. 2015. "What Matters Most for Children: Influencing Inequality at the Start of Life." *American Institutes for Research*, July. www.air.org/sites/default/files/downloads /report/Early-Childhood-Education-Equity-Howard-August-2015.pdf.

Kuhl, Patricia K. 2011. "Early Language Learning and Literacy: Neuroscience Implications for Education." *Mind, Brain, and Education* 5 (3): 128–42.

Landry, Susan H., Tricia A. Zucker, Heather B. Taylor, P. R. Swank, Jeffrey M. Williams, Michael Assel, April Crawford, and Weihua Huang et al. 2014. "Enhancing Early Child Care Quality and Learning for Toddlers at Risk: The Responsive Early Childhood Program. *Developmental Psychology* 50 (2): 526–41.

La Paro, Karen M., Amy C. Thomason, Joanna K. Lower, Victoria L. Kintner-Duffy, and Deborah J. Cassidy. 2012. "Examining the Definition and Measurement of Quality in Early Childhood Education: A Review of Studies Using the ECERS-R from 2003 to 2010." *Early Childhood Research and Practice* 14 (1). ecrp.uiuc.edu/v14n1/laparo.html.

La Paro, Karen M., Amy C. Williamson, and Bridget Hatfield. 2014. "Assessing Quality in Toddler Classrooms Using the CLASS-Toddler and the ITERS-R." *Early Education and Development* 25 (6): 875–93.

La Paro, Karen M., and Lissy Gloeckler. 2016. "The Context of Child Care for Toddlers: The 'Experience Expectable Environment.'" *Early Childhood Education Journal* 44 (2): 147–53.

Laughlin, Lynda. 2010. "Who's Minding the Kids? Child Care Arrangements: Spring 2005/ Summer 2006." *Current Population Reports*, August. US Census Bureau. www.census.gov /prod/2010pubs/p70-121.pdf.

———. 2013. "Who's Minding the Kids? Child Care Arrangements: Spring 2011." *Current Population Reports*, April. US Census Bureau. www.census.gov/prod/2013pubs/p70-135.pdf.

Matthews, Hannah, and Rhiannon Reeves. 2014. "Infants and Toddlers in CCDBG: 2012 Update." *CLASP*, August. www.clasp.org/resources-and-publications/publication-1 /Infants-and-Toddlers-in-CCDBG-2012-Update.pdf.

NAEYC (National Association for the Education of Young Children). 2011. "Code of Ethical Conduct and Statement of Commitment." *National Association for the Education of Young Children*, May. www.naeyc.org/files/naeyc/image/public_policy/Ethics%20Position %20Statement2011_09202013update.pdf.

———. 2017. "DAP with Infants and Toddlers." Accessed May 23. www.naeyc.org/dap /infants-and-toddlers.

National Scientific Council on the Developing Child. 2008/2012. *Establishing a Level Foundation for Life: Mental Health Begins in Early Childhood: Working Paper 6*. Updated Edition. www.developingchild.harvard.edu/wp-content/uploads/2008/05/Establishing -a-Level-Foundation-for-Life-Mental-Health-Begins-in-Early-Childhood.pdf.

Nores, Milagros, and W. Steven Barnett. 2014. "Access to High Quality Early Care and Education: Readiness and Opportunity Gaps in America." *Center on Enhancing Early Learning Outcomes*, May. http://ceelo.org/wp-content/uploads/2014/05/ceelo_policy_report_access _quality_ece.pdf.

Panfile, Tia M., and Deborah J. Laible. 2012. "Attachment Security and Child's Empathy: The Mediating Role of Emotion Regulation." *Merrill-Palmer Quarterly* 58 (1): 1–21.

Ruprecht, Karen, James Elicker, and Ji Young Choi. 2016. "Continuity of Care, Caregiver-Child Interactions, and Toddler Social Competence and Problem Behaviors." *Early Education and Development* 27 (2): 221–39.

Ruzek, Erik, Margaret Burchinal, George Farkas, and Greg J. Duncan. 2014. "The Quality of Toddler Child Care and Cognitive Skills at 24 Months: Propensity Score Analysis Results from the ECLS-B." *Early Childhood Research Quarterly* 29 (1): 12–21.

Sabol, Terri J., and Robert C. Pianta. 2012. "Recent Trends in Research on Teacher-Child Relationships." *Attachment and Human Development* 14 (3): 213–31.

Slot, Pauline L., Paul P. M. Leseman, Josje Verhagen, and Hanna Mulder. 2015. "Associations between Structural Quality Aspects and Process Quality in Dutch Early Childhood Education and Care Settings." *Early Childhood Research Quarterly* 33 (4): 64–76. www.sciencedirect.com/science/article/pii/S0885200615000599.

USDHHS (US Department of Health and Human Services). 2006. "The NICHD Study of Early Child Care and Youth Development: Findings for Children up to 4½ Years." National Institutes of Health: National Institute of Child Health and Human Development. www.nichd.nih.gov/publications/pubs/documents/seccyd_06.pdf.

USDOE (US Department of Education). 2015. "A Matter of Equity: Preschool in America." www2.ed.gov/documents/early-learning/matter-equity-preschool-america.pdf.

USDOL (US Department of Labor) Women's Bureau. 2016. "Working Mothers Issue Brief." www.dol.gov/wb/resources/WB_WorkingMothers_508_FinalJune13.pdf.

Vandell, Deborah Lowe, Jay Belsky, Margaret Burchinal, Nathan Vandergrift, and Laurence Steinberg. 2010. "Do Effects of Early Childcare Extend to Age 15 Years? Results from the NICHD Study of Early Childcare and Youth Development." *Child Development* 81 (3): 737–56.

Vernon-Feagans, Lynne, Mary E. Bratsch-Hines, and The Family Life Project Key Investigators. 2013. "Caregiver-Child Verbal Interactions in Childcare: A Buffer against Poor Language Outcomes When Maternal Language Input Is Less." *Early Childhood Research Quarterly* 28 (4): 858–73. www.ncbi.nlm.nih.gov/pmc/articles/PMC3947639/.

Weilin, Li, George Farkas, Greg J. Duncan, Margaret R. Burchinal, and Deborah Lowe Vandell. 2013. "Timing of High-Quality Child Care and Cognitive, Language, and Preacademic Development." *Developmental Psychology* 49 (8): 1440–51.

Yoshikawa, Hirokazu, Christina Weiland, Jeanne Brooks-Gunn, Margaret R. Burchinal, Linda M. Espinosa, William T. Gormley, Jens Ludwig, Katherine A. Magnuson, Deborah Phillips, and Martha J. Zaslow. 2013. "Investing in Our Future: The Evidence Base on Preschool Education." Foundation for Child Development, October. www.fcd-us.org/assets/2016/04/Evidence-Base-on-Preschool-Education-FINAL.pdf.

Chapter 2

Bagdi, Aparna, John Vacca, and Kendra N. Waninger. 2007. "The Importance of Sensory Functioning: Guidelines for Infant and Toddler Caregivers. *Dimensions of Early Childhood* 35 (2): 13–22. www.southernearlychildhood.org/upload/pdf/Spring_Dimenions_2007.pdf.

Bernstorf, Elaine. 2012. "Parten's Levels of Social Play in Kodály Teaching Contexts." *Kodaly Envoy* 39 (1): 7–11.

Bull, Danielle. 2015. "Demystifying Sensory Processing." *Educating Young Children: Learning and Teaching in the Early Childhood Years* 21 (1): 32–33.

Parks, Louise. 2014. "Sensorimotor Development: Hands-On Activities for Infants and Toddlers." *Texas Child Care Quarterly* 37 (4): 19–28. www.childcarequarterly.com/pdf/spring14_infants.pdf.

Parten, Mildred. B. 1932. "Social Participation among Preschool Children." *Journal of Abnormal and Social Psychology* 27 (3): 243–69.

Pate, Russell R., and Jennifer R. O'Neill. 2012. "Physical Activity Guidelines for Young Children: An Emerging Consensus." *Archives of Pediatrics and Adolescent Medicine* 166 (12): 195–96.

Ruxton, Carrie. 2012. "Toddler Milestones Match Marathon Effort." *Online PR Media*, September 5. www.onlineprnews.com/news/259317-1346830588-toddler-milestones-match-marathon-effort.html.

White, Jan. 2013. "Somersaults and Spinning." *Exchange* 211: 76–78.

Chapter 3

AAP (American Academy of Pediatrics). 2016. "Media and Young Minds." *Pediatrics* 138 (5): 1–8. https://pediatrics.aappublications.org/content/pediatrics/early/2016/10/19/peds.2016-2591.full.pdf.

Akhtar, Nameer, and Morton Ann Gernsbacher. 2007. "Joint Attention and Vocabulary Development: A Critical Look." *Language and Linguistic Compass* 1 (3): 195–207.

American College of Pediatricians. 2016. "The Impact of Media Use and Screen Time on Children, Adolescents, and Families," November. www.acpeds.org/the-college-speaks /position-statements/parenting-issues/the-impact-of-media-use-and-screen-time-on -children-adolescents-and-families.

Bodrova, Elena, and Deborah J. Leong. 2007. *Tools of the Mind: The Vygotskian Approach to Early Childhood Education.* 2nd ed. Upper Saddle River, NJ: Pearson.

Chonchaiya, Weerasak, and Chandhita Pruksananonda. 2008. "Television Viewing Associates with Delayed Language Development." *Acta Paediatra* 97 (7): 977–82.

Daly, Laura A., and Linda M. Perez. 2009. "Exposure to Media Violence and Other Correlates of Aggressive Behavior in Preschool Children. *Early Childhood Research and Practice* 11 (2). http://ecrp.uiuc.edu/v11n2/index.html.

Erikson, Erik H. 1993. *Childhood and Society.* New York: W. W. Norton and Company.

Honig, Alice Sterling. 2006. "What Infants, Toddlers, and Preschoolers Learn from Play: 12 Ideas." *Montessori Life* 18 (1): 16–21.

Kwon, Kyong-Ah, Gary Bingham, Joellen Lewsader, Hyun-Joo Jeon, and James Elicker. 2013. "Structured Task versus Free Play: The Influence of Social Context on Parenting Quality, Toddlers' Engagement with Parents and Play Behaviors, and Parent-Toddler Language Use." *Child and Youth Care Forum* 42 (3): 207–24.

Landry, Susan H., Tricia A. Zucker, Heather B. Taylor, et al. 2014. "Enhancing Early Child Care Quality and Learning for Toddlers at Risk: The Responsive Early Childhood Program." *Developmental Psychology* 50 (2): 526–41.

NAEYC and Fred Rogers Center (National Association for the Education of Young Children and the Fred Rogers Center for Early Learning and Children's Media at Saint Vincent College). 2012. "Technology and Interactive Media as Tools in Early Childhood Programs Serving Children from Birth through Age 8," January. www.naeyc.org/files/naeyc/PS _technology_WEB.pdf.

Nathanson, Al, Fashina Aladé, Molly L. Sharp, Eric E. Rasmussen, and Katheryn Christy. 2014. "The Relation between Television Exposure and Executive Function among Preschoolers." *Developmental Psychology* 50 (5): 1497–1506.

Parent, Justin, Wesley Sanders, and Rex Forehand. 2016. "Youth Screen Time and Behavioral Health Problems: The Role of Sleep Duration and Disturbances." *Journal of Developmental and Behavioral Pediatrics* 37 (4): 277–84.

Prairie, Arleen Pratt. 2013. "Supporting Sociodramatic Play in Ways That Enhance Academic Learning." *Young Children* 68 (2): 62–69.

Recchia, Susan, and Jeesun Jung. 2013. "Scaffolding Infants' Play through Empowering and Individualizing Teaching Practices." *Early Education and Development* 24 (6): 829–50.

Reich, Stephanie M., Joanna C. Yau, and Mark Warschauer. 2016. "Tablet-Based eBooks for Young Children: What Does the Research Say?" *Journal of Developmental and Behavioral Pediatrics* 37 (7): 585–91.

Schmidt, Marie Evans, Tiffany A. Pempek, Heather L. Kirkorian, Anne Frankenfield Lund, and Daniel R. Anderson. 2008. "The Effects of Background Television on the Toy Play Behavior of Very Young Children." *Childhood Development* 79 (4): 1137–51.

Shin, Minsun. 2012. "The Role of Joint Attention in Social Communication and Play among Infants." *Journal of Early Childhood Research* 10 (3): 309–17.

Shochat, Tamar. 2012. "Impact of Lifestyle and Technology Developments on Sleep." *Nature and Science of Sleep* 4:19–31.

Shrimpi, Priya, Nameera Akhtar, and Chris Moore. 2013. "Toddlers' Imitative Learning in Interactive and Observational Contexts: The Role of Age and Familiarity of the Model." *Journal of Experimental Child Psychology* 116 (2): 309–23.

USDA (United States Department of Agriculture). 2016. "Limit Screen Time: Nutrition and Wellness Tips for Young Children. Provider Handbook for the Child and Adult Care Food Program." www.fns.usda.gov/sites/default/files/limitscreen.pdf.

Chapter 4

AAP, APHA, and NRC (American Academy of Pediatrics, American Public Health Association, and National Resource Center for Health and Safety in Child Care and Early Education). 2011. *Caring for Our Children: National Health and Safety Performance Standards; Guidelines for Early Care and Education Programs*, 3rd ed. Elk Grove Village, IL: American Academy of Pediatrics; Washington DC: American Public Health Association. http://cfoc.nrckids.org/webfiles/CFOC3_updated_final.pdf.

Bock, Renee. 2016. "Lighting a Musical Fire in Children." *Exchange* 232:52–55.

Collins, Anita. 2014. "Music Education and the Brain: What Does It Take to Make a Change?" *Applications of Research in Music Education* 32 (2): 4–10.

Foran, Lucille M. 2009. "Listening to Music: Helping Children Regulate Their Emotions and Improve Learning in the Classroom." *Educational Horizons* Fall (88) 1: 51–59. http://files.eric.ed.gov/fulltext/EJ868339.pdf.

Hemmeter, Mary Louise, Michaelene M. Ostrosky, Kathleen M. Artman, and Kiersten A. Kinder. 2008. "Moving Right Along: Planning Transitions to Prevent Challenging Behavior." *Beyond the Journal: Young Children on the Web.* http://journal.naeyc.org/btj/200805/pdf/BTJ_Hemmeter_Transitions.pdf.

Hodges, Eric A., Susan L. Johnson, Sheryl O. Hughes, Judy M. Hopkinson, Nancy F. Butte, and Jennifer O. Fisher. 2013. "Development of the Responsiveness to Child Feeding Cues Scale." *Appetite* 65: 210–19.

McCrory, Eamon, Stephane A. De Brito, Essi Viding. 2010. "Research Review: The Neurobiology and Genetics of Maltreatment and Adversity." *Journal of Child Psychology and Psychiatry* 51 (10): 1079–95.

McNally, Janet, Siobhan Hugh-Jones, Samantha Caton, Carel Vereijken, Hugo Weenen, and Marion Hetherington. 2016. "Communicating Hunger and Satiation in the First 2 Years of Life: A Systematic Review." *Maternal and Child Nutrition* 12 (2): 205–28.

Parlakain, Rebecca, and Claire Lerner. 2010. "Beyond Twinkle, Twinkle: Using Music with Infants and Toddlers." *Young Children* 65 (2): 14–19.

Pérez-Escamilla, R., S. Segura-Pérez, and M. Lott, on behalf of the RWJF HER Expert Panel on Best Practices for Promoting Healthy Nutrition, Feeding Patterns, and Weight Status for Infants and Toddlers from Birth to 24 Months. 2017. *Feeding Guidelines for Infants and Young Toddlers: A Responsive Parenting Approach. Guidelines for Health Professionals.* Durham, NC: Healthy Eating Research. http://healthyeatingresearch.org/wp-content/uploads/2017/02/her_feeding_guidelines_report_021416-1.pdf.

Rauduvaitė, Asta, and Živilė Virganavičienė. 2015. "Peculiarities of Expression of Leadership of Pre-Primary Children in Musical Activities." *Pedagogy Studies* 117 (1): 118–32.

Saarikallio, Suvi. 2009. "Emotional Self-Regulation through Music in 3–8-Year-Old Children." August 8, 2009. Proceedings of the 7th Triennial Conference of European Society for the Cognitive Sciences of Music (ESCOM 2009), Jyväskylä, Finland.

Smith, Andrea D., Moritz Herle, Alison Fildes, Lucy Cooke, Silje Steinsbekk, and Clare H. Llewellyn. 2017. "Food Fussiness and Food Neophobia Share a Common Etiology in Early Childhood." *Journal of Child Psychology and Psychiatry* 58 (2): 189–96.

Winsler, Adam, Lesley Ducenne, and Amanda Koury. 2011. "Singing One's Way to Self-Regulation: The Role of Early Music and Movement Curricula and Private Speech." *Early Education and Development* 22 (2): 274–304.

Winter, Elaine. 2014. "The Important Role of Music in Early Childhood Learning." *Applications of Research in Music Education* 32 (12): 4–10.

Chapter 5

Allen, Josephine R., and Kristofer Kinsey. 2013. "Teaching Theory of Mind." *Early Education and Development* 24 (6): 865–76.

Becker, Derek R., Megan M. McClelland, Paul Loprinzi, and Stewart G. Trost. 2014. "Physical Activity, Self-Regulation, and Early Academic Achievement in Preschool Children." *Early Education and Development* 25 (1): 56–70.

Blair, Clancy, and Rachel Peters Razza. 2007. "Relating Effortful Control, Executive Function, and False Belief Understanding to Emerging Math and Literacy Ability in Kindergarten." *Child Development* 78 (2): 647–63.

Blair, Clancy, Alexandra Ursache, Roger Mills-Koonce, et al., and Family Life Project Investigators. 2015. "Emotional Reactivity and Parenting Sensitivity Interact to Predict Cortisol Output in Toddlers." *Developmental Psychology* 51 (9): 1271–77.

Brock, Laura L., and Timothy W. Curby. 2016. "The Role of Children's Adaptability in Classrooms Characterized by Low or High Teacher Emotional Support Consistency." *School Psychology Review* 45 (2): 209–25.

Buss, Kristen E., Jeffrey M. Warren, and Evette Horton. 2015. "Trauma and Treatment in Early Childhood: A Review of the Historical and Emerging Literature for Counselors." *The Professional Counselor* 5 (2): 225–37. http://tpcjournal.nbcc.org/wp-content/uploads/2015/03/Pages%20225%E2%80%93237.pdf.

CDC (Centers for Disease Control and Prevention). 2016. "Violence Prevention: Adverse Childhood Experiences (ACEs)." www.cdc.gov/violenceprevention/acestudy/index.html.

Center on the Developing Child at Harvard University. 2011. "Building the Brain's 'Air Traffic Control' System: How Early Experiences Shape the Development of Executive Function" https://developingchild.harvard.edu/resources/building-the-brains-air-traffic-control-system-how-early-experiences-shape-the-development-of-executive-function/.

Denham, Susanne A., Heather K. Warren-Khot, Hideko Hamada Bassett, Todd Wyatt, and Alyssa Perna. 2012. "Factor Structure of Self-Regulation in Preschoolers: Testing Models of a Field-Based Assessment for Predicting Early School Readiness." *Journal of Experimental Child Psychology* 111 (3): 386–404.

Eisenberg, Nancy, Tracy L. Spinrad, and Natalie D. Eggum. 2010. "Emotion-Related Self-Regulation and Its Relation to Children's Maladjustment." *Annual Review of Clinical Psychology* 6: 495–525.

Graziano, Paulo A., Susan P. Keane, and Susan D. Calkins. 2010. "Maternal Behaviour and Children's Early Emotion Regulation Skills Differentially Predict Development of Children's Reactive Control and Later Effortful Control." *Infant and Child Development* 19 (4): 333–53.

Gunnar, Megan R., Erin Kryzer, Mark J. Van Ryzin, and Deborah A. Phillips. 2010. "The Rise in Cortisol in Family Day Care: Associations with Aspects of Care Quality, Child Behavior, and Child Sex." *Child Development* 81 (3): 851–69.

Gus, Licette, Janet Rose, and Louise Gilbert. 2015. "Emotion Coaching: A Universal Strategy for Supporting and Promoting Sustainable Emotional and Behavioral Well-Being." *Educational and Child Psychology* 32 (1): 31–41.

Heberle, Amy E., Yolanda M. Thomas, Robert L. Wagmiller, Margaret J. Briggs-Gowan, and Alice S. Carter. 2014. "The Impact of Neighborhood, Family, and Individual Risk Factors on Toddlers' Disruptive Behavior." *Child Development* 85 (5): 2046–61.

Kersey, Katharine, and Marie Masterson. 2013. *101 Principles for Positive Guidance: Creating Responsive Teachers.* Boston: Pearson.

Knafo, Ariel, Carolyn Zahn-Waxler, Carol Van Hulle, JoAnn L. Robinson, and Soo Hyun Rhee. 2008. "The Developmental Origins of a Disposition toward Empathy: Genetic and Environmental Contributions." *Emotion* 8 (6): 737–52.

Kuo, Alice A., Ruth A. Etzel, Lance A. Chilton, Camille Watson, and Peter A. Gorski. 2012. "Primary Care Pediatrics and Public Health: Meeting the Needs of Today's Children." *American Journal of Public Health* 102 (12): e17–e23.

Laible, Deborah, Tia Panfile, and Drika Makariev. 2008. "The Quality and Frequency of Mother-Toddler Conflict: Links with Attachment and Temperament." *Child Development* 79 (2): 426–43.

Liew, Jeffrey. 2012. "Effortful Control, Executive Functions, and Education: Bringing Self-Regulatory and Social-Emotional Competencies to the Table." *Child Development Perspectives* 6 (2): 105–11.

Lisonbee, Jared A., Jacquelyn Mize, Amie Lapp Payne, and Douglas A. Granger. 2008. "Children's Cortisol and the Quality of Teacher-Child Relationships in Child Care." *Child Development* 79 (6): 1818–32.

Mäntymaa, Mirjami, Kaija Puura, Ilona Luoma, Reija Latva, Raili K. Salmelin, and Tuula Tamminen. 2012. "Predicting Internalizing and Externalizing Problems at Five Years by Child and Parental Factors in Infancy and Toddlerhood." *Child Psychiatry and Human Development* 43:153–70.

Margetts, Kay. 2005. "Responsive Caregiving: Reducing the Stress in Infant Toddler Care." *International Journal of Early Childhood* 37 (2): 77–84.

Moilanen, Kristin L., Daniel S. Shaw, Thomas J. Dishion, Frances Gardner, and Melvin Wilson. 2010. "Predictors of Longitudinal Growth in Inhibitory Control in Early Childhood." *Social Development* 19 (2): 326–47.

Mongillo, Elizabeth A., Margaret Briggs-Gowan, Julian D. Ford, and Alice S. Carter. 2009. "Impact of Traumatic Life Events in a Community Sample of Toddlers." *Journal of Abnormal Child Psychology* 37 (4): 455–68.

Morasch, Katherine C., and Martha Ann Bell. 2011. "The Role of Inhibitory Control in Behavioral and Physiological Expressions of Toddler Executive Function." *Journal of Experimental Child Psychology* 108 (3): 593–606.

National Scientific Council on the Developing Child. 2005/2014. "Excessive Stress Disrupts the Architecture of the Developing Brain: Working Paper 3." Updated Edition. www.developingchild.harvard.edu/wp-content/uploads/2005/05/Stress_Disrupts _Architecture_Developing_Brain-1.pdf.

Paul, Kaleigh E. 2014. "Baby Play Supports Infant and Toddler Social and Emotional Development." *Young Children* 69 (1): 8–14.

Schwartz-Henderson, Ileen. 2016. "Trauma-Informed Teaching and Design Strategies: A New Paradigm." *Exchange* 231:36–40.

Shonkoff, Jack P. 2016. "Capitalizing on Advances in Science to Reduce the Health Consequences of Early Childhood Adversity." *JAMA Pediatrics: Clinical Review and Education* e1–e5. www.acesconnection.com/fileSendAction/fcType/0/fcOid/451808762877317332 /filePointer/452793993453277360/fodoid/452793993453277357/CapitalizingonAdvances .pdf.

Spinrad, Tracy, Nancy Eisenberg, Bridget Gaertner, Tierney Popp, Cynthia L. Smith, Anne Kupfer, Karissa Greving, Jeffrey Liew, and Claire Hofer. 2007. "Relations of Maternal Socialization and Toddlers' Effortful Control to Children's Adjustment and Social Competence." *Developmental Psychology* 43 (5): 1170–86.

Tanyel, Nur E. 2009. "Emotional Regulation: Developing Toddlers' Social Competence." *Dimensions of Early Childhood* 37 (2): 10–14.

Valiente, Carlos, Nancy Eisenberg, Rg Haugen, Tracy L. Spinrad, Claire Hofer, Jeffrey Liew, and Anne Kupfer. 2011. "Children's Effortful Control and Academic Achievement: Mediation through Social Functioning." *Early Education and Development* 22 (3): 411–33.

Vygotsky, Lev S. 1978. *Mind in Society*. London: Harvard University Press.

Warren, Heather K., Susanne A. Denham, and Hideko H. Bassett. 2008. "The Emotional Foundations of Social Understanding." *Zero to Three* 28 (5): 32–39.

Watamura, Sara Enos, Deborah A. Phillips, Taryn W. Morrissey, Kathleen McCartney, and Kristen Bub. 2011. "Double Jeopardy: Poorer Social-Emotional Outcomes for Children in the NICHD SECCYD Experiencing Home and Child-Care Environments That Confer Risk." *Child Development* 82 (1): 48–65.

Wilson, Steven R., Felicia Roberts, Jessica J. Rack, and Julie E. Delaney. 2008. "Mothers' Trait Verbal Aggressiveness as a Predictor of Maternal and Child Behavior during Playtime Interactions." *Human Communication Research* 34 (3): 392–422.

Yeary, Julia. 2013. "Promoting Mindfulness: Helping Children with Separation." *Young Children* 68 (5): 110–12.

Zero to Six Collaborative Group, National Child Traumatic Stress Network. 2010. "Early Childhood Trauma." www.nctsn.org/sites/default/files/assets/pdfs/nctsn_earlychildhoodtrauma _08-2010final.pdf.

Zero to Three. 2016. "Tuning In: Parents of Young Children Tell Us What They Think, Know, and Need." Accessed October 24, 2017. www.zerotothree.org/resources/series/tuning-in -parents-of-young-children-tell-us-what-they-think-know-and-need.

Chapter 6

Adams, Gina, Kathryn Tout, and Martha Zaslow. 2007. "Early Care and Education for Children in Low-Income Families: Patterns of Use, Quality, and Potential Policy Implications." June 21. Urban Institute. www.urban.org/UploadedPDF/411482_early_care.pdf.

Aguiar, Cecília, and Robin A. McWilliam. 2013. "Consistency of Toddler Engagement across Two Settings." *Early Childhood Research Quarterly* 28 (1): 102–10.

Bandura, Albert. 1982. "Self-Efficacy Mechanism in Human Agency." *American Psychologist* 37 (2): 122–47.

Blair, Clancy. 2013. "Promoting the Development of Self-Regulation in Young Children: Emotion, Attention, Stress, and Executive Functions." Lecture presented at the NAEYC professional development conference, San Francisco, June 9.

Bruno, Holly Elissa. 2011. "Using Our Brain to Stay Cool under Pressure." *Young Children* 66 (1): 22–27.

Camilli, Gregory, Sadako Vargas, Sharon Ryan, and W. Steven Barnett. 2010. "Meta-analysis of the Effects of Early Development of Academic Language, and Literacy Skills." *Applied Developmental Science* 12:113–27.

Claffey, Anne E., Laura J. Kucharski, and Rene R. Gratz. 1994. "Managing the Biting Child." *Early Child Development and Care* 99 (1): 93–101.

Duncan, Greg J., Katherine Magnuson, W. Thomas Boyce, and Jack P. Shonkoff. 2013. *The Long Reach of Early Childhood Poverty: Pathways and Impacts.* Boston: Harvard University.

Fuller, Bruce, John W. Gasko, and Rebecca Anguiano. 2010. "Lifting Pre-K Quality: Caring and Effective Teachers." www.elcmdm.org/Knowledge%20Center/reports /Fullerhighquality.pdf

Gershoff, Elizabeth T. 2010. "More Harm Than Good: A Summary of Scientific Research on the Intended and Unintended Effects of Corporal Punishment on Children." *Law and Contemporary Problems* 73 (31): 31–56.

Gershoff, Elizabeth T., and Susan H. Bitensky. 2007. "The Case against Corporal Punishment of Children: Converging Evidence from Social Science Research and International Human Rights Law and Implications for U.S. Public Policy." *Psychology, Public Policy, and Law* 13 (4): 231–72.

Mashburn, Andrew. 2008. "Quality of Social and Physical Environments in Preschools and Children's Education Interventions on Cognitive and Social Development." *Teachers College Record* 112 (3): 579–620.

NAEYC (National Association for the Education of Young Children). 2011. "Code of Ethical Conduct and Statement of Commitment." National Association for the Education of Young Children, May. www.naeyc.org/files/naeyc/image/public_policy/Ethics%20Position %20Statement2011_09202013update.pdf.

———. 2016. "Understanding and Responding to Children Who Bite." Accessed October 24, 2017. https://families.naeyc.org/learning-and-development/child-development /understanding-and-responding-children-who-bite.

Osher, David, George G. Bear, Jeffrey R. Sprague, and Walter Doyle. 2010. "How Can We Improve School Discipline?" *Educational Researcher* 39 (1): 48–58.

Phillips, Deborah. 2010. "10 Years Post–*Neurons to Neighborhoods*: What's at Stake and What Matters in Child Care?" Keynote address at the celebration of the twentieth anniversary of CCDGB, Washington, DC, October 19.

Phillips, Deborah A., and Mary Elizabeth Meloy. 2012. "High-Quality School-Based Pre-K Can Boost Early Learning for Children with Special Needs." *Exceptional Children* 78 (4): 471–90.

Saint-Onge, Hubert, and Debra Wallace. 2003. *Leveraging Communities of Practice for Strategic Advantage.* Boston: Butterworth-Heinemann.

Sterns, Peter N., and Clio Sterns. 2017. "American Schools and the Uses of Shame: An Ambiguous History." *History of Education* 46 (1): 58–75.

Straus, Murray A. 2010. "Prevalence, Societal Causes, and Trends in Corporal Punishment by Parents in World Perspective." *Law and Contemporary Problems* 73 (1): 1–30.

Chapter 7

Cunha, Flavio, and James J. Heckman. 2010. "Investing in Our Young People. NBER Working Paper No. w16201." https://ssrn.com/abstract=1641577.

Denham, Susanne A., and Chavaughn Brown. 2010. "'Plays Nice with Others': Social-Emotional Learning and Academic Success." *Early Education and Development* 21 (5): 652–80.

Espinoza, Linda M., and Miriam Calderon. 2015. "State Early Learning and Development Standards/Guidelines, Policies, and Related Practices: How Responsive Are They to the Needs of Young Dual Language Learners?" October. http://buildinitiative.org/Portals/0 /Uploads/Documents/BuildDLLReport2015.pdf.

Fernald, Anne, Virginia A. Marchman, and Adriana Weisleder. 2013. "SES Differences in Language Processing Skill and Vocabulary are Evident at 18 Months." *Developmental Science* 16 (2): 234–48.

Fox, Sharon E., Pat Levitt, Charles A. Nelson. 2010. "How the Timing and Quality of Early Experiences Influence the Development of Brain Architecture." *Child Development* 81 (1): 28–40.

Gloeckler, Lissy R., Jennifer M. Cassell, and Amy J. Malkus. 2013. "An Analysis of Teacher Practices with Toddlers during Social Conflicts." *Early Child Development and Care* 184 (5): 749–65.

Hallam, Rena A., Hillary N. Fouts, Kaitlin Bargreen, and Lauri A. Caudle. 2009. "Quality from a Toddler's Perspective: A Bottom-Up Examination of Classroom Experiences." *Early Childhood Research and Practice* 11 (2). http://ecrp.uiuc.edu/v11n2/hallam.html.

Head Zauche, Lauren, Taylor A. Thul, Ashley E. Darcy Mahoney, and Jennifer L. Stapel-Wax. 2016. "Influence of Language Nutrition on Children's Language and Cognitive Development: An Integrated Review." *Early Childhood Research Quarterly* 36:318–33.

King, Sarah E., and Julie E. Dockrell. 2016. "Investigating Affordance of Opportunity for Young Children's Language Interactions in a Nursery Setting: How Can Small Group Talk Act as a Forum for Language Learning?" *Journal of Early Childhood Research* 14 (4): 351–69.

Kuhl, Patricia K. 2011. "Early Language Learning and Literacy: Neuroscience Implications for Education." *Mind, Brain, and Education* 5 (3): 128–42.

Landry, Susan H., Tricia A. Zucker, Heather B. Taylor, et al. 2014. "Enhancing Early Child Care Quality and Learning for Toddlers at Risk: The Responsive Early Childhood Program." *Developmental Psychology* 50 (2): 526–41.

Magnuson, Katherine, and Greg J. Duncan. 2014. "Can Early Childhood Interventions Decrease Inequality of Economic Opportunity?" Paper prepared for the Federal Reserve Bank of Boston conference on inequality of economic opportunity in the United States, Boston, October 17–18. www.bostonfed.org/inequality2014/papers/magnusun-duncan.pdf.

Rowe, Meredith L. 2012. "A Longitudinal Investigation of the Role of Quantity and Quality of Child-Directed Speech in Vocabulary Development." *Child Development* 83 (5): 1762–74.

Semingson, Peggy, Kathryn Pole, and Jodi Tommerdahl. 2015. "Using Bilingual Books to Enhance Literacy around the World." *European Scientific Journal* 3:132–39.

Shonkoff, Jack P. 2010. "Building a New Biodevelopmental Framework to Guide the Future of Early Childhood Policy." *Child Development* 81 (1): 357–67.

Suskind, Dana. 2016. *Thirty Million Words*. New York: Random House.

Suskind, Dana, Patricia Kuhl, Kristin R. Leffel, Susan Landry, Flavio Cunha, and Kathryn M. Neckerman. 2013. "Bridging the Early Language Gap: A Plan for Scaling Up." White paper prepared for the White House meeting on "Bridging the Thirty-Million-Word Gap." Chicago, IL, September.

Vygotsky, Lev. 1978. "Interaction between Learning and Development." In *Mind in Society*, edited by Michael Cole, 79–91. Cambridge, MA: Harvard University Press.

Weisleder, Adriana, and Anne Fernald. 2013. "Talking to Children Matters: Early Language Experience Strengthens Processing and Builds Vocabulary." *Psychological Science* 24 (11): 2143–52.

Weldon, Arianne. 2014. "Language Nutrition: Filling the Word Opportunity Gap." Speech presented at the National Meeting of State Leads for the National Campaign for Grade-Level Reading, Washington, DC, January 9.

Chapter 8

AAP (American Academy of Pediatrics). 2017. "Promoting Resilience." Accessed August 1. www.aap.org/en-us/advocacy-and-policy/aap-health-initiatives/resilience/Pages/Promoting-Resilience.aspx.

APA (American Psychological Association). 2017. "Parents and Caregivers Are Essential to Children's Healthy Development." Accessed October 24, 2017. www.apa.org/pi/families/resources/parents-caregivers.aspx.

Center on the Developing Child at Harvard University. 2014. *A Decade of Science Informing Policy: The Story of the National Scientific Council on the Developing Child*. http://46y5eh11fhgw3ve3ytpwxt9r.wpengine.netdna-cdn.com/wp-content/uploads/2015/09/A-Decade-of-Science-Informing-Policy.pdf.

Eichner, Jerrold M., and Beverley H. Johnson. 2012. "Patient- and Family-Centered Care and the Pediatrician's Role." *Pediatrics* 112 (3): 691. http://pediatrics.aappublications.org/content/129/2/394.

Forry, Nicole D., Shannon Moodie, Shana Simkin, and Laura Rothenberg. 2011. *Family-Provider Relationships: A Multidisciplinary Review of High Quality Practices and Associations with Family, Child, and Provider Outcomes*, Issue Brief OPRE 2011–26a. Washington, DC: Office of Planning, Research and Evaluation, Administration for Children and Families, US Department of Health and Human Services. www.acf.hhs.gov/sites/default/files/opre/family_provider_multi.pdf.

Halgunseth, Linda C., Gisela Jia, and Oscar A. Barbarin. 2013. "Family Engagement in Early Childhood Programs: Serving Families of Dual Language Learners." In *California's Best Practices for Young Dual Language Learners*, edited by Linda Espinosa, 119–71. Sacramento: California Department of Education.

Hill, Nancy E., and Diana F. Tyson. 2008. "Excavating Culture: Ethnicity and Context as Predictors of Parenting Behavior." *Applied Developmental Science* 12 (4): 188–97.

Köster, Moritz, Lilia Cavalcante, Rafael Vera Cruz de Carvalho, Briseida Dôgo Resende, and Joscha Kärtner. 2016. "Cultural Influences on Toddlers' Prosocial Behavior: How Maternal Task Assignment Relates to Helping Others." *Child Development* 87 (6): 1727–38.

Lang, Sarah N., Angela R. Tolbert, Sarah J. Schoppe-Sullivan, Amy E. Bonomi. 2016. "A Cocaring Framework for Infants and Toddlers: Applying a Model of Coparenting to Parent-Teacher Relationships." *Early Childhood Research Quarterly* 34 (1): 40–52.

Mah, Janet W. T., and Charlotte Johnston. 2012. "Cultural Variations in Mothers' Acceptance of and Intent to Use Behavioral Child Management Techniques." *Journal of Child and Family Studies* 21 (3): 486–97.

Masten, Ann S. 2007. "Resilience in Developing Systems: Progress and Promise as the Fourth Wave Rises." *Development and Psychopathology* 19 (3): 921–30.

Masterson, Marie, and Katharine Kersey. 2016. *Enjoying the Parenting Roller Coaster: Nurturing and Empowering Your Children through the Ups and Downs*. Lewisville, NC: Gryphon House.

NCCP (National Center for Children in Poverty). 2017. "Young Child Risk Calculator." Accessed August 1. www.nccp.org/tools/risk/.

NCPFCE (National Center for Parent, Family and Community Engagement). 2014. "Family Connections to Peers and Community." https://eclkc.ohs.acf.hhs.gov/sites/default/files /pdf/rtp-family-connections-to-peers-and-community.pdf.

NSCDC (National Scientific Council on the Developing Child). 2005/2014. *Excessive Stress Disrupts the Architecture of the Developing Brain: Working Paper No. 3*. Updated edition. www.developingchild.harvard.edu/resources/wp3/.

Ruprecht, Karen, James Elicker, and Ji Young Choi. 2016. "Continuity of Care, Caregiver-Child Interactions, and Toddler Social Competence and Problem Behaviors." *Early Education and Development* 27 (2): 221–39.

Schwartz, Mallary I., and Ann M. Easterbrooks. 2014. "The Role of Parent, Provider, and Child Characteristics in Parent-Provider Relationships in Infant and Toddler Classrooms." *Early Education and Development* 25 (4): 573–98.

Shonkoff, Jack P., and Andrew S. Garner. 2012. "The Lifelong Effects of Early Childhood Adversity and Toxic Stress." *Pediatrics* 129 (1): e232–e246. http://pediatrics.aappublications.org /content/pediatrics/129/1/e232.full.pdf.

Vélez-Ibañez, Carlos G. 1988. "Networks of Exchange among Mexicans in the U.S. and Mexico: Local Level Mediating Responses to National and International Transformations." *Urban Anthropology and Studies of Cultural Systems and World Economic Development* 17 (1): 27–51.

Vinall, Jillian, Rebecca Pillai Riddell, and Saul Greenberg. 2011. "The Influence of Culture on Maternal Soothing Behaviors and Infant Pain Expression in the Immunization Context." *Pain Research and Management* 16 (4): 234–38.

Wolf, Eric R. 1966. *Peasants*. Englewood Cliffs, NJ: Prentice-Hall.

Appendix

La Paro, Karen M., Bridget K. Hamre, and Robert C. Pianta. 2012. *Classroom Assessment Scoring System (Class) Manual, Toddler*. Baltimore: Paul H. Brookes Publishing.